TRANSNATIONAL PROSTITUTION

Changing Patterns in a Global Context

EDITED BY SUSANNE THORBEK
AND BANDANA PATTANAIK

Zed Books
LONDON · NEW YORK

Transnational Prostitution: Changing Patterns in a Global Context
was first published by Zed Books Ltd, 7 Cynthia Street, London
N1 9JF, UK and Room 400, 175 Fifth Avenue, New York, NY
10010, USA in 2002.

www.zedbooks.demon.co.uk

Cover designed by Andrew Corbett
Set in Monotype Fournier by Ewan Smith, London
Printed and bound in the United Kingdom by Biddles Ltd,
Guildford and King's Lynn

Distributed in the USA exclusively by Palgrave, a division of
St Martin's Press, LLC, 175 Fifth Avenue, New York, NY 10010.

A catalogue record for this book is available from the British
Library.

US CIP data has been applied for from the Library of Congress.

ISBN 1 84277 030 6 cased
ISBN 1 84277 031 4 limp

Contents

About the Contributors

Ryan Bishop is senior fellow in the Department of English Language and Literature at the National University of Singapore. He is co-author, with Lillian S. Robinson, of *Night Market: Sexual Cultures and the Thai Economic Miracle* (Routledge 1998), and co-editor, with John Phillips and Yeo Wei Wei, of *Perpetuating Cities: Postcolonial Urbanism in Southeast Asia* (Routledge 2002) and *Beyond Description: Singapore, Space, Historicity* (Routledge 2002). He has published articles on critical cultural studies, literary theory and the production of knowledge.

Marieke van Doorninck is a historian and works as a researcher, policy consultant and spokesperson at the Mr A. de Graaf Foundation, the Dutch institute for prostitution issues. This is the national centre for research, policy development and information on prostitution and related issues. The foundation's central objective is to diminish the (social) problems connected to prostitution. One of the principal items is to improve the juridical and social status of sex workers.

Arthur Gould is reader in Swedish social policy in the Department of Social Sciences, Loughborough University. He has written extensively on the Swedish welfare state and Swedish drug policy. His books include *Conflict and Control in Welfare Policy: The Swedish Experience* (1988), *Capitalist Welfare Systems: Japan, Britain and Sweden* (1993) and *Developments in Swedish Social Policy: Resisting Dionysus* (2001).

Ana Lopez Lindstrom is a researcher in the Taller de Estudios Internacionales Mediterraneos in the Universidad Autonoma de Madrid, Spain. She is a graduate in Arabic and Islamic Studies in the Universidad Complutense de Madrid. She is currently finishing her PhD in the Department of Social Anthropology of the UAM on 'Moroccan Women in Madrid: Marriage Strategies in a Multicultural Context'.

Anders Lisborg has been working since 1997 with issues of human trafficking and migrant sex-workers. He has had a six-month internship at the International Organization for Migration (IOM) in Southeast Asia on the counter-trafficking programmes in the region. He is currently affiliated to the Centre for Development Research (CDR) in Copenhagen, where he is writing his thesis on human smuggling and the migration patterns among spontaneous asylum seekers.

Linda Meaker has worked as an educator and counsellor with sex workers from culturally and linguistically diverse backgrounds since 1990. She is currently supervisor of a non-governmental organization funded to provide support and health services to sex workers in Queensland.

Prapairat R. Mix has been a social worker since 1993. She is a member of Amnesty for Women e.V, an organization based in Hamburg, Germany, a migrant centre to combat the trafficking of women and forced prostitution. It mainly helps women and transsexuals from Southeast Asia (especially Thailand and the Philippines), Latin America and Eastern Europe.

Bandana Pattanaik currently works as the programme coordinator of research and training at the Global Alliance Against Traffic in Women, Bangkok. Her work experience include teaching English language and literature at the tertiary level in India, developing community-based English language teaching programmes for Somali and Palestinian students in India, working as a research associate with the Australian Women's Research Centre, and coordinating an electronic network of small women publishers in the Asia Pacific region at Spinifex Press, Australia. Bandana has been involved with several non-governmental organizations since her student days, specifically with women's groups.

Joan L. Phillips is currently postdoctoral fellow at University of London, Royal Holloway. Her research focus is in tourism, gender, sexuality and race in the Caribbean, about which she has written a number of publications.

Lillian S. Robinson was a founder of the field of women's studies in the United States. She is the author/co-author of five academic books, including *Night Market: Sexual Cultures and the Thai Economic Miracle*, with Ryan Bishop (Routledge, 1998). Currently principal-directrice of the Simone de Beauvoir Institute, the women's studies department of Concordia University, Montreal, Robinson has taught at a number of American institutions, from MIT to the University of Hawai'i, as well as the University of Paris.

Pataya Ruenkaew is a Thai scholar living and working in Germany. She completed her doctoral study in sociology at the University of Bielefeld, Germany. She has undertaken research on Thai women in Germany at the Interdisciplinary Women's Study Centre, Bielefeld University (1990) and also on the marriage migration of Thai women to Germany at the Faculty of Sociology, Bielefeld University. She is one of the founders and currently chairperson of the THARA Association, an organization intended to help Thai women in Germany and to protect their rights.

Marlene Spanger's MA thesis examined transnational prostitution in Denmark, focusing on black female migrants. She is employed as research assistant for co-ordination for gender studies at Copenhagen University. She is co-editor on the journal *Kvinder, Køn og Forskning*, theme: 'Sex til Salg', 3/2001, and co-organizer of the conference Sex til Salg: Prostitution, Køn, Magt og Ligestilling (Sex for Sale: Prostitution, Gender, Power and Equality)

Noulmook Sutdhibhasilp, a PhD graduate from the University of Toronto, worked as an adult educator and a social worker with local and international non-governmental organizations for several years in Thailand. In Canada, she conducted two research studies on the issues of the human rights violations of Asian migrant workers and trafficking in women. Her academic and activist interests include adult education for social transformation, women migrant workers' rights, sexual identities and politics.

Susanne Thorbek (DPhil) is employed as senior lecturer at Aalborg University, Denmark, where she is a member of the Centre for Feminist Research and of the Centre on Development and International Relations.

She has worked with prostitution, especially in the Third World, in recent years. She has published the books *Voices from the City, Women of Bangkok* (Zed Books 1987), and *Gender and Slum Culture in Urban Asia* (Vistaar Publications 1994)

Chitraporn Vanaspong was born in Thailand, and received a master of journalism from Chulalongkorn University in Bangkok, Thailand. She was a journalist for more than seven years in Thailand. Since 1997 she has worked with the international NGO ECPAT International (End Child Prostitution, Child Pornography and Trafficking of Children for Sexual Purposes) as regional officer for Asia and the Pacific.

INTRODUCTION

Prostitution in a Global Context: Changing Patterns

SUSANNE THORBEK

§ Prostitution across borders has increased in the last twenty to thirty years. More and more men go abroad as tourists or to military or UN camps (Enloe 1989) and many of them buy sexual satisfaction from local women. In the last twenty years the number of women who migrate to richer countries from poorer and work in prostitution has also grown (see chapters by Ruenkaew and Lisborg).

The differences in the circumstances of migrant prostitutes are vast. Some may have been cheated or forced into the trade; others have chosen it voluntarily, knowing what the work entails; and some have had experience of prostitution both at home and abroad before travelling to Europe (Ruenkaew). There are differences in 'legal status': some have citizenship, others not. Some are married to a fake husband who is often well paid for his hire. Others are illegal migrants. The type of employment and the existence of women's networks are important elements in the amount of autonomy an individual woman has. Income levels and the degree to which women are exploited vary so much that some women barely survive while others earn double the minimum wage (Lisborg).

All this means that living conditions and prospects for the future also vary considerably. This makes it difficult to generalize from case studies, but case studies do show that other generalizations are doubtful: for example, the habitual naming of sex-workers of foreign origin as sex-slaves, debt-slaves or trafficked women is inaccurate. Case studies can also show differences and nuances much better than most other methods of study. They indicate the complexity involved in the choices the women make (Ruenkaew, Mix). In this volume the case studies were undertaken either by researchers or staff in NGOs who work with prostitutes. Some of them utilize the statistics of their NGOs and in this way give a more general picture (Meaker, Ruenkaew). So, with careful consideration of the context, it is possible to generalize and to raise new issues.

Many of the studies in this anthology concern Thai women in prostitution, and the reader may well be tempted to make the generalization that Thailand has more prostitution than other countries. Vanaspong argues in her chapter that this is not the case and demonstrates how media handling of the theme has created such an impression. Lim (1998) has shown that prostitution is widespread in four Southeast Asian countries, and is little influenced by either its legal status or by religion. Lim, however, was concerned with prostitution for the home market and in this area Thailand is in no way exceptional; but it is probably the country which has the greatest tourist-related prostitution involving straight men. At the same time, Thailand is the focus of better and more research than other countries, housing as it does a well-known international organization that works with trafficking (GAATW).

MEN IN PROSTITUTION: THE CUSTOMER

Men as customers in prostitution have historically been ignored both in public debates and in legislation. In recent years, however, several studies have been undertaken. The two studies of men in prostitution in this anthology explore mainly tourist-related prostitution in Thailand (Bishop and Robinson, Thorbek). Both argue that the men combine old notions on race, class and gender with very modern (postmodern?) conditions of life and personalities. It can be argued that the image of the tourist is an idiom of postmodernism (Bauman 1996), and that the sex tourist in this sense becomes an image of postmodern man (Thorbek). Bishop and Robinson analyse men's travel reports on the Internet and show how these men are alienated from their own sexuality but also from society in general through their obsession with the Internet.

The increase in the male demand for paid sex is logical in the sense that 'privileges' which were formerly restricted by class, race and gender are now available to everybody; there is no need to be rich to exploit women in very poor countries.

The customers and their relationships with prostitutes come in many forms. Much has been written about the so-called 'open-ended' relation-ships at some prostitution resorts, for instance in Thailand. O'Connell Davidson (1998) pointed out the inbuilt contradiction in the trade in sex: many men search for something more than a fuck – maybe male bonding and respect or maybe some sort of feeling of being alive in the meeting with another human being. In a clear-cut business relationship around sex neither of these aims is achieved.

Male customers are numerous and they may be served by male and female prostitutes, and children. Male prostitutes who serve female customers exist in some tourist resorts. The 'open-ended' relationship is characteristic of the latter in Barbados as well, Phillips argues here. She shows also how the male prostitutes see themselves as entrepreneurs. They create themselves in the image of the white world, fulfilling their female customers' fantasies with their hairstyles, their young, well-trimmed bodies, virility and sex-drive as well as their lack of inhibitions.

Even if the women who buy their services and give them gifts exploit their poverty as men do with female prostitutes in other circumstances, the relationships between them seem to be based on 'normal', maybe now old-fashioned, gender relations. The male prostitutes choose their customers carefully, they flatter and entertain them, take them on boat trips, teach them to enjoy seaside sports, and so on. And their motives are those of an entrepreneur: to earn money, to invest and to take risks.

Many female prostitutes can also be seen as entrepreneurs. Spanger shows how some black female prostitutes have marketing strategies similar to those of the Barbados 'beach boys'. They re-create their image in terms of European/American clichés about black women's sexuality: their sex-drive, loose morals and lack of inhibitions.

Migrant women who work as prostitutes can in many cases also be seen as entrepreneurs in an economic sense: they take risks and invest in order to earn good money. They are not just victims.

MIGRANT WOMEN IN PROSTITUTION

The case studies in this book show that migrant women in pros-titution are not only able to make money, at least after a period of time, but are also able to create a life under new circumstances.

A case study in which the life histories of prostitutes are used as material shows that the migrant women are, on average, twenty-eight years old when they arrive, although they may have entered prostitution when they were much younger. Many are mothers and the education of their children is a strong motive for taking the risk of going abroad (Ruenkaew). The ways in which they structure their lives in the new country differ. Some compartmentalize their lives and keep their work a secret even from their closest family (Spanger). Some live in a re-created Thai group with Thai food, videos, friends and gambling (Mix, Lisborg); others become part of the local community, where one exists.

The most obvious dividing line between prostitutes separates those who are free and able to take new citizenship and those who work to pay off their debts. In Brisbane, Australia, the debt contract workers had to service between 400 and 700 men to get free (Meaker); in the German study they had to work for periods of between six months and four years to pay off their debts. Their legal status has far-reaching consequences, especially when it comes to violence, for it has a bearing on whether or not women are willing to call the police. In an illegal massage parlour in Denmark, knives were hidden under the bed and at the door.

In studies of diasporas, migrant women who work as prostitutes are seldom if ever included. This anthology shows that they keep in contact with family, friends and kin both in their country of origin and in other countries. They are part of a chain migration (Lisborg), using telephones, money remittances, and travel to maintain contacts (Spanger, Lisborg) and they are part of the creation of transnational social space.

TRAFFICKING AND MIGRATION

Trafficking has been defined in several ways; here, though, it seems logical to reserve the term for a situation in which a person is lured, cheated or forced into travelling to another country and to work there. Case studies in this anthology show that many women who decide to go abroad already know the risks. Only in one case was a woman lured into the business. She managed to escape (Lisborg). Trafficking does exist but there is less of it than the police, politicians, some feminist organizations and the media assume.

In the public debate at present, all women who work as prostitutes abroad are considered to be victims of trafficking, but this perception is wrong. In fact, it is very difficult to distinguish between who is trafficked and who is not. A woman may decide to go abroad, knowing she will work as a prostitute, and then find the conditions under which she has to work and the payment of the debt and the interest rates charged unacceptable; in this sense she may be considered a victim of trafficking. Another woman may be lured or cheated into the trade but decide that, in the circumstances, her best option is to go on. Has she been trafficked if she does not want to be liberated?

Those people who organize travel, papers and jobs may charge very high prices.[1] It is not only women who go in order to work as prostitutes who pay dearly. Workers from Asia who go to the Middle East to work as domestics or labourers certainly pay dearly too. As do refugees, as an old Danish example from the Second World War shows. When the Jews in Denmark were fleeing to Sweden, the Danish fishermen who sailed them across Øresund charged 1,500 kroner per person on the days when demand was highest, but less before and after (Mogensen 2001). These fishermen are today seen as heroes by both Jews and Danes.

Prices charged by smugglers or traffickers today also depend on demand and on the difficulties and dangers they anticipate. Traffickers and smugglers are seen by prostitutes, for instance, as both exploitative and as helpers (like travel agents, only rather more expensive).

It is common in the rich world today to define anyone who arranges for a prostitute to travel to work in a richer country as a trafficker, regardless of whether the prostitute has chosen to travel herself or has been forced or lured into the situation. If she is found by the police, the woman is often sent home immediately; the traffickers are prosecuted where possible but receive relatively mild sentences. In several countries the police are reluctant to use prostitutes as witnesses.

The hypocrisy of the public debate becomes very clear at this point. If the prostitutes who pay high prices to come to Europe (or Australia, Canada, USA) were seen as victims, we might expect that they should receive compensation and help. But the policy in the West is to send them home at a day's notice, to the same situation they had left behind, but now often in debt to the trafficker as well. And since few creditors take their losses without any action, many may choose or be forced to leave again, this time in a more clandestine, more vulnerable and probably more expensive way.

The whole policy is argued in terms of the human rights of the prostitutes by the media, the police, by politicians in some countries and by several feminist and humanitarian organizations. If these people and institutions were concerned about the women's plight, they would find many good ideas proposed by NGOs, among them SQWISI (Meaker), as well as in a draft for a reform by the EU Commission (1995) where it is proposed that prostitutes who are willing to be witnesses or to bring a case should be allowed to stay in the country until the trial is finished. They should have medical and legal support during this period. Police and staff in the juridical system should be trained to understand the conditions and the lives of prostitutes.

It seems that what is of concern in public policies today is the question of immigration, not the human rights of prostitutes.

POLICIES ON PROSTITUTION

From a feminist perspective, it is important to see prostitution in its social, economic and political context, and equally important to consider the power relations involved.

There is little doubt about the influence of economic and social conditions on prostitution. The main motive of women who choose prostitution is poverty, the desire to attain those goods – among them education and medical services – that others take for granted in a modern society. Global inequalities and the exploitation of poor nations are of course of paramount importance in the spread of transnational prostitution (Kempadoo and Doezema 1998). Personal factors may play a role, too, in particular family crises, including violence.

Julia O'Connell Davidson (1998) argues that women who work as prostitutes are involved in three sets of power relationships: with the customer, with 'third parties', such as owners of brothels, massage parlours, bars and nightclubs, escort agencies and so on, with society at large, most directly with the courts and the police. These three power relations influence each other: the law and the police's implementation of it places limits on the actions of 'third parties', and prostitutes' relations with their customers are influenced by both the others.

In the debate on prostitution today, there are two different lines of thought. The first is put forward by the abolitionists who want to get rid of prostitution. They argue that relations with the customers are by nature demeaning and harmful for the prostitute, as are relations with the 'third parties'. They seldom argue for broader economic and social reforms but campaign for more legislation against prostitution. In some cases (as in Denmark) it is not criminal to sell sexual satisfaction but it is criminal to pay a 'third party' for it. In practice this means that Danish-born prostitutes, who are not supposed to pay 'third parties', can work legally, especially indoors, but women who arrive from other countries cannot, since they must pay for travel, for a 'hired' husband and to be part of a massage parlour or brothel.

The other line of thought argues that the main problems for prostitutes are related to legislation and police harassment, and that the solution is to legalize prostitution, including payment to brothel owners and the like. According to this thinking, sex-work will then be considered similar to other kinds of work and women will be able to form trade unions, will be taxed and have access to social security, pensions and the like. This argument is concerned with adult women who choose to go into prostitution.

Noulmook Sutdhibhasilp shows in detail in her chapter how both legislation and implementation on in-migration and prostitution make the lives of migrant prostitutes (and poor women) very difficult in Canada, and how strong discrimination against them is.

An implicit argument in favour of the second line of thinking can be found in the newly implemented laws on prostitution in Holland, with legalized brothels, with strict rules about hygiene and condom use, and the allocation of sites for street prostitutes outside the cities. However, Dorninck states that the law will still not legalize the work of migrant prostitutes or of prostitutes who work in less capital-intensive brothels. So the probable result will be a division in prostitution, with one section of workers legalized and another still operating in a black market. The outcome of this reform for the legal prostitutes will also depend very much on an individual's ability to organize.

The new Swedish law that prohibits men from buying sex but allows women to sell it is analysed in the chapter by Gould. He shows in detail how the idea of a gender equal society and the presence of feminists both in public services and in organizations has contributed to the new law. He argues, too, that fear of the immigration of women who work as prostitutes has been the chief driving force. Previously, prostitution had been dealt with mainly in relation to policies on equality, unemployment, social services and so on, and this was in fact very successful.

In the concluding chapter questions of feminist methodology are taken up and Pattanaik discusses several of the concepts which are central to the debate.

CONCLUSION

The problematic of prostitution is full of political overtones. The word prostitute, or for that matter sex-worker, is not acceptable to most women who work in the sex trade. Their devaluation and stigmatization are strongly felt and many probably share society's opinion of their work. They see their identities as separate from their work, refusing to accept the generalizations implied in the term 'sex-work' (Spanger).

The life of a prostitute is harsh and beset by many problems of different kinds. It is a telling comment on the current global, as well as national, economic and social situation that women choose this work as the least unacceptable in a series of unattractive choices. In this sense the in-migration of women from poor countries who work as prostitutes is the new globalization that strikes back at the West.

Legalizing prostitution, making it a business like any other, is problematic too. So far the market has not solved questions of inequality, or for that matter conditions of work or even slavery (in its new forms). The legalization of pornography has resulted in an explosion in this trade, a proliferation of pictures that demean women and teach youngsters and adults a rather absurd sort of sexuality. The legalization of prostitution may very well have similar results.

The best solution might be to concentrate on finding the real traffickers – those who coerce children and women into the business and keep them there by force. Simultaneously, a more lenient policy could be formulated (keeping one eye closed, as a Danish policeman described it) to deal with more 'normal' prostitution. And support would be available from NGOs or GOs without registration for women seeking help for medical, juridical, social and other problems.

These two forms of policies may very well turn out to be complementary. Support groups and the lack of police persecution and public stigmatization may contribute to the creation of trust between prostitutes and specific people and society at large, including the juridical system and the police. Some degree of trust is vital if women who work as prostitutes are going to bring charges against traffickers.

The principal aim of a more humane policy should be to contribute to a less exploitative world order and to make the plight of prostitutes, including migrant prostitutes, less taxing.

NOTE

1. 'Traffickers' are the organizers of travel, papers and jobs for migrants. They are paid after arrival, usually from the trafficked people's earnings. 'Smugglers' organize only travel, and sometimes papers, and are paid in advance.

REFERENCES

Bauman, Z. (1996) 'From Pilgrim to Tourist or a Short History of Identity', in S. Hall and P. du Gay (eds), *Identity* (London: Sage).

Enloe, C. (1989) *Bananas, Beachers, Bases* (London: Pandora).

European Commission (1995) *The Ministerial Conference's Guidelines on Proposals for a New Treaty on Trafficking in Women with the Purpose of Sexual Exploitation* (The Hague: EC).

Kempadoo, K. and J. Doezema (1998) *Global Sex-workers: Rights, Resistance and Redefinition* (New York: Routledge).

Lim, L. L. (1998) *The Sex Sector. The Economic and Social Bases of Prostitution in Southeast Asia* (Geneva: ILO).

Mogensen, M. (2001) Lecture, Centre for Holocaust and Genocide Studies (Copenhagen).

O'Connell Davidson, J. (1998) *Prostitution, Power and Freedom* (London: Polity).

Skrobanek, S. et al. (1997) *The Traffic in Women – Human Realities in the International Sex Trade* (London: Zed Books).

PART ONE

Men in Prostitution

ONE

Travellers' Tails: Sex Diaries of Tourists Returning from Thailand

RYAN BISHOP AND LILLIAN S. ROBINSON

§ From the clipboard to the chatroom to the bulletin board, the meta-language of electronic communication has adapted – indeed, appropriated – its terminology from a wide range of other media. As rapidity of communication, interactive capability and hypertextualization become features of the phenomenon, use of the reverse-formation 'snail-mail' to specify what used to be known simply as 'mail' suggests a massive, even a revolutionary shift, one with the power to transform what is meant by 'reading' and 'writing'. At the same time, the content carried by these new modalities frequently turns out to be all too familiar and conservative, as technological development outstrips real social change at each stage.

This contradiction is nowhere so apparent as in the various forms of sexual communication that the Internet makes possible. On the one hand, both sexual discourse and sexual acts have been redefined by the institutionalization of virtual sex talk and virtual sex acts. Not only can the Net make 'writing' and 'reading' signify different experiences, but it also has the capacity to create new definitions of every sexual event from flirtation to intercourse and orgy. Yet, for many users, the post-modern medium is little more than a means of electronically globalizing such reactionary sites of sexual discourse as the wall in the men's toilet, the locker room, and the bridegroom's stag party, sometimes without so much as the most perfunctory recourse to the Net's interactive potential.

The World Sex Guide's rubric 'Prostitution by Country' thus makes it possible for men, mostly white residents of Europe, North America and the Antipodes, to share information and stories about commercial sex without making any use of the new sexual institutions created by the technology, much less challenging the traditional ways that these men imagine, experience and represent sexuality, starting with their own.

For most of the countries represented on the World Sex Guide website, the entries are rather perfunctory: information, often provided by local men, about the legal status of prostitution, the age of consent, current prices for various acts, and, perhaps, an indication of what sex-workers in that country typically refuse to do for any amount of money. Locations of the red-light districts in the major cities and addresses of professionals providing specialized services complete the entry. If there is any interaction, it takes the form of updating or 'correction' of this information, with personal accounts limited to remarks such as 'I went to that street and there was nothing happening [or the girls were ugly or too expensive], but I got lucky a few blocks over, on … '

Whereas almost all the other listings occupy a few pages each, 'Thailand' goes on for hundreds of pages, some of them devoted to commentary from people who take a critical position towards the Thai sex industry. Most of the verbiage, however, comes from returning sex-tourists who make use of the Net to share their experiences. As we indicated in our book, *Night Market: Sexual Cultures and the Thai Economic Miracle* (1998), tourism to Thailand, motivated largely by the sex industry, brings in more than $4 billion a year to the national economy. Millions of travellers, 70 per cent of them men travelling alone, arrive in Thailand annually to purchase at bargain rates the sexual services of teenage workers from historically poor regions of the king-dom, regions that have been further impoverished in recent decades by deliberate national policies influenced by the demands of international planning and lending agencies. In lieu of the customary holiday slides and home movies, many of these returning tourists extend and relive their vacations by logging on to the Net and producing texts.[1]

These texts fall into three categories, echoing familiar genres in the non-virtual world: the travel guide, the etiquette book, and the diary. Although there is an increasing self-reflexiveness about *being* on the Net and even about having learned from reading about it beforehand what to expect in Thailand, these documents follow certain conventions without otherwise responding to what anyone else has written. The guidebooks supplement the ones that talk about temples, palaces, hotels and restaurants by providing a *vade mecum* to the brothels, go-go bars and massage parlours. One of them even creates a map of the sex districts

using dots on a grid. Naturally, as with any other guide, these emphasize
the best (literal) bang for the buck and are larded with warnings about
how to avoid being exploited while engaged in the act of exploitation.
In keeping with the conventions of the genre, they neglect the existence
of similar documents on the Web; but, whereas there is a commercial
motive for one standard published guidebook to ignore the others, here,
where the information is provided gratis, apparent unawareness of the
others is a reflection of the isolation and alienation that characterize
these customers' approach to the sex industry and to sex itself.

The documents we have called 'etiquette' guides rarely mention
specific names and addresses, confining themselves to descriptions of
the way 'you' should negotiate transactions in the different sex venues.
'Sex in Thailand: The Basics', posted 23 August 1994, after explaining
how best to get laid in Thailand and stressing the mutuality of the
relationship in which each partner has something to give that the other
desires, concludes by revealing the limits of this reciprocity:

> Almost without exception in my experience, these girls are very, very
> good at what they do. That said, it would be well to remember that what
> these girls 'do,' each for their own reasons, is not what they are ... [I]f
> you never cease to remember that they are, before anything else, human
> beings with human feelings, chances are good you'll truly enjoy yourself,
> and you will have made her life, for a moment ... *not as completely
> horrible as it might have been.* (emphasis added)[2]

The most extensive genre in the Thailand section, however, is the
travel diary or journal, with its obsessive orientation towards explicit
descriptions of the conjoined sexual and monetary minutiae of each
transaction. From the amount paid for ground transportation into town
after landing in Thailand, there is a price tag on every experience
described and, since the diaries gloss over any daytime sightseeing with
some terse phrase like 'mostly temples', that means a price-tag on every
suck, stroke and fuck, each of them characterized as a great bargain, a
waste of money, or a splurge that paid off big-time.

Once the invariable economic framework is established, the material
connections become even more revealing. One correspondent, not a
native speaker of English, complains in his July 1995 posting about a
'dumb' masseuse who didn't know she was supposed to massage muscles,
not bones. When the couple get into bed, she's also a dud in the blowjob

department, because *he* can't get an erection. He observes, 'I thought about helping her with thinking at something REALLY nice, but then I thought, "what for do I pay?"' She is supposed to do all the work, after all, so why should he participate in his own arousal, which is to say, be part of his own sexuality, even to the extent of conjuring up an erotic fantasy?

This is a mentality that leads to narratives in which, as in one posting, dated 27 March 1995, the loss of a credit card and the wait for its replacement becomes a suspense-enhancing motif and where romance is destroyed and 'heartbreak' ensues when a prostitute becomes 'greedy' – that is, when she tells the customer she has been seeing 'steadily' for several days that, according to her roommate, 1,000 baht, not 500 (at the time, $40, instead of the $20 he'd been paying), should be the price for an all-night session. He whines to the reader that he is really disappointed because he thought 'good-will' had been established and that 'she was different'.

This narrator shows rather more emotion, although hardly less self-righteousness, than the author of a long sexual travelogue dated 5 August 1997. Having failed at some half-hearted bargaining on his last night in Chiang Mai, he is 'too tired to care', but is pursued by a girl who wants to go back to his hotel:

> Not thinking straight in my fatigue, I bring her back without agreeing to any terms. We're both naked on my bed, she a darker skinned one with her pussy shaved, when she brings up wanting an exorbitant amount with an early hour leave. Not caring for the *change in her personality*, decide to abort this one, dress, and tell her to leave now. I manage to keep the situation fairly cool, choosing to just quietly sit in a chair until she gets the message, and am rid of her *without violence and at a cost of only 390 baht*. I breath [sic] a sigh of relief after closing the door behind her and go to bed. (emphasis added)[3]

It is only fitting, in such a context, that a lengthy diary posting, dated 19 September 1996, bears the heading, in lieu of a title, 'The following is a true account of my trip to Thailand; Note: $1 = 25 Baht'. And that the ultimate experience is getting something for nothing.

The 'freebie', however, is the exception, in these accounts, rather than the rule, and, more often, the narratives provide not only extensive information about money and quantified descriptions of sexual activity, but a sense of never relaxing one's guard against the possibility of being overcharged or even robbed. Whence the wonderful typo from another non-native speaker, writing about a December 1996 trip, who explains that, not having shared a bed with anyone for a long time, he had trouble sleeping after his first sexual contact on arrival and, besides, 'I ... did not thrust her very much'.

More recent postings tend to reflect some minimal awareness about the way the commercial nature of the interaction informs the experience. Thus, while the narrator who helpfully provides the exchange rate in lieu of an epigraph crows over how many orgasms he gives the women, making it clear that the illusion of so doing is what arouses him, the December '96 tourist says things like:

> I tipped her 200 Baht, because she made me a lot of compliments about my style of fucking her. She said she enjoyed it etc. (a lot of lies but who cares) ...
>
> It's all acting there is no real love in return for money. If you believe in it you are a fool. All they think of is money ...
>
> This might be the ultimate freedom for some people for the other it was the ultimate immorality and perversion. I enjoyed it since everything [sic] could have what they wanted without interfering with others.

Recent correspondents also reflect some consciousness of the medium itself. Although there is no acknowledgement that his own story is virtually identical to all the others, this last narrator even includes the fact of updating his diary in the account of the day-by-day (not to say blow-by-blow) events, a self-reflexivity that gives new meaning to Samuel Pepys's recurrent 'and so to bed'. Indeed, on 25 February 1998, a diary begins:

> I owe the WSG for helping lay the groundwork for a great vacation and lots of help on numerous business trips so I felt that it was time for my own post. This is an update of information on Thailand. I will not repeat the volumes of detail already available on the WSG on Thailand, this is just to provide an update as of February 21, 1998. This was my first trip to Thailand and because of the WSG I was able to make the most of every minute.

Although, as promised, this narrator spares us some of the detail, his entry is still substantial because it blurs the otherwise discrete Internet genres of travel guide and etiquette book into that of diary, deploying, in the process, a certain limited use of the second-person point of view in acknowledgement of the reader's presence (albeit both temporary and virtual) within the space of his personal sexual narration.

Paralleling the economic confessionals that make up the 'Prostitution by Country' entries for Thailand is an apparently newer site called the 'Banker's World Sex Guide', accessed by substituting dot com for dot org after worldsexsguide and following the electronic trail to Thailand. Here, although each posting, called a 'Travel Report', is brief, most occupying only a single paragraph, it, too, combines the functions of diary and guidebook, with recommendations for 'you' on 'your' own trip. Thus, a correspondent with the seemingly inappropriate moniker 'Cranky' writes on 8 July 1998 that he went

> 'out back' with a transsexual prostitute on Kho Samui and was given a fantastic blow-job for the equivalent of US$5. Another wanted to come back to our hotel with my wife and I [sic] and we were sorely tempted as this one, though beautiful, still had a dick and was happy with men or women. It was the trip of a lifetime and I would recommend it to anyone. I will definitely be returning there.

'Darklord' introduces an action-packed report on a Pattaya massage parlour by announcing, 'I went to Thailand on [sic] June 1998 with a few of my friends. I had a great time in Pattaya and I wish to share that wonderful experience with you and hope you get that wonderful treatment.' But on that same day, 22 June, 'The Whole Shebang' turns melancholy at the end, explaining, 'The whole session did not last the promised one and a half hour. 60 minutes at the most. Which suited me quite fine. I left the place with the usual mixed feelings: happy for having been with one more woman, unsettled by her cheat and her ill-concealed hatred.' 'Stranger in the Night' describes his climax this way:

> ... [W]e arrived in due time at the right thing, a good lengthy orgasm inside her body. Paun, elf girl of the tropical night, let me come thoroughly, her fine face turned towards mine, half covered with streams of thick jet black hair, eyes closed in beautiful imitation of sensual ecstasy while her belly performed the slow motion pumping moves that drew out every sparkle of electricity from glowing nerve threads.

Then, in a move not replicated, as far as we know, anywhere in this genre, he apostrophizes the sex-worker: 'Thank you, Paun! In spite of your ability to extract much more money than negotiated from this farang, I do not regret having met you'.

Why do these men feel compelled to write about their experiences? What drives them to articulate their movements and acts, the costs and benefits, the frustrations and pleasures? To do so in such a public but also anonymous forum? To do so in such excruciating detail? To do so in such a monologic manner? Perhaps the notion of totalizing alienation that we formulated in the concluding chapter of *Night Market* can help explain these public/private declarations and make sense of their distinctive discursive traits.

The commercial sex encounter that occurs under the purview of international sex tourism is a completely alienating experience, in both material and psychological senses of the term. For the sex-worker, the work itself is alienated labour in the material sense, in that its value is appropriated, and also in the emotional sense, in that it is separated from and causing separation from authentic feelings, giving rise to isolation and revulsion.

These postings make clear that the customers' own fetishized mentality often causes them to experience the transaction as alienated as well. The constant praise or derision of the purchased product *as* a product reveals this point, especially since the quality fluctuates dramatically according to cost and perceived economic value. Similarly, when the customer's experience is good, the sex-worker is described with a synecdoche: 'the tightest pussy', 'the fullest lips', 'the most pert breasts' and so on. But when the client's experience does not satisfy, then the worker-qua-worker is to blame: her whole being is conflated with her job performance and is at fault due to incompetence, inattention or greed. The slippage, of course, is that the customer's discourse always already constitutes the worker metaphorically, either as synecdoche in the first instance or metonymy in the second. Either way, no fully human sex-worker exists for the client. Marx and Engels neatly articulated this slippage as emerging from different relations to and comfort levels with alienation itself:

The property-owning class and the class of the proletariat represent the same human self-alienation. But the former feels at home in this self-alienation and feels itself confirmed by it; it recognises alienation as its own instrument and in it possesses the semblance of a human existence. The latter feels itself destroyed by this alienation and sees in it its own impotence and the reality of an inhuman existence.[4]

Although the most blatant and prevalent characteristic in these documents is the constant, unsurprising linkage between money and sex, with the invocation of one being essentially an invocation of the other, no simple substitution is at work here, nor is there even a clear analogy of money for sex or vice versa. Instead, a more complicated connection between the two occurs and is implicated in the discursive practices of the Web itself – its representation of itself and how it functions on the techno-cusp of the new millennium.

On the Net, talk is ever-abundant, ever-pervasive and ever-in-process. But despite its democratic and utopian proclamations, discourse on the Net is also ever-unidirectional, ever the domain of the privileged, ever-self-referential, and ever-emanating from the dominant subject position. The 'you' addressed in the various etiquette guides is really only the 'I' entering the piece on his keyboard. No substantial differences exist between the self who is writing and the other who is reading. Even if the 'I' is showing off for an imagined reader – showing off in terms of knowledge or experience – the reader is simply a version of the authorial 'I' in homunculus. All of the I's assumptions about the self-in-the-world and how the world works are projected on to any 'other' who might read the posting, which is hardly the self/other or I/thou relationship envisioned by Buber or Levinas.

That only a very few of these many postings ever refer to any of the others clearly reflects the self-contained, solipsistic and masturbatory (in that it is non-interactive) nature of discourse on the Web – again contrary to the claims it makes for itself. Although, as the massive repetition in form, content and organization among the pieces reveals, each author has read the other postings, the marked lack of reference to the writing of others (especially others so like the authorial self) is at once baffling and enlightening; it reveals the deep deception operating in cyberspace's co-optation of the liberal ideals of democracy, free choice, free will, autonomous actors, free markets and self-fulfilment that characterize our *fin-de-siècle* world of transnational capital and global marketplaces. Despite being so much about the self, these postings reveal a profound lack of self-awareness. In this twenty-four-hour-a-day, convenience-store world of sex chatter, sex shopping and private monologue lobbing, the yobs fingering the keyboard seem unaware of the systems that create the even-larger net that ensnares their comfortable Net. The magnetic pull of tourist to tourist site, of sex-worker to client, of supply to meet demand, and of specific modes of desire to specific types of satiation may be more programmed all the way around than the side of the ledger espousing freedom and autonomy would admit. (The authors have, after all, used their 'free' time from work to enter this information of their own 'free' will to be disseminated 'free' for the greater good of all.) The locus of the Net is clearly one that emanates from their dominant subject position, which like all dominant subject positions gets cast as progressive, liberating, commonsense, unquestioned, natural, logical and unmarked. And the Web functions in their world in this way.

Consider, for example, the author who rushes from a plane to a red-light district at three in the morning to enact immediately what he had read on the Net, and, having found a girl who wanted 1,000 baht for the whole night, gave her 750 rather than the 500 she would have taken because he is 'not a cheap bastard'. When the sex-worker expresses disbelief when he claims that he has never been in the bars before (a cynical claim made by sex patrons and just as cynically dismissed by sex-workers), he follows by saying, 'Of course there was no point in telling her about the Internet etc.' His own sense of being at home in electronic transactions could be gleaned from his reading of these postings, but his application of virtual reality to peopled reality is something he assumes is clearly beyond the prostitute's ken. His electronic world of openness, free flow of information, democracy, unfettered dialogue and so on is one that he is sure the sex-worker he hired could not even begin to conceptualize.

Not only does the Net allow one to move between sites, it also allows one to achieve movement without moving (a version of royal omnipotence past) and it does so by concealing the various global economic and labour-driven systems required for all this liberation of the dominant subject to manifest itself. These authors perch behind their glowing screens and hurl their missives into the cybervoid without considering the consequences of their behaviour or language practices. Writing itself becomes one more in a series of actions whose consequences and effects occur conveniently and tidily elsewhere. The global market and technology take care of that, not unlike the video confirmation of a missile striking a target in our post-Gulf War military moment. And not unlike any purchase made on the free market, whether it is a sex-worker's time and labour or the oil for the electricity necessary to keep the Net from vanishing in the click of a mouse, the causes leading to the purchase, as well its effects, are hidden from the consumer/ author who readily participates in its concealment.

Thus, the financial crisis in Southeast Asia that has wrecked national economies and left hundreds of thousands starving, with millions more teetering on the brink of abject poverty, merely translates for the Internet diarists into making Thailand an even better bargain for the sex-shopper. For them, the devaluation of the baht means only cheaper goods and a greater array of choice as more and more people are forced into this portion of the service sector. A posting dated February 1998 makes the point abundantly clear when the author discusses his trip's cost as amounting to only a third of what he'd originally planned: 'Because of the devaluation of the baht ($1 = baht 45) this turned out to be a very cheap vacation. I spent half of the money that I budgeted to spend, and I was not especially trying to save money as I went.'

Heightening the all-inclusive alienation, the author who calls himself 'The Whole Shebang' seems confused about the 'ill-concealed hatred' of the sex-worker who bargained for more money and reduced his contact time with her. The interactive potential of the Internet may emerge in a post-colonial moment and institutions, but it is by no means post-imperial in its material manifestations.

Stephen Tyler has argued that the Internet is the next logical application of the Cartesian grid: the presumed triumph of mind over body and space over time, as well as the separation of the knowing subject from knowledge.[5] In this grid, all thoughts and things can dwell in a space free of human intervention or contact. The Net likes to characterize itself as just such a repository, and its admirers like to invoke these Enlightenment claims of liberation. For all its forward thinking and claims to staking out whole new frontiers, the tropes and ideals that drive the Net's claims to legitimacy and hegemony are the same ones that have driven manifold western desires for several centuries. So the joys of morphing and virtual identity formations can materialize as sending one's dick on vacation by itself. And the disembodied pleasures of the grid can, and in fact do, result in fully bodied violence of the totalizing alienation experienced by sex-workers and clients alike.

NOTES

1. Our collaborative study, *Night Market: Sexual Cultures and the Thai Economic Miracle* (New York and London: Routledge, 1998) discusses some examples of the sex diaries. This extended look at the genre was originally prepared for the session 'Postmodern Site, Prose Medium: Money, Sex, and Gender on the Internet', sponsored by the Division on Non-Fiction Prose at the Modern Language Association's December 1998 annual meeting in San Francisco. It was also presented by Robinson as a keynote paper at the 1999 conference, 'Prostitution in a Global Context – Intertwined Histories, Present Realities', at Aalborg University, Denmark.

2. These diaries may be accessed at www.worldsexguide.org and thence following the cues to the rubric 'Prostitution by Country: Thailand'. We provide dates for all postings quoted, but material is periodically removed from the site and may not still be there for readers to follow up.

3. This and the other citations from the later 1990s come from the alternative site mentioned later in the article, the Banker's World Sex Guide: www. worldsexguide.com

4. Karl Marx and Friedrich Engels, *The Holy Family or Critique of Cultural Critique* (1844), Chapter 4, as cited in Georg Lukács, *History and Class Consciousness: Studies in Marxist Dialectics*, trans. Rodney Livingstone (Cambridge, MA: MIT Press, 1971). This version is less awkward than the standard translation by R. Dixon (Moscow: Foreign Languages Publishing House, 1956). We are grateful to Gerald P. Kavanagh, III, for calling this line and Lukács' version of it to our attention.

5. Stephen A. Tyler, 'Vile Bodies: A Mental Machination', presented at the conference 'The Body in Knowledge', University of Amsterdam, June 1993.

TWO

The European Inheritance: Male Perspectives

SUSANNE THORBEK

§ This chapter explores male views of prostitutes. I shall concentrate on the European experience, especially on the modernists, those men who, in the period around 1900 and especially in Vienna and Paris, believed in science and (some) progress. My findings are that they constructed the idea of prostitution by combining the concepts or stereotypes they inherited or developed around gender, class and race. I shall compare these views with the perspectives that foreign customers have of prostitutes today, as expressed in recent studies of sex-tourists in Thailand. These men's experiences are partly expressed in the idioms of the modernists.

At the turn of the last century, the structural arrangements that framed these views were colonialism and the debates on slavery. These structures have changed and I have taken the new structures of globalization into account. The chapter ends with some speculation about the social changes that have led to an increased demand for paid sex and the interest in money that the customers express.

MODERNISTS' DEFERENCE AND FASCINATION

The following gives some examples of science, art and literature in the world of the modernists.

Race In his work *Difference and Pathology*, Sander L. Gilman (1985) analysed the modernists' beliefs about science and their perspectives on gender, race, class and prostitution, especially in Vienna and Paris, in the second half of the nineteenth century; and in an article written with

Nancy Leys Stepan, he analysed the criticism of scientific racism (Leys Stepan and Gilman 1993). Scientific racism with its measurements and biological reductionism was created in the late nineteenth century. The scientific paper with its empirical material, its conclusions on this basis, and its eradication of all religious and moral arguments became a major form of communication. Scientific racism gained importance in the years after the prohibition of slavery, during the expansion of empire-building.

When scientific racism is seen through our eyes, its most obvious flaws are the weak empirical bases for its conclusions, its biological reductionism and the absence of any moral or political considerations. It led to a belief in the mental and moral superiority of whites, to evolutionary thinking and essentialist perspectives. Contemporary critiques of this sort of science came *only* from Jewish and black scientists, some of them hospital doctors, who could provide much more convincing statistics. None of the criticism came from white scientists. Scientific racism allied itself with Darwin by extending his theory of evolution to the social behaviour of human beings. Scientific racism was officially rejected only in the early 1930s.

Essential to this science was Saartje Baartman, a young woman from South Africa, exhibited in Europe in the first part of the nineteenth century. Later, and until very recently, her dissected body was exhibited in the Musée de l'Homme in Paris. The result was an image of black women with protruding buttocks, somewhat fat, and with an over-developed clitoris and genitals. The anomaly of black women's sexuality and their bodily signs was taken seriously by Havelock Ellis in *Studies in the Psychology of Sex* (1905) and by Darwin (1871). It was generally believed that the childish or animal-like sexuality of black women, and potentially all women, could be deduced from the shape of their genitals and the rest of their bodies. On the basis of such descriptions, black women were supposed to have a wild, untamed and, in some accounts, naturally uninhibited sexuality; they were also promiscuous.

Gender and Sex In a sense, this fitted in nicely with the general view of women as presented in Sigmund Freud's analysis. In *Three Essays on the Theory of Sexuality* he wrote:

In this respect children behave in the same way as an average un-cultivated woman in whom the same polymorphous perverse disposition persists. Under ordinary conditions she may remain normal sexually, but if a clever seducer leads her on, she will find every sort of perversion to her taste and will retain them as part of her own sexual activities. Prostitutes exploit the same polymorphous, that is, infantile disposition for the purpose of their profession; and considering the immense number of women who are prostitutes or who must be supposed to have an aptitude for prostitution without being engaged in it, it becomes impossible not to recognize that this disposition to perversion of every kind is a general and fundamental human characteristic. (quoted in Gilman 1985: 38)

Freud saw such sexual traits as being present in all women, at least potentially. In reality, of course, education and class were major dividing lines. For Lombroso, on the other hand, there were two kinds of women: the Madonna and the whore.

A later analysis of Freud's private correspondence with his friend Wilhelm Fliess, in which he developed the Oedipus theory on the basis of an analysis of his dreams, shows that Freud's dreams were neither about his mother nor his father, but about a servant in the house. He wrote: 'My prime originator was an ugly elderly but clever woman. She was the first to raise (me) up and the first to humiliate me as clumsy' (Swan 1974; quoted from McClintock 1995: 87). Thus sexuality became a sign of class and, potentially, gender as well.

Prostitution and blacks   These notions were clearly combined in the study of prostitutes. Best known is probably the work of Lombroso (1893), who showed that the bodily characteristics of prostitutes were their facial features, fatness and protruding buttocks. Parent-Duchachelet (1836) showed how tumours and abscesses made their labia thicker. These features, as Gilman (1985) argued, are remarkably similar to the early image of the so-called Hottentot, Saartje Baartman.

In the art of the period, illicit sexuality was signalled through black servants. Manet's (1832–82) painting called 'Olympia' created a scandal. It showed a naked woman on a bed, looking directly at the observer. In the background a black female servant can be seen with flowers in her hands and wearing a headscarf. At the time of the painting (1865), this was interpreted in the usual way – she is a 'primitive' black, a symbol of illicit sexuality, an interpretation still maintained by, among others,

Gilman (1985). However, this is open to question. Pollock (1999) points out that the black woman is painted as a Parisian servant, wearing, as did most servants at the time, second-hand clothes. The headscarf is not painted in the bright contrasting colours that indicate 'primitiveness' but in gentle colours. So to a degree Manet may have been attempting to break with the common view of blacks as sexually uninhibited primitives.

This seems, however, not to have been the case in an earlier painting by Manet ('Nana', 1877) in which a white prostitute is fat and has protruding buttocks. The painting was inspired by a minor character in a novel by Emile Zola. According to Gilman (1985), Zola saw the painting in Manet's studio and decided to write a novel about its subject, which he also called *Nana* (1880). Since then *Nana* has become a colloquial term in France. A biographer and translator of Zola, George Holden, argued that the book (and earlier titles in the Rougon-Macquart sequence) is an exploration of the question of inheritance contra environment. Emile Zola had high expectations that science could create a better life for people, and thought that literature might do the same. Zola summarized *Nana* as follows: 'A whole society hurling itself at the cunt. A pack of hounds after a bitch, who is not even on heat and makes fun of the hounds following her. The poem of male desire' (Holden 1972: 11).

Questions of race and gender are to the fore in the novel. It begins with Nana, who is an actor, throwing a party; rumour has it that six naked male Negroes are to serve the food. More important, though, is the question of male lust; rich men and descendants of the nobility ruin themselves in order to fulfil her whims.

> She had finished her labor of ruin and death. The fly that had come from the dunghill of the slums, carrying the ferment of social decay, had poisoned all these men simply by alighting on them. It was fitting and just. She had avenged the beggars and outcasts of the world and while, as it were, her sex rose in a halo of glory and blazed down on her prostrate victims like a rising sun shining down on a field of carnage, she remained as unconscious of her actions as a splendid animal, ignorant of the havoc she had wreaked and as good-natured as ever. (Zola 1972)

In this masculine view of a prostitute (or a woman), the metaphor of the animal is paramount. Throughout the novel the men are animals too, but on her initiative. She extracts a large amount of money from men and in this sense, too, destroys them. Not only does *Nana* portray the destructive influence of a woman from the slums who is attractive to men from the finest families, but it also shows the destructive power of wealth and male lust. The riches they heap on Nana, her demands and the degradation they create for each other are without limits in Zola's eyes.

The Orientalist or racist perspective of Europe is thus old and well known. More remarkable is the race, class and sex (gender) construction of the modernist reformer's views. They prolonged the older concepts but also changed them by giving them scientific respectability.

The prostitute becomes a point of intersection of the concepts of women, of female sexuality, of race(s) and of class. She is the image of the sexualization and racialization of women, of colonial people, and of working-class people.

Zola shares these ideas of prostitutes as childish, animal-like and whimsical, but his novel is also about men's lust which leads to degradation and the destruction of society. In the last passages of *Nana*, her death from smallpox is described by Zola as a parallel to the war, which men entered singing.

Colonial history In the colonies of European countries the questions of race, class and gender were as urgent as in the metropoles. These concepts, ideas and stereotypes were not developed only in the metropoles and exported to the colonies, however, but arose in both places and influenced each other. A.B. King (1991) has even argued that the colonial cities were rather forerunners of the modernity that developed later in the metropoles, or laboratories of modernity.

In a theoretical work on Foucault (1988), Ann Laura Stoler (1995) has argued that sexuality or the education of desire became a main dividing line not only for class, but for race too. In one line of colonial historical thinking, the colonies have marked a place beyond the inhibitions or the bourgeois culture of Europe. 'In this repressive model of history the colonies were sites of unfettered economic and sexual opportunity where masculine self-indulgence could be given free vent' (Stoler 1995: 5).

Stoler, however, also showed how vulnerable the ideas of class, race and gender were in the colonies. They might work when the differences between colonists and colonized were clearly defined but they might not. Educated men or men with good businesses in the colonies raised demands for political rights and citizenship. A great number of white men had legitimate or illegitimate offspring with colonized women. The way in which these children were to be classified raised a problem: were they white like their fathers, or were women more important in influencing the identity of their children? Such ways of thinking involved breaking with stereotypes of race and gender.

Stoler showed how fear of degeneracy and ideas of white supremacy were challenged by these developments. This was also true of the poor whites, who often lived more like the indigenous populations. In the years 1900 to 1920, biological racism could not account for these groups and in debates and eventually in legislation other dimensions came to the fore: cultural racism was developed in (what is now) Indonesia, in Vietnam and less so in the British colonies.

At different points in time, and sometimes with different arguments, a consensus in thought, legislation and political measures was created. The management of sexuality, parenting and morality was at the heart of the late imperial project. 'Cohabitation, prostitution, and legally recognised mixed marriages slotted women, men, and their progeny differently in the social and moral landscape of the colonised society. These sexual contracts were buttressed by pedagogic, medical, and legal evaluations that shaped the boundaries of European membership and the interior frontiers of the colonial state' (Stoler 1995: 226). Biological differences as created by imperial ideas were still in force, but became increasingly difficult to maintain. Arguments based on cultural (and climatic) differences took over and became increasingly important: laziness, sloppiness, loose sexual behaviour, poor upbringing of children, lack of language and education and the like. All the above are still prevalent in Europe and the USA today.

Gender was important in the sense that a tighter control of women's sexuality and desires was demanded, and became so important that legal and political standards depended on it. Marriage or cohabitation with a colonized or mixed-race man meant that a woman lacked any sense of nation or civilization, whereas men held on to their nationality/race, sometimes conferring it on their mixed-race children, depending on the child's education, the father's feelings, and so on. The idea of male middle-class superiority was thus kept intact even when biological concepts of race had to be disavowed and a cultural concept established.

CONDITIONS FOR INTERNATIONAL PROSTITUTION TODAY

The conditions for prostitution across borders have changed a great deal over the last hundred years. We are now talking about independent countries, at least in principle, and a great part of international prostitution today is tourist-related or related to military staff abroad, to large male workplaces and to migrant labour.

Globalization is, of course, an important factor. It entails new forms of international relations with open financial markets, more television and other means of communication, migration between countries and, to a lesser degree, between continents, as well as increased business across borders. If other kinds of business turn global, why not prostitution?

A new language, or perhaps not so new, has been developed in recent history. Today, only a few people speak openly of the superiority of particular races, classes or gender. If they do they are careful to explain such superiority or inferiority in terms of culture, not biology, which is what Stoler has termed cultural racism. However, in the field of development discourse, important influences of global relations on international prostitution can be detected. In *Sex, Money and Morality* (1990), Thandam Truong has shown how the tourist industry was developed after the Second World War in part as a response to the falling demand for American aircraft. In the development industry, tourism has been seen as a major possibility for economic growth. This strategy has been criticized by many authors for not providing much in terms of foreign currency, since nearly everything consumed by tourists is owned or controlled by foreign companies, from aircraft to whisky. Prostitution, which has increased in conjunction with the increase in tourism, may be one of the few indigenous businesses involved. Perhaps more important in mainstream development research, no one has discussed the prostitution which has followed tourism – it has become a 'non-topic'.

Development policies in the last twenty or thirty years have, however, had another important role to play. One main drive has been to get women into the market: to make them take jobs, never mind how low paid, to make them sell their work on the market, thus eroding subsistence production,to make them take loans and so on. However, quite a few women have little to sell besides their bodies. These policies may very well be part of the explanation why an increasing number of women have turned to prostitution.

At bottom, of course, is the structuring of the global labour market. People in the Third World generally, especially if they have little education, earn much less than people in Europe, America and elsewhere. And women everywhere earn less than men. To use Judith Walkowitz's comment about society in Victorian England: 'There is perhaps no more telling commentary to the exploitative character of Victorian society than the fact that some working women regarded prostitution as the best in a series of unattractive alternatives' (Walkowitz 1980: 31).

MALE CUSTOMERS' PERCEPTIONS OF THAI PROSTITUTES TODAY

The male customers' view of Thai prostitutes today has some similarities with the European modernist view around 1900. It is hard to find out exactly how much has changed, and I will leave it partly to the reader to draw conclusions.

The views of sex-tourists to Thailand have been examined in, among others, the following works: *Hello My Big Honey!* (Walker and Ehrlich 1992), a selection of letters written by customers to Thai prostitutes (and interviews with the Thai prostitutes, most of whom have a poor grasp of English); *Travels in the Skin Trade* (Seabrook 1996), a book of interviews with (mostly) long-term travellers to Thailand; and *The Night Market* (Bishop and Robinson 1998), a discussion of foreigners who buy prostitutes in Thailand. Davidson and Taylor (1994) have written a series of booklets analysing prostitution in different countries, mainly child prostitution. Their seventh booklet, *Sex Tourism, Thailand*, is about British customers in Pattaya.[1]

Both *Hello My Big Honey!* and *Travels in the Skin Trade* focus on tourists who have a long association with Thailand, either because they have visited several times or because they have moved there. The majority of sex-tourists or travellers – one-time visitors going for the fucking – are underrepresented in these books. Perhaps the variety of experiences can be illustrated by one or two examples.

In *Travels in the Skin Trade* we find an older man who explains: 'I don't know what will happen. I'm not a pessimist, but Loi is 25 years younger than I am ... But Loi is the best thing that ever happened to me. I miss my children of course; but I've found something that has made life a thousand times better than I ever thought it could be'

(Seabrook 1996: 20). Another, more common, relationship is one in which an older white man now and again sends small sums of money to a much younger Thai woman, and writes to her, advising her to stop going to the bar, expresses his fear of AIDS and promises money in the future; such men are both stingy and patronizing, deliberately refusing to acknowledge the reality of the women's lives. These letters also reveal the men's loneliness.

Seabrook (1996) also presents a man from Germany with a Thai wife whom he sent to work in the streets of Hamburg. Eventually, she escaped from him but he then set out to find another woman to work for him.

The Night Market (Bishop and Robinson 1998) looks at the men who go to Thailand apparently just to fuck. Bishop finds himself a guide to the bar-scene who stresses the many opportunities for blowjobs or quick fucks. Likewise, the Internet reports discuss blowjobs, and various types of encounter with Thai prostitutes, all the while weighing the pleasure against the price. Here there are no romantic affairs, and no humanity, not even fantasies in the minds of the travellers (see Bishop and Robinson in this volume).

Echoing Zola's novel *Nana*, a sex-tourist describes his relationship with a Thai prostitute as follows: 'For the first few months I was in a kind of fever ... If I'd been at home I would never have caught fire like I did' (Seabrook 1996: 35). Most of the interviewees in Seabrook's book, however, are concerned with how women cheat and ruin men. For instance: 'You don't realise in the beginning. In fact as long as we had money everything was fine. She sure could spend it' (Seabrook 1996: 24). This man recounts how he bought a Thai prostitute a house and a car, but she sold or mortgaged them. Then, when he wanted to retire, she left him. Complaints range from the story of a woman who asked for more money for a one-night stand, to complaints about more costly losses:

> In Thailand money is the big aphrodisiac ... I've often thought about it in the bars. Some of the blokes are repulsive, old, fat, ugly. Yet these women gaze into their eyes, pat their pot belly, caress their baldness, as though this is what they really want ... I want to know what they would make of me if I had nothing. (Seabrook 1996: 21)

These customers reveal a quite astonishing attitude towards prostitution. They go out to buy love. They search bars and hotels, and when they realize that the women really are working for money, that love is not that easily bought, they become depressed and frustrated. The feeling that they have been cheated is, in some cases, extended to include all women in Thailand; sometimes the feeling is generalized to cover the entire population: 'They are a treacherous lot. Don't believe a word they tell you and you may survive, but I wouldn't bank on it. They're good at acting. Don't get involved. They're arseholes' (Seabrook 1996: 22).

The customers in Thailand count their money immediately. Zola's men, however, seem to find that the more they pay the better the chances of a good relationship. Modern customers seem to count it a success to get a cheap fuck, blowjob or whatever; even better if they can get it for free. This becomes most clear in Bishop and Robinson's (1998) analysis of the Thai travellers' website:

> The obsession becomes a compulsion in the personal narratives. Since all the minutiae of the trip are recorded, the payment for ground trans-portation from the airport, hotel rooms, and souvenirs are often part of the account – but so is the price of each sexual encounter with details of the particular services purchased. At the height of ecstasy – experienced or recollected in virtuality – these guys remain aware of how much it costs and whether each ejaculation was a rip-off, a relative bargain, a wise investment, or a splurge that paid off a big time. (Bishop and Robinson 1998: 246)

Davidson and Taylor divide British sex-tourists to Pattaya into three groups: 'The Macho Lads, mostly relatively young. For these young men Pattaya is a kind of Macho theme park with beer, motorbikes, go-go bars, kick boxing, live sex shows, pool tables in English-style pubs and guaranteed access to dolly birds to posture and have sex' (Davidson and Taylor 1994: 2). The second group is made of men described as 'Mr Average', somewhat older, often married or divorced men who go to Pattaya on a package tour, often for singles. 'He prides himself on being an ordinary bloke and is mostly interested in simulating some kind of emotional or romantic affair with either one or a series of women' (Davidson and Taylor 1994: 3). The third group is made up of what the authors call 'Cosmopolitan Man'. These men deny that they are sex-tourists; they are really on business, or spending a few months on a Southeast Asian tour. They stay longer in Bangkok as well as in more remote places, and go to Pattaya only for a few days of relaxation. They are worldly wise and would (normally) never visit a prostitute.

The Internet customers and those who frequent the bar-scene could be characterized as 'Macho Lads', whereas the majority see themselves as 'Mr Average'. Of course, this classification was devised for Pattaya and may not cover the Bangkok scene. Nevertheless there is considerable overlapping.

THE WESTERN INHERITANCE: CONTINUITY AND CHANGE

In the first chapter of *Culture and Imperialism*, Edward W. Said reflected on the past and the present: 'The main idea is that even as we must fully comprehend the past-ness of the past, there is no just way in which the past can be guaranteed from the present. Past and present inform each other, each implies the other and each co-exists with the other' (Said 1994: 2).

Orientalist, even racist, views are expressed by the men quoted in the books mentioned earlier. For example:

Call me Simple if you like ... but that is my opinion. We have had to have emigration control in Britain, because all the scum of Asia would come flooding in if we didn't. When I come here I'm not taking anybody else's job away. If they come there they are. Then at the same time, they hold their hand out for anything that is going. (Seabrook 1996: 33)

Seabrook adds: 'In many of the wanderers of Asia there is a strong vein of imperialism.'

Bishop and Robinson (1998) have a whole chapter on imagining the sexual Other, in which they show how old European ideas or fantasies are repeated in modern texts. Furthermore, Davidson and Taylor stress British sex-tourists' disgust for and criticism of men of Arab, Japanese or Thai origin and their excitement about Thai prostitutes. All the men with whom they spoke stressed the cleanliness of the Thai women: 'They wash ... their neat and tidy appearance. Their scrupulously clean and manicured nails ... They are also held to be more affectionate, loyal, innocent, and natural than white women' (Davidson and Taylor 1994: 13). Thus, the authors deonstrate how fantasies of the exotic Other come into play.

[handwritten annotations in top margin: "Thai pros completely diff meaning for selling themselves! Eventually lead 35 2 marriage if a relaship is made with lust."]

It is clear to the customers that the availability of sexual satisfaction in Thailand is due to the poverty of the women involved and the relative wealth of the customers. The guide to the bar-scene expresses this quite clearly: 'You could never get this at home.' Yet the very cheapness of the sexual, and sometimes domestic and tourist guide, services that the customers are buying from Thai prostitutes is a continuous source of worry, alleviated by comparisons between white men and other men. Customers find relief in the fact that these young Thai women 'prefer' them, regardless of age or appearance.

> British sex tourists are convinced that, despite their own exotic charm and beauty, Thai women recognise the superiority of whites. Sex tourists continually assert that Thai women prefer white men ('white skin turns them on ... white men treat them better than Arabs and their own kind') and that Thai women would actually like to be white themselves. (Davidson and Taylor 1994: 14)

The combination of fascination and desire on the one hand and disgust on the other that the customers exhibit is characteristic of the discourse on racism between Us and the Other, as Hall and Bieben (1992) have shown. These split feelings are certainly visible. The disgust and/or deference shown by tourists towards Thai prostitutes, and towards Thai women in general, are the outcome of a combination of the different strands in the western heritage. Many customers have had unhappy marriages. Bishop and Robinson show the irritation of these men at white women's subjectivity. It is mostly when the Thai prostitutes, their kindness notwithstanding, start to talk about their own lives that relations start to break down. Or are customers disgusted by the poverty of the women? Their under-class position seems to legitimize nearly everything, although only the guide to the bar-scene and the Internet writers express this directly. It is often hidden behind a language of equal exchange and equal benefits. Or is it the different race and skin colour (or, in modern parlance, culture) of the women that is at the root of these reactions?

Customers' consciousness of the unequal economic relations between them and the women is clear. So too is the combination of admiration for natural, sexy, beautiful women and disgust for cunning, cheating women; Thai women are seen as both noble savages and inferior people. The men believe that women should be there for men to use for their pleasure. There are very few men who talk about the wishes and desires of the women.[2]

The prostitute became an idiom of class, race and sex differences for the modernists, and this seems to be true today. The Thai prostitutes, perhaps prostitutes in general, are still a point of condensation of the old ideas of gender, race and class.

GLOBALIZATION, MODERNITY AND THE SEX-TOURIST

We could thus argue that the old ideas about the Other – sexualized and racialized – are still in force, but important changes have occurred. Globalization and what is sometimes called a post- or late modern society are among them. By globalization I mean the new forms of international relations that have been characterized by the erosion of state power. This has happened more in some countries than in others; less, it seems, in the USA, and in Europe it has taken the form of the building of the European Union, itself an emerging state. This erosion of state power is concomitant with a less restricted market, preferably a global market, and the marketing of more and more areas of life.

Over the last forty years or so, what was formerly 'women's work' has become subject to the market: cleaning, food production, to a degree childcare, healthcare and the care of old people. Sexual relations seem to be the last area in which women's work is marketed.

Globalization has also strengthened institutions such as the IMF, the World Bank, the WTO, some regional banks, and state organizations such as the EU. The most notable fact about the most powerful of these organizations is their lack of any semblance of democracy; they are beyond the reach not only of individuals, but of nation-states too, as Chomsky (1994) has argued. The exception is the UN, which has lost influence, partly as a result of the USA's (and other nations') unwillingness to accept that enemies should be negotiated with, not just attacked.

Another outcome of globalization is the expansion of the tourist industry and related prostitution. There is also increasing migration between nation-states and, to some degree, between continents. A number of authors have pointed to a weakening of social relations and local cultures – working-class cultures, gender cultures, neighbourhood cultures – but to the continued existence of class, race and gender structures (Sernhede 1996). The enlarging of the market and, to some extent, the erosion of nation-states both contribute to the disappearance or loosening of 'given' cultures or communities in the neighbourhood (increased geographical mobility), of trade unions (which lose influence when the state is weakened) and, for the same reason, of political parties (Hobsbawm 1997).

So there is simultaneously a change in the direction of buying services which were formerly given or exchanged on a neighbourhood, kin or workplace basis, and a decrease in the relevance of the state for people which loosens the organizations. Thus there seems to be a growing search for some point of identification, a voluntarily created and not necessarily geographically defined common interest group or network.

Inasmuch as 'natural' or 'given' social relations and cultures have been weakened and have become things that have to be actively strived for, this must imply that some, perhaps many, people do not find these new networks. Many studies, for instance in Denmark, indicate a high degree of loneliness, especially among older or ill people.

In terms of prostitution, the changes in lifestyle and family forms are remarkable. In Denmark more than half the adult population live alone, but four out of five children live with their biological parents. This seems to imply that those who live in 'old-fashioned' families are, by and large, those who have children. There are thus many single adults, and not all of them are integrated into local networks.

The public debate around sexuality has changed a lot too. Ehrenreich et al. (1986) argued that the so-called sexual revolution was mainly a women's revolution: men have always fooled around, but now women are demanding orgasms and feel more or less free to fool around themselves too. This may not be the whole story, however, because the sexual revolution has resulted in sex being marketed more than ever before. The public debate is now more concerned with sexuality. In many western societies, pornography has entered the mainstream: advertisements, the Internet, television, videos and films show nudity and sexual activity. In this sense sexual satisfaction, sexual play and intercourse have become legitimate subjects of public debate, are highly valued and are now things that can be sold and bought.

MODERNITY AND THE GLOBAL SEARCH FOR PAID SEX

The (late) modern experience of many single people who know little about communality might be expected to raise the demand for paid sex, especially since public debate has virtually made orgasm a right for the individual, and the whole public sphere is permeated, directly or indirectly, by sex.

Since communities are no longer a given and loneliness is common, and since (as Thai prostitutes point out) many people work very long hours and have little time for a social life, the need has arisen for organized relaxation, packaged tours, and for sex to be available on demand, preferably at a very low price.

The stinginess displayed by sex-tourists stems from their perspective on sex: it is a commodity like any other. They also seem to feel that Thai women 'owe' white men something, however curious this may sound. The white man feels he has a right to get sex.

The rising demand for sex and the exploitative forms this takes are thus a result of the combination of the global structuring of labour markets, the promotion of tourism, and of old ideas about sex, race and class expressed in a new, sometimes not so new, form.

Let me end this chapter with a note on modernity, or, as the early twenty-first century has been characterized, post- or late modernity (referring to the socio-psychological forms of identity developed in the last thirty to forty years). In 'From Pilgrim to Tourist – a Short History of Identity', Baumann (1996) discussed the difference in identity between modern and 'postmodern' society, suggesting images that might express these changes. Identity, he argued, has always been a project, not something given, but it has changed considerably: 'The catchword of modernity was creation, the catchword of postmodernity is recycling. If the modern "problem of identity" was how to create an identity and keep it solid and stable, the Post-modern "problem of identity" is primarily how to avoid fixation and keep the options open' (Baumann 1996: 18).

Baumann argued that the central image of identity in modernity was the pilgrim: 'The protestants, as Weber told us, accomplished a feat unthinkable for the lonely hermits of yore: They became innerworldly pilgrims. For these men time and space were stable concepts, designating stretches which lay ahead and should be used as the basis for creation and continuing their lives' tasks.' Today, space has become something easily passed through and does not necessarily designate homeliness. Time is no longer a stream or a river but is fragmented into episodes and is without inner cohesion.

> No consistent and cohesive life strategy emerges from the experience which can be gathered in such a world – none remotely reminiscent of the sense of purpose and the rugged determination of the pilgrimage. Nothing emerges from that experience but certain, mostly negative, rules of thumb: do not plan your trips too long, the shorter the trip the greater the chance of completing it; do not get emotionally attached to people you meet at the stop-over, the less you care about them, the less it will cost you to move on; do not commit yourself too strongly to people, places, causes – you cannot know how long they will last or how long you will count them worthy of your commitment ...
>
> The tourist thus becomes one of the main images of post-modern identity. The tourist seeks new and exciting experiences as the joy of the familiar wears off. The tourist wants to immerse himself in a strange and bizarre element ... on condition, though, that it will not stick to the skin and thus can be shaken off whenever they wish. In the tourist's world the strange is tame, domesticated, and no longer frightens. (Baumann 1996; 25, 29)

I have quoted Baumann's article at length because it seems to me that his thinking shows us the sex-tourist to Bangkok as the quintessential postmodern man, and contributes to our understanding of why the demand for bought sexual satisfaction has increased. The episodic character of the encounters, the lack of emotional involvement, the search for something different without commitment but still safe seem to be characteristic of tourists who are searching for sex and adventure. (Although the safety is somewhat superficial: Davidson remarks that many sex-tourists believe that frequent washing eliminates the risk of AIDs.)

Thus, although the sex-tourist carries a heavy baggage of earlier ideas on race, class and gender, he seems to dress it up in modern language in which culture stands for biology, but the duality of deference and fascination with the Other is very visible. While carrying around the baggage of earlier ideas and stereotypes, he seems to behave as the postmodern man *par excellence*.

NOTES

1. This series was kindly sent to me by Chitraporn Vanaspong.

2. Interestingly, a Danish man who has been very active in the gender debate has argued several times in print and on television that if he was not married, he would prefer to go to prostitutes whom he did not have to charm, talk to, listen to, or, in fact, relate to as another person, but with whom he could have sex straight away.

REFERENCES

Baumann, Z. (1996) 'From Pilgrim to Tourist – or a Short History of Identity', in Hall and du Gay (eds) *Cultural Identity* (London, Thousand Oaks and New Delhi: Sage).

Bishop, R. and L. S. Robinson (1998) *The Night Market: Sexual Cultures and the Thai Economic Miracle* (New York and London: Routledge).

Chomsky, N. (1994) *World Orders, Old and New* (London: Pluto Press).

Darwin, Charles (ed.) (1974) *The Origisn of Species by Means of Natural Selection or the Preservation of Favoured Races in the Struggle for Life*, with an introduction by J. W. Burrow (London: Penguin Books).

Davidson, J. O'Connell and S. J. Taylor (1994) *Sex Tourism – Thailand* (ECPAT).

Ehrenreich, B. et al. (1986) *The Remaking of Love* (New York: Anchor Doubleday).

Ellis, Havelock (1905) *Studies in the Psychology of Sex* (New York: Random House).

Foucault, M. (1988) *The History of Sexuality I* (New York: Vintage).

Freud, S. (1963) *Three Essays on the Theory of Sexuality*, trans. and ed. James Strachey (New York: Basic Books).

Gilman, S. L. (1985) *Difference and Pathology, Stereotypes of Sexuality, Race and Madness* (New York: Cornell University Press).

Hall, Stuart and P. du Gay (eds) (1996) *Cultural Identity* (London, Thousand Oaks, New Delhi: Sage).

Hall, Stuart and B. Bieben (eds) (1992) 'The West and the Rest: Discourse and Power', in *Formations of Modernity* (London: Open University Press).

Harding, S. (ed.) (1993) *'Racial' Economy of Science: Towards a Democratic Future* (Bloomington: Indiana University Press).

Hobsbawm, E. (1997) *The Age of Extremes, the Short Twentieth Century 1914–1991* (London: Abacus).

Holden, G. (1972) 'Introduction' to E. Zola, *Nana* (Harmonsworth: Penguin).

King, A. B. (1991) 'Introduction: Spaces of Culture, Spaces of Knowledge', in A. B. King (ed.) (1991) *Culture, Globalisation and the World-System* (London: Macmillan).

Leys, Stepan and S. L. Gilman (1993) *Appropriating the Idioms of Science: the Rejection of Scientific Racism*, in Harding (ed.), *'Racial' Economy of Science: Towards a Democratic Future* (Bloomington: Indiana University Press).

Lombroso, C. and G. Ferrero (1893) *La donna delinquente* (Turin: Roux) (quoted from Gilman 1985, pp. 98–9).

McClintock, Anne (1995) *Imperial Leather* (New York: Routledge).

Parent-Duchachelet, A. J. B. (1836) *De la prostitution dans la ville Paris* (Paris: J. B. Baillière) (quoted from Gilman 1985, p. 94).

Pollock, G. (1999) *Differencing the Canon: Feminist Desire and the Writing of Art Histories* (London and New York: Routledge).

Røgilds, F. (ed.) (1996) 'Rejser i Nutiden, etniciet, modernitet, etnicitet', *Social kritik*, 45/46, Copenhagen.

Said, E. W. (1994) *Culture and Imperialism* (New York: Vintage).

Seabrook, J. (1996) *Travels in the Skin Trade* (London and Chicago: Pluto Press).

Sernhede, O. (1996) *Det fremmede, Fascination og rædsel*, in Røgilds (ed.), *Social kritik*, 45/46.

Stolcke, V. (1993) 'Is race to ethnicity as sex to gender', in T. del Valle (ed.), *Gendered Anthropolgies* (London and New York: Routledge).

Stoler, A. L. (1995) *Race and the Education of Desire* (Durham, NC, and London: Duke University Press).

Swan, J. (1974) *Master and Nannie: Freud's Two Mothers and the Discovery of the Oedipus Complex* (American Imago).

Truong, Than-dam (1990) *Sex, Money and Morality* (London and New Jersey: Zed Books).

Walker, D. and R. S. Ehrlich (1992) *Hello My Big Honey!: Love Letters to Bangkok Bar Girls* (Bangkok: Dragon Dance Publications).

Walkowitz, J. R. (1980) *Prostitution and Victorian Society: Women, Class and the State* (Cambridge: Cambridge University Press).

Ware, Vron (1992) *Beyound the Pale, White Women, Racism and History* (London and New York: Verso).

Zola, E. (1972) *Nana*, trans. with an introduction by George Holden (London: Penguin Books).

Beach Boys of Barbados: Post-colonial Entrepreneurs

JOAN L. PHILLIPS

§ Academic discourse on sex tourism, described as one of the most emotive and sensationalized issues in the study of tourism (Hall 1994), has focused on the white, western, male heterosexual's image of the sexualized Other (Morgan and Pritchard 1998). The articulation of this image has been that of a (white) western male travelling to have sex with Third World women who are endowed with a perceived El Dorado of femininity (Cohen 1982; Enloe 1989; Phillips and Dann 1998; Thruong 1990).

Women within this androcentric discourse are the objects of the male gaze (Urry 1990). They are the servicers of the tourism industry: exotic markers, meeting both the sexual and domestic needs of men (Morgan and Pritchard 1998), victims of both economic circumstances and the overtures of drunken men (MacCannell 1989). However, the introduction of gender, like race/ethnicity and class, as a significant variable within tourism discourse (Richter 1995) has resulted in a deconstruction of the tourist experience as being essentially male. Moreover, it has confirmed that tourism, as Enloe (1989) argued, is profoundly gendered, is based on notions of masculinities and femininities, and shapes tourism marketing, guests' motivations and hosts' actions (Swain 1995). With gender, one is able to view the tourist as female, newly endowed with economic power and feminist liberation ideology: 'They [women] work, they have leisure time and money, and they have the personal, political and social freedom to travel (often with one another) abroad' (Leneheny 1995: 379). As Swain argues, 'researchers may study only one or both sexes together, theorising how behaviours and roles are given gendered meanings, how labour is divided to express gender and gendered differences symbolically, and how social structures incorporate gender values and convey gender advantages in hierarchical relationships' (Swain 1995: 253).

In this vein, this ethnographic research[1] focuses on the gendered interaction between female tourists in Barbados and the male beach boy. The study focuses on insider interpretation of the beach boy's perception of this gendered interaction. The fieldwork began in 1997 and continued intermittently until June 1999. Ethnographic techniques such as systematic lurking (Dann et al. 1988: 25), semi-participant observation, in-depth interviews and focus groups were utilized.

Male tourism prostitution is not a new phenomenon. Certainly, studies such as Cohen (1971) focused on the interactions between Arab boys and Scandinavian female tourists; and Turner and Ash (1975) remarked on the existence of the phenomenon in the Caribbean. Press (1977), and Karch and Dann's (1981) insightful study of the phenomenon in Barbados focused on an insider interpretation for the beach boy and viewed it through the lens of post-colonial discourse. Sporadic studies have continued to find their way into mainstream tourism literature from fieldwork. For example, Wagner (1977); Wagner and Yamba (1986) on Gambian males and their interaction with Scandinavian female tourists; Pruitt and LaFont's (1995) controversial study on 'romance tourism' in Jamaica; de Albuquerque's (1998) anecdotal foray into the Jamaican and Barbadian tourist sex industry; Phillips (1999) on the Barbadian beach boy; and Dahles and Bras (1999) on the Indonesian beach boy.

Research in this arena has highlighted the fact that the interaction between these gendered actors is based on racialized sexual fantasies stemming from a post-colonial discourse (Said 1978). Stereotypical constructions of the sexual Other – the black man by the western world – have resulted in a type of prostitution based on these mythical constructions. This study attempts to build on such research which focuses on the tourist's gaze (Urry 1990) as female, and the construction of this image through neo-colonialism which also articulates a 'fixity' of this ideological construction of Otherness (Bhabha 1983).

The black man has been socially constructed in binary opposition to the white man. Early studies have attempted a unitary pathological construction of black masculinity and pointed to the impact of slavery and continued institutional racism on the development of black masculinity, and its inability to adopt the traditional patriarchal masculine role

(Rutherford 1988; Segal 1990; Staples 1982). The literature on the marginality of the black man has explained his Otherness construction in a way that parallels Said's Oriental (Phillips 1999). Segal (1990) traces this colonial construction of the white man's Other in colonial literature where the black man was referred to as a 'beastly savage', a 'hypersexual animal'. The literature contends that these binary representations of primitive, sexual and violent blacks and civilized, cerebral and restrained whites are internalized by the former because of the dominance of white social institutions in society (Fanon 1970; Hernton 1965; Segal 1990; Staples 1982). Mercer and Julien (1988) argue that black men internalize these attributes in response to the definitions of dependency and powerlessness that racism and racial oppression enforce, and therefore the black man bases his masculinity on the stereotypes of being macho, hypersexual and athletic. In this gaze, we can see how black sexuality has been constructed as masculine, animalistic, elemental and unrestrained (Morgan and Pritchard 1998: 177).

Further, a plethora of research exists on the analogy of tourism as neo-colonialism (Britton 1982; Crick 1989; Karch and Dann 1981; Morgan and Pritchard 1998; Nash 1989; Van den Berghe 1980). It has been argued that tourism further reinforces the unequal divide between rich and poor countries, and continues the colonial social structures that are based on racism. Certainly, an industry based on the construction of an indigenous Other (Urry and Rojek 1997) has little to offer in the way of race and gender equity. Therefore, any study focusing on tourism in Barbados must do so within the context of the broader framework of neo-colonialism. From this point of departure we can gather an insider understanding of the black man in Barbados, and his new bid for entrepreneurship.

THE SETTING

Barbados is a 166-square-mile island in the Caribbean. Its main industry is tourism: nearly half a million tourists visited in 1996, and revenues amounted to US$684.9 million (CTO 1996). The island is known for its hospitable people, beautiful beaches and what Karch and Dann (1981) and de Albuquerque (1998) see as 'close encounters of the Third World'.

Prostitution invariably forms part of sex tourism (de Albuquerque

1998; Oppermann 1999; Phillips and Dann 1998). The 'prostitution as work' model can be extended to view prostitution as entrepreneurship (Jenness 1990; Rosenblum 1975). While several authors have used the model of entrepreneurship to understand prostitution (for example Heyl 1977; Day 1990), limited use of this model has been employed with regard to sex tourism. With a few exceptions (for example Phillips and Dann 1998; Dahles and Bras 1999), researchers have, however, alluded to the entrepreneurial spirit of those engaging in sex tourism work (Cohen 1982, 1993; Odzer 1990; Wagner and Yamba 1986). The intention is to define the beach boy as an entrepreneur using the definition offered by Phillips and Dann: 'An individual drawn from a minority group of low socio-economic status in society, who in an effort to find alternative avenues of employment, consciously decides to undertake an innovative enterprise assuming risk for the sake of profit' (Phillips and Dann 1998: 65).

THE BEACH BOY

The beach boy, or hustler as he is also known, is usually a dreadlocked youth between fifteen and thirty-five years old. He works within the informal beach economy renting jet-skis, sail boats, banana boats, lounge chairs and umbrellas, or selling coconuts, aloe vera, coral and handcrafted jewellery and drugs (de Albuquerque 1998; Phillips 1999). In order to supplement his income the hustler acts as a gigolo, defined as 'men who receive material compensation for the social or sexual services they render to women' (Press 1978: 111). These services may include sexual intercourse, companionship, arranging tours of the island, finding cheaper accommodation, as well as food. The material compensation can range from free club admissions, drinks, food, taxi fares, duty-free items, shopping sprees for brand-name clothing, airline tickets and cash.

The beach boy is a well-known figure on the beach, ostentatiously dressed in the latest beach fashion – Tommy Hilfiger beach shorts worn pulled down a little to show a tantalizing peep of his well-muscled buttocks. He is a well-built individual usually sporting a gold necklace or bracelet (of at least 18-carat gold). His appearance, an obvious marketing strategy, is based on the western female's notion of the quintessential hypersexual black male: the exotic appeal of blue-black skin proclaiming his pride in his ancestry, hair often dreadlocked, to suggest an untamed, primitive nature (Phillips 1999). As one informant[2] explained:

> You know why some of the girls like the knot-up hair? When some girls send photos and stuff up to England, you don't see any clean-cut men. They send a picture of a Rasta. So when a girl come down here they think a Rasta is a real Caribbean man, so that is why they go for the Rasta. But some of them does get fool, them does get an impostor.

When asked why he works on the beach within an informal labour market that is seasonal at best, one beach boy responded: 'Because the beach is where the money is.' Another put it thus:

> 'cause the guys like the open area, no hassle, we are our own bosses. It is nice being in an open area to work, we can do our own thing. Not in an office stuck up. The boss telling you to do this and do that. We come out here and get the money. I like it here, you meet people from all over the world. You learn different things, get friends that treat you real good. So ain't like back in the office sitting down doing paper work stress out, the boss telling you a bunch of shit everyday. I like the beach 'cause I can work when I feel like, I ain't gotta pay no taxes.

Another asserted: 'I does make my money about here and I sticking out here, you understand.'

Most of the beach boys interviewed left school with few or no qualifications, so gaining entry into the formal labour market would prove very difficult. Many started out in the construction business as labourers or unskilled manual workers. As one beach boy maintained: 'Most of the people in water sports basically left school, sad to say ain't really had no educational background and they use water sports as a form of escape.'

Big Dog, as he is affectionately known on the beach, is typical of many in the host country.[3] He has been working on the beach for seven years, and he 'does all sorts of things, darling, jet skis, glass bottom boat, anything darling, anything to make money'. At 21 years old he has lost count of the number of white women he has slept with. He is a self-styled ghetto youth and comes from a family of fisher folk: 'My grandmother was a fish vendor, my mother is a fish vendor, my father is a fisherman, my grandmother husband is a fisherman, I was a fisherman.' Big Dog finished school at fourteen because, 'I don't like fucking school darling. I could read and count very well, though. I would rather be on the beach, though.'

Economically, the beach boy can be defined as a risk-taker, leaving a (low-paying) job of US$100 per week within the formal labour market to partake in a seasonal but successful activity which might earn him US$500 per day. The litany of 'we are our own bosses' is a common one; they seek economic and social independence in a bid to rid themselves of the marginality of being a black working-class man (Brathwaite 1983). This can be perceived as an entrepreneurial step to self-advancement.

Health-wise the beach boy can also be defined as a risk-taker. Cohen (1993) and Phillips and Dann (1998) have focused on sex tourism and the threat of AIDS. Certainly, Bangkok stands out as a sex tourism destination where there has been an endemic rise in AIDS (Hall 1994). The link between beach boy prostitution and AIDS has not yet been established in Barbados. However, one can still infer that there is some risk to both beach boy and client in their mutual sexual behaviour. One beach boy gave this philosophical answer:

> I don't know that is a personal question, that is just like asking if a black man here did working a normal job, and he meet a normal girl and you ask him if he uses condoms what is he going to tell you? He is going to tell you yeah. This is an obvious answer to an obvious question, but behind closed doors, it is a different story. Life is a chance, the first time you might use, but the second time ...

According to Malibu: 'If I meet you today and sleep with you today I must use a condom.' Derek, though, admits that 'You might make a mistake one or two times and go out partying and your head full.'[4] Big Dog maintains that 'the majority of the white girls does want condoms'. The risk of HIV and AIDS among the beach boys is very real, particularly given their sporadic use of condoms.

The beach boys' motivation for engaging in sexual relations with white tourist women is the desire to supplement their already high incomes, thus reinforcing the image of the 'highflying' lifestyle of beach boys (de Albuquerque 1998). As one beach boy argued: 'If you out here and you don't have ownership of a boat, the most thing that you are going to focus on is to get a piece of crotch, you know, get some money.' As Malibu said: 'I don't shag for fun neither. If them come that sort a way they gotta to give me cash.' Material benefits include: 'I like to travel, I stop and go to Canada for four, five months and when it get too cold I back in Barbados again'; or 'a plane ticket to England with six months' spending money'; or US$15,000; or an 18-carat diamond ring. Then there are the shopping sprees, the apartment rentals, the jet-skis, and the repatriation of money towards their general subsistence.

Even the selection of potential partners speaks to the pecuniary nature of these arrangements. According to Peter: 'Tourists carry you to dinners. When I was on the sand (beach) I used to eat food at Sandy Lane.[5] I still eating food there me and my girl at Sandy Lane. I don't spend anything. I don't spend a cent. They invite you out, they going to treat you nice.' Ted claimed that: 'Bajan[6] women always looking for somebody to support them. I looking for somebody to support me too, what is wrong with that? I happy.' One key informant put it even more succinctly: 'I like to get involved with executive ladies. My women are lawyers, own their own companies, are executives of other companies … technically speaking I love women who love money.' Don was angry about the number of charter flights coming to Barbados: 'Man, the girls here broke now, girls coming about here broke, coming on a lot of cheap flights, the men in for business they ain't want broke girls.' Two of his colleagues discussed the merits of getting married:

> BB1: Whoever wanta marry me could marry me for about three grand.
> BB2: I got a woman that want to marry me for ten grand.
> BB1: Well you could do that but, you hear the best man is get more than the man that get marry.
> BB2: If I marry ten grand, I ain't mind.

These relationships are not chosen on the basis of mutual attraction but of economic allure, i.e. profit for the beach boy. Even Pruitt and Lafont's (1995) study on the romance element in sex tourism still admits that many of the young men view these interactions as a way to get ahead. There is even a strategy to ascertain the degree of wealth of a potential client:

> It is a matter of getting into the computer … when you socialising you ask what do you do? How you spend your time. Also, of a matter of interest, if you meet someone and they [female tourists] say they like you they will return shortly, like next week. Not many people can do

that, if you save for the vacation usually they come two, three times a year.

However, some admit to being fooled by the credit card gimmick: 'When you see them putting down the credit card for everything, you know that they ain't got a cent, that you got more money then them, man.' Dave expressed disgust at the lack of discernment shown by some of his colleagues:

I am not like the rest of them targeting those piss-ass Irish girls who come here on those charters with 300 dollars who ain't got no money. I head for the wine bars on the West Coast, them is the ones with the money. They should learn to hold a conversation, like me too. I go about it clinical that you would never know it. Them men ain't serious, man, they are jokers, they after the price of a rum and coke that's what them after, 'buy me drink'. Hello, after the drink gone you go and fuck all night, break down yourself, them girls go on the beach all day, and you fagged out [tired] all day, and you ain't earning no money still, you pimping.

The selection of a potential client is also a skill learned from personal experience and the acknowledged existence of a hierarchy of preferred nationalities, age and attractiveness (de Albuquerque 1998; Karch and Dann 1981; Press 1978). From the evidence, the preferred group is French Canadians. Generally, Europeans are higher on the list than Americans in terms of lack of sexual inhibitions and availability of money, since 'Americans too cheap and got too much attitude. Also the older they are the more grateful they are.' English girls, however, are considered to be the most sexually aggressive and promiscuous.

The beach boys spoke of the need to retain a muscular body. One informant said:

These women is some funny women, they don't check fat guys, you know what I mean. We Bajan guys don't carry a lot of fat, you under-stand. We don't carry a lot of fat working with the boats, you get fit. The first couple of days you might find that you got a little fat on you, then you going to find that your body begin to tone. You going to start doing a little swimming before you start work and after work and then your body going to come to order.

Being an innovator is part of any entrepreneurial activity. This situation may involve working long hours and undertaking activities in new and better ways (Phillips and Dann 1998). For the beach boy this involves initiating a relationship with a white female tourist and extending this relationship to receive remuneration over a period of time.

Usually the potential client is approached on the beach as she sunbathes. The beach boy uses such standard lines (de Albuquerque 1998; Karch and Dann 1981) as 'Hello, is this your first visit to Barbados?' 'How are you enjoying your stay?' 'How do you like the beach?' 'Would you like some aloes on your skin?' 'Can I have a cigarette?' 'Would you like me to rub some suntan lotion on you?' According to beach boys, the most successful gambit is, 'My goodness, you are getting brown'. If this ploy is successful, an invitation is extended to show her the island, or go to a club.[7]

The new client is usually taken to a club frequented by beach boys and their tourist girlfriends (Karch and Dann 1981) so that she feels at home. It is at the club that the beach boy can demonstrate his expertise. Here he can emphasize his masculinity, thus reinforcing racial stereotypes; he becomes the exotic Other giving the female tourist what she expects (Phillips 1999). He begins by showing his 'natural rhythm', gyrating wickedly to the latest calypso and reggae tunes, sometimes shaking his dreadlocks or nubbies[8] or just running his hands through them to emphasize his 'passion' for the music. When the music changes to a slower beat, he will hold 'his woman' and croon in her ear showing his 'natural ability' to sing. He holds her even closer so that she can feel the strength of his 'masculine body' and he whispers what he intends to do with her tonight, sometimes in her own language so great is his repertoire. By this time, the female tourist is so overcome by the rum and cokes, the music, the heat and by this skilled performance of this Barbadian Lothario that the lovemaking begins there and then on the dance floor. This is a skill based on his indigenous masculinity based upon his reputation (Wilson 1969), not constructed like his Jamaican counterpart as Pruitt and Lafont (1995) argued.

He is the black man of the female gaze. It does not end here; the romance must continue. A car is rented so that the beach boy can show his 'love' the sites. Often he moves into her apartment or a more liberal hotel for the duration. A former client described the plight of the female tourist:

They get here and all of a sudden they are on a beach wearing next to nothing, and up and down the beach parading are all of these gorgeous men like peacocks coming up to you and saying, you are so beautiful, you are so gorgeous, can I take you out tonight, can I do this, can I do that. Before you know it the girls are intoxicated … the usual scenario is this… she spends money on him, she pays for the taxi … she buys the clothes … she mistakes sex for love.

A key informant explained why the female tourists are mistakenly caught up:

They does get into us and do everything with us, everything. We does carry them places, island tours, sailing and so on. We does be with them showing them everything, giving them a good time, making sure they enjoy their holiday. So they are going devote time with us, they ain't going to look for another person right.

Another argued: 'I guess that it is pretty stressful, the guys back home don't have much time for them and stuff you know, so when they come down here we show them such a good time within two, three weeks they fall in love pretty quick with us.'
Another said:

You give them attention that they are not accustomed to back home. You know the women tend to like the attention, the loving, the touching, the holding hands, the kissing. Women like that kind of attention shown that is one thing that I know about women. They don't get it where they are from. I guess they probably subdues within their cultures because that is not something that comes, when it comes you know is something that you like and it is there and you go for it. It is something that you remember and you want to repeat. The romance, the courtship seems to be something that they are not privy too in their own environment, they can go to the islands and get it for two weeks with their Bajan man.

Another skill claimed by many is the beach boy's ability to satisfy a white woman: 'They [white men] ain't up to the mark, so when them come to Barbados and see that we black boys healthy and looking good, they [white women] want to try something new. You can't beat that. I have seen women divorce their husbands, get divorce you know what I mean.'

Another spoke of the stereotypical images white females have with regard to black male sexuality: 'White women come from overseas come to live out a fantasy and walk away. A man might take advantage of that situation … some women may be telling themselves, I like these jungle pictures, all of these big, strong men. I want to go down there and get fuck in the bush and thing, all kinda fantasies.'

Such is the skill and innovation of the beach boy that the female tourist returns. A similar situation occurs with bar girl prostitution in Bangkok (Phillips and Dann 1998). Many beach boys are offered plane tickets, others receive feverishly written letters. One beach boy said:

> She does write me and say the weather up here is this and that. I does get fun out of that, writing me long letters, when I write back I does write like ten lines and done. If I feel like what I does so is get a phone card or if I home call and talk with them for awhile. But when I get them letters … I mean, them people does tell you about everything, where they went partying, what them do. It does be fun though.

Like any entrepreneurial activity, competition is fierce, not only among beach boys, but from other male Barbadians who recognize the lucrative nature of the business. Having a white woman is a status symbol in a post-colonial society. As Derek maintained:

> I find that a lot of guys working in the banks and thing now looking to hustle the white women, but they hassle the white women, we don't do that. For us it is a business, so eventually we come into contact with white women everyday, so eventually they end up liking us, you know. We don't have to go out there like the business guys, like the bank guys trying to hassle them and trying to sweet talk them. What is for a man he will get, 'cause you will find that the beach guys is go out tonight with a lady and leave her alone for a couple of minutes, go to the bathroom or go for a drink, and on your way back to the woman you will find one of the office guys up in she ear whispering things, trying to tell her bad things about the guy that she is with.

Among beach boys, the complaint is similar: 'Man, they would cut one another throat. Men does go and tell women all kind of things about the next one and thing. I tell the woman I gotta talk to you, and I wait until you go to the bathroom and I go and tell the woman that you like boys all of that sort of thing.'

CONCLUSION

This skill of the beach boy to package the western female gaze of black male sexuality and offer it to her at a price is truly the work of an entrepreneur. Through this enterprise he is able to maintain a measure of independence, status and material goods that as a working-class, black youth he would never have been able to achieve. He is, in fact, adamant about the significant role he plays within the tourism industry (Phillips 1999). He has constructed an arena into which the liberated western female can come to sample the archetype of the post-colonial black man; the black man does bear the burden of exploitation but also the rewards of profit and entrepreneurship.

This can be viewed as a case in which the empire truly fights back. However, we must still be aware of the unequal relationship that operates between host and guest, forcing this type of prostitution arrangement. If there is such a thing as 'dependent development', then a similar view can be extended to regard beach boys' actions as 'dependent entre-preneurship'.

NOTES

1. This research is part of an ongoing PhD study. It was initially commissioned as part of a funded project focusing on sex work in the Caribbean co-ordinated by the Women's Studies Program at the University of Colorado, the Caribbean Association for Feminist Research and Action (CAFRA), and the Instituto Latino-americano de Servicios Legales Alternativos (ILSA).

2. Excerpts from some of the interviews with beach boys will be utilized throughout this chapter.

3. Pseudonyms are used to guarantee anonymity.

4. Barbadian slang for being inebriated.

5. An exclusive resort on the west coast of Barbados.

6. Colloquial term for Barbadian.

7. Historically, all hotels had clubs attached in title and in policy. Those hotels that retain the 'club' title still continue to operate under a colour bar, of which the beach boy is well aware. He would never suggest a drink within the hotel bar as a first date.

8. A shorter version of dreadlocks.

REFERENCES

Bhabha, H. (1983) 'The Other Question – the Stereotype and Colonial Discourse', *Screen*, 24, 18–36.

Brathwaite, F. (1983) *Unemployment and Social Life. A Sociological Study of the Unemployed in Trinidad* (Bridgetown: Antilles Publications).

Britton, S. (1982) 'The Political Economy of Third World Tourism', *Annals of Tourism Research*, 9: 331–58.

Cohen, E. (1971) 'Arab Boys and Tourist Girls in a Mixed Jewish Community', *International Journal of Comparative Sociology*, 12: 217–33.

— (1982) 'Thai Girls and Farang Men: the Edge of Ambiguity', *Annals of Tourism Research*, 9: 403–28.

— (1993) 'Open-ended Prostitution as a Skilful Game of Luck, Opportunity, Risk And Sexuality among Tourist-oriented Prostitutes in a Bangkok Soi', in M. Hitchcock, V. King and M. Parnell (eds), *Tourism in South-East Asia* (London: Routledge), pp. 155–78.

Crick, M. (1989) 'Representations of International Tourism in the Social Sciences: Sun, Sex, Sights, Savings and Servility', *Annual Review of Anthropology*, 18: 307–44.

CTO (Caribbean Tourism Organisation) (1996) *Statistical Report*.

Dahles, H. and K. Bras (1999) 'Entrepreneurs in Romance. Tourism in Indonesia', *Annals of Tourism Research*, 26(2): 267–93.

Dann, G., N. Nash and P. Pearce (1988) 'Methodology in Tourism Research', *Annals of Tourism Research*, 15: 1–28.

Day, S. (1990) *Prostitute Women and the Ideology of Work in London* (New York: Praeger Publishers), pp. 93–110.

de Albuquerque, K. (1998) 'Sex, Beach Boys and Female Tourists in the Caribbean', *Sex Work and Sex Workers. Sexuality and Culture*, 2: 87–112.

Enloe, C. (1989) *Bananas, Beaches, Bases: Making Feminist Sense of International Politics* (Berkeley: University of California Press).

Fanon, F. (1970) *Black Skin, White Masks* (London: Paladin).

Hall, M. (1994) 'Gender and Economic Interest in Tourism Prostitution: the Nature, Development and Implications of Sex Tourism in South-East Asia', in V. Kinnaird and D. Hall (eds), *Tourism: a Gender Analysis* (Chichester: Wiley), pp. 142–63.

Hernton, C. (1965) *Sex and Racism in America* (New York: Doubleday).

Heyl, B. (1977) 'The Madam as Entrepreneur', *Sociological Symposium*, 11: 545–55.

Jenness, V. (1990) 'From Sex as Sin to Sex as Work – COYOTE and the Reorganization of Prostitution as a Social Problem', *Social Problems*, 37(3): 403–20.

Karch, C. and G. Dann (1981) 'Close Encounters of the Third World', *Human Relations*, 34(4): 249–68.

Leneheny, D. (1995) 'A Political Economy of Asian Sex Tourism', *Annals of Tourism Research* 22(2): 367–84.

MacCannell, D. (1989) *The Tourist: a New Theory of the Leisure Class*, 2nd edn (New York: Schocken Books).

Majors, R. (1986) 'Cool Pose: the Proud Signature of Black Survival', *Changing Men: Issues in Gender, Sex and Politics*, 17: 5–6.

Mercer, K. and I. Julien (1988) 'Racism and the Politics of Masculinity', in R. Chapman and J. Rutherford (eds), *Male Order* (London: Lawrence and Wishart), pp. 97–164.

Morgan, N. and A. Pritchard (1998) *Tourism, Promotion and Power: Creating Images, Creating Identities* (Chichester: Wiley).

Mueke, M. (1992) 'Mother Sold Food. Daughter Sells her Body: The Cultural Continuity of Prostitution', *Social Science Medical Journal*, 35(7): 891–901.

Nash, D. (1989) 'Tourism as a Form of Imperialism', in V. Smith (ed.), *Hosts and Guests* (Philadelphia: University of Pennsylvania Press).

Odzer, C. (1990) *Patpong Prostitution: Its Relationship to, and Effect on, the Position of Thai Women in Thai Society*, unpublished PhD thesis (New York: School for Social Research).

Oppermann, M. (1999) 'Sex Tourism', *Annals of Tourism Research*, 26(2): 251–66.

Phillips, J. (1999) 'Tourist-oriented Prostitution in Barbados: the Case of the Beach Boy and the White Female Tourist', in K. Kempadoo (ed.), *Sun, Sex and Gold: Tourism and Sex Work in the Caribbean* (Boulder: Rowan & Littlefield), pp. 183–200.

Phillips, J. and G. Dann (1998) 'Bar Girls in Central Bangkok: Prostitution as Entrepreneurship', in M. Oppermann (ed.), *Sex Tourism and Prostitution: Aspects of Leisure, Recreation, and Work* (New York: Cognizant Communication Corporation), pp. 60–70.

Press, C. (1978) 'Reputation and Respectability Reconsidered: Hustling in a Tourist Setting', *Caribbean Issues*, 4(1): 109–19.

Pruitt, D. and S. LaFont (1995) 'For Love and Money: Romance Tourism in Jamaica', *Annals of Tourism Research*, 22(2): 422–40.

Richter, L. (1995) 'Gender and Race: Neglected Variables in Tourism Research', in R. Butler and D. Pearce (eds), *Change in Tourism, People, Places, Process* (London: Routledge), pp. 71–91.

Rosenblum, K. (1975) 'Female Deviance and the Female Sex Role: a Preliminary Investigation', *British Journal of Sociology*, 26(2): 169–85.

Rutherford, J. (1988) 'Who that man?', in R. Chapman and J. Rutherford (eds), *Male Order. Unwrapping Masculinities* (London: Lawrence and Wishart), pp. 21–69.

Said, E. (1978) *Orientalism* (London: Penguin Books).

Segal, L. (1990) *Slow Motion: Changing Masculinities. Changing Men* (London: Virago Press).

Staples, R. (1982) *Black Masculinity* (San Francisco: Black Scholar Press).

Swain, M. (1995) 'Gender in Tourism', *Annals of Tourism Research*, 22(2): 247–66.

Thruong, T. (1990) *Sex, Money and Morality: Prostitution and Tourism in South-East Asia* (London: Zed Books).

Turner, L. and J. Ash (1975) *International Tourism and the Pleasure Periphery* (London: Constable).

Urry, J. (1990) *The Tourist Gaze* (London: Sage).

Urry, J. and C. Rojek (1997) *Touring Cultures: Transformations of Travel and Theory* (London: Routledge).

Van den Berghe, P. (1980) 'Tourism as Ethnic Relations: a Case Study of Cuzco, Peru', *Ethnic and Racial Studies*, 3(4): 375–92.

Wagner, U. (1977) 'Out of Time and Place: Mass Tourism and Charter', *Ethnos*, 42: 38–52.

Wagner, U. and B. Yamba (1986) 'Going North and Getting Attached', *Ethnos*, 51: 3–45.

Wilson, P. (1969) 'Reputation and Respectability: a Suggestion for Caribbean Ethnology', *Man*, 4(1): 70–84.

PART TWO

Migrant Women in Prostitution

FOUR

A Social Response to Transnational Prostitution in Queensland, Australia

LINDA MEAKER

§ Over the last two decades, the number of migrant women working in the sex industry throughout Australia has increased significantly. Several studies have highlighted the characteristics of transnational prostitution in Sydney (Brockett and Murray 1994), but there has been little research examining the complex and non-homogeneous nature of transnational prostitution in Queensland. This chapter will consider transnational prostitution as it occurs throughout Queensland, particularly in Brisbane, where two distinct groups of migrant sex-workers can be identified. These two groups are resident migrant workers and contract workers, for whom there is a marked polarity in self-determination.

The information presented in this chapter has been collected through working directly with sex-workers accessing SQWISI, a community-based organization funded to provide health and support services to the sex industry. In the past four years the multicultural project has had in excess of 1,500 contacts with sex industry workers from diverse cultural backgrounds.[1] From these contacts this paper has been developed.

THE BACKGROUND TO TRANSNATIONAL PROSTITUTION AND ASIAN SEX WORK IN AUSTRALIA

The majority of transnational or migrant sex-workers in Australia come from neighbouring countries in the Asia Pacific region, in particular Thailand and the Philippines. Increasingly, women from mainland China are also entering the Australian sex industry.

In Sydney and Melbourne, an established Asian sex industry has existed for some time, with Asian women providing commercial sex services to local clients. Asian sex establishments are numerous and, according to sex-workers, the majority of clients are men from local migrant communities, particularly Vietnamese and Chinese (Brockett and Murray 1994). According to the Australian Federal Police (1995), some of these establishments are connected to organized syndicates responsible for recruiting and contracting sex-workers throughout Southeast Asia. Debt contract operations dominate the market in Sydney and Melbourne, and most of the women working under these conditions are illegal immigrants, vulnerable to deportation if discovered by authorities.

Contact with health service providers in other states, such as the Australian Capital Territory, Western Australia and South Australia, has indicated a considerable increase in the number of Asian women in the sex industry over the last few years.[2] This is consistent with the increasing mobilization of female migrant labour throughout the region in general, and may also reflect an expansion of international illegal operations. In these states, contact with the women has been problematic, as language and cultural barriers make communication difficult. In Melbourne, Sydney, Brisbane and more recently Western Australia, the health and welfare needs of migrant sex-workers have been significant enough to prompt state government health departments to fund specific projects targeting these women. It may be that such programes will be initiated in other states in the future.

THE ASIAN SEX INDUSTRY IN BRISBANE AND QUEENSLAND

In Queensland the Asian sex industry is concentrated in Brisbane and the Gold Coast, with an increasing flow northwards to satellite cities such as Townsville and Cairns. Brisbane differs from some of the other capital cities in that the majority of Asian sex-workers are permanent residents or Australian citizens, perhaps because Queensland's harsh prostitution laws and heavy policing have been a deterrent to illegal operators. It is only recently that raids by local police have revealed the presence of Asian women working under debt-contract.[3]

In the past twelve months proposed prostitution law reform has attracted interest from brothel and massage parlour owners in other states, and may have encouraged illegal operations to move northwards in anticipation of these changes. Whatever the reason, the current situation in Queensland provides an interesting case study of migrant

Have to due to debt.

prostitution as it facilitates an examination of the experiences of debt-contract workers as compared with those of Asian women who are self-employed.

DEBT-CONTRACT WORK AND RESIDENT SEX-WORKERS: THE DIFFERENT EXPERIENCES OF ASIAN WOMEN

Most debt-contract workers are women from Southeast Asia, particularly Thailand, who come to work in Australia under a contract arrangement with an agent/owner, possibly connected to a syndicate (Australian Federal Police 1995). Typically, contract workers have their air fares, accommodation and employment provided in exchange for sexual services equivalent to a predetermined amount. Ten years ago this was somewhere in the vicinity of AU$20,000 (Brockett and Murray 1994), but these days contracts are often based on a quota system, i.e. with sex-workers having to see between 500 and 700 clients to repay the debt.

Contrary to much of the anti-trafficking discourse, the majority of women know they will be working in the sex industry and often decide to come to Australia in the belief that they will be able to make a substantial amount of money. Fortunately, cases of deceptive coercion[4] are rare in Australia (Brockett and Murray 1994). While it has been argued in some of the research, and certainly in the popular press, that migrant prostitution is sex slavery, the fact that most women have consented to this work indicates that this view is somewhat oversimplified and misguided. Indeed, abuse of human rights is more likely to occur as a result of the work being illegal and informal, than through deceptive coercion and lack of consent. Consenting to sex work does not mean that the women agree to poor working conditions. However, the criminal nature of the debt-contract system often leaves migrant women vulnerable to exploitation. Usually travelling on false passports and visas, perhaps assuming another nationality and identity, many of the women are afraid to seek help and support outside the brothel environment.

The disadvantages of debt-contract work are considerable. Women have complained of the lack of autonomy, long working hours, poor working conditions and unsafe sex. In recent years, following the public response to HIV/AIDS in Australia and an alarmingly high rate of

STD infection among Asian sex-workers, health-workers have managed to gain access to some Asian brothels in order to provide condoms and safe-sex education and information (Donovan et al. 1993). However, such safe-sex practice is only possible if supported by other stakeholders, such as clients and bosses, and this is not always the case.

Why do women enter a debt-contract? Most women enter a debt-contract because of economic necessity, compounded by family dependence. Limited access to education and viable employment opportunities in their home countries often prompt women to look for work further afield. Despite significant social change and industrialization, many women in developing countries do not receive an income comparable to that of their male counterparts. Farm, factory and domestic work continue to be the major sources of employment for women in many parts of the world. Sex work offers the potential for far greater financial rewards, particularly overseas, and for this reason transnational prostitution has become a vitally important source of remittances in Southeast Asia. Stringent immigration laws make it difficult for women from Southeast Asia to work legally in Australia and therefore debt-contracts are agreed to in exchange for protection and promises of work. Many women tolerate their circumstances with the philosophical attitude that a little suffering now will lead to financial security in the future.

RESIDENT MIGRANT SEX-WORKERS

The second group of sex-workers are those who have permanent or temporary residency or citizenship. Very little research has focused on this group of sex-workers, even though they constitute a significant proportion of the sex industry throughout Brisbane and Queensland. These women are self-employed, usually from Thailand, the Philippines or Malaysia, and have entered sex work through a number of avenues.

The largest group of women have become permanent residents through marriage to Australian men, either organized through a mail-order/pen-pal network or through having met their husbands in their home countries, where they frequently work as entertainers, bar staff or sex-workers. Others are students, or have secured permanent residency through family migration programmes. Some women may have originally arrived under a debt-contract in Sydney or Melbourne and later married and moved to Queensland. There is also a significant group of women who have professional qualifications not recognized in Australia, and who have never worked in the sex industry in their home country.

Discussions with resident migrant sex-workers indicate that there are a number of reasons why sex work is such an attractive option. First, work in the sex industry is highly lucrative and for migrant women with few options other than factory work or domestic work it makes economic sense. Second, working in another country has distinct advantages. Most women conceal their work from their families as sex work is stigmatized in many cultures. Despite the increased acceptance of prostitution as a source of overseas income, prostitution remains the work of the 'bad girl' in many communities.

It some cases, this sense of deviance is attractive to migrant sex-workers accessing SQWISI. The expression of sexuality can be empowering for women from cultures where sexual expression is often suppressed. Some women have described the process of becoming a sex-worker as liberating, explaining that it provides them with power, independence and self-confidence. This is particularly so for those women who work independently, and is often the case for Asian women who have entered the industry as a conscious decision to take charge of their lives. Few of the women would ever consider themselves sex slaves and, in fact, many laugh and state, 'Not me, darling, it is the man that is the sex slave ... after all I am the one who gets the money.'

For Asian sex-workers there is a strong sense of community and peer support and sex-workers from similar cultural backgrounds tend to spend a lot of time together socially. There may be arguments and problems, but there is undeniably a wellspring of mutual support. Asian sex-workers who work independently tend to look out for each other; this is very important in Queensland where the current laws encourage women to work under dangerous circumstances. For example, it is illegal to own, operate or work for a sex establishment or escort agency. Street soliciting is illegal and private sex-workers are not permitted to employ any security personnel or work with a friend to share expenses. The only legal option is to work as a sole operator, which in practice means that sex-workers are providing services without protection, often resulting in an increase in violence. SQWISI estimated a 300 per cent increase in violence since the current laws were enacted in 1992. The implications of these stringent laws are far-reaching for the safety of all sex-workers and sex-workers from non-English-speaking backgrounds in particular. They are vulnerable targets for extortion and violent assault.[5]

Interestingly, these tough laws have not deterred Asian women from setting up in business on their own. The number of Asian women working autonomously as sex-workers in Queensland is considerable and continues to grow despite the tough laws, increased policing and emergence of debt-contract. This is because sex work offers financial security and independence for many Asian women. Given that so many Asian women willingly enter the sex industry, it may be argued that sex work itself is not oppressive. However the social, legal and economic frameworks that marginalize sex-workers certainly contribute to the creation of exploitative work conditions.

DEVELOPING A SOCIAL RESPONSE TO TRANSNATIONAL PROSTITUTION IN QUEENSLAND

As a community responding to the needs of Asian sex-workers in Queensland, our first priority is to challenge the frameworks which perpetuate exploitation and impact upon health and wellbeing. The following recommendations for a social response are based on the identified and expressed needs of sex-workers and support services throughout Queensland.

Provision of health services, testing and treatment The provision of appropriate clinical services and health education is vital. This involves developing foreign-language resources, employing bilingual staff and conducting ongoing needs assessment with the target group. SQWISI has recently commenced a Thai-specific health clinic, where bilingual staff assist the target group and medical staff. This clinic is based on a successful model operating in the Sydney Sexual Health Centre and the Melbourne Sexual Health Clinic. It is also envisaged that a Chinese clinic will be operational within the next year. The success of such clinics is dependent upon confidentiality and accessibility. The clinics are free, do not require a Medicare card, medical insurance or personal identification and therefore they are accessible to all within the community. In terms of public health, it is important that treatment and care be available regardless of legal status.

Provision of confidential welfare, counselling and support services
Asian sex-workers often face difficulties in their work and personal
lives and the provision of emotional support is very important. This
support includes developing referral networks, the provision of counselling and welfare assistance, as well as consulting with government
departments for assistance in areas such as accommodation, emergency
relief, legal matters and court support. Asian sex-workers accessing
SQWISI have presented a broad range of emotional concerns, including
but not exclusively domestic violence, depression, self-harm, anxiety,
drug and alcohol problems, loneliness and eating disorders.

Provision of outreach services Outreach to sex establishments and the
street sex industry is an important strategy for contacting men and
women who may be working in illegal environments. Often outreach is
the only method for contacting transitory Asian sex-workers who may
not be aware that free, confidential assistance is available. Outreach to
brothels allows health services to have contact with clients and owners
and provides a non-threatening environment in which to discuss issues
such as health and safe sex.

Lobbying for legal reforms and networking with policing bodies Most
debt-contract workers are working illegally in Australia and conse-
quently there are few avenues for appeal on humanitarian grounds. At
the federal level, immigration laws prevent any consideration or review
of circumstances for a person found to be working illegally. In all but
very few cases, the authorities detain illegal immigrants until arrangements are made for the sex-worker to be sent home. This means that
sex-workers on debt-contract are summarily deported without consideration of the risks they may face when they return home before
completing their debt-contract. This punitive approach fails to take into
account the particular circumstances of individuals, such as their health
status. On several occasions women being treated for serious sexually
transmitted diseases (STDs) have been deported before treatment had
been completed, allowing no opportunity for follow-up or referral. An
effective social response must encompass factors such as health and
safety regardless of the immigration status of the sex-worker.

The enactment and enforcement of federal laws, including those governing immigration, depend largely on the political agenda of the government. Scarlet Alliance, the national sex-worker body in Australia, has argued that issuing work visas for sex-workers would allow migrant sex-workers greater freedom and autonomy and deter syndicates from operating debt-contracts (Scarlet Alliance 1998). Unfortunately, the political reality is that work visas are unlikely to be introduced. Therefore, the first tangible step in developing a social response may be to lobby the Australian government to reconsider the blanket policy of compulsory deportation in favour of individual case assessments. Temporary visas may be issued in order to review the facts of the case and the associated risks to the health and wellbeing of each individual person.

At the state and local level, lobbying for law reform that increases workplace health and safety for the sex industry in general will also benefit migrant sex-workers. Furthermore, lobbying the government for increased funding to provide outreach education programes to sex establishments will increase the access of Asian sex-workers to essential services and information. Currently the legislation and budget available to SQWISI make it difficult for outreach programes to be delivered on a regular basis.

Developing a working relationship with local police has also proven to be beneficial. Discussions with state police have been helpful in raising awareness and understanding of the issues facing Asian sex-workers. In Queensland, the appointment of a police sex-worker liaison officer on the Gold Coast has also proved helpful in encouraging Asian women to come forward and report incidences of violence, extortion and exploitation. Recently SQWISI has begun providing training to officers in the police academy regarding the needs of sex-workers, and requests have been made for training on the specific needs of migrant sex-workers in Queensland. Additionally, SQWISI regularly advocates on behalf of clients with other government departments such as the Department of Family Services and the Department of Immigration.

Provision of education and training assistance for migrant women wishing to leave the sex industry Much of the academic discourse discusses migrant female labour, exploitative work conditions and prostitution with little recourse to practical alternatives. If women do not have access to education or skills training, it is very difficult to find employment in the formal sector. This is why sex work, domestic service and factory work are the mainstay of migrant women's work. Governments need to commit money and energy to alternative work options before there will be any significant shift in the numbers of women working in transnational prostitution.

Many of the Asian women accessing SQWISI would like to leave the sex industry. However, illiteracy and lack of formal training make it difficult to break away from the cycle of prostitution. Even though some women leave the industry and join the formal sector, they often return to sex work because they can work fewer hours and make more money. SQWISI runs an education, training and support project that assists in the retraining of sex-workers wishing to leave the industry. However, recent funding cuts have restricted the training and job placement assistance available to sex-workers. Without this financial support it is difficult to provide sustainable assistance to those wishing to leave the sex industry. Lobbying for funding to assist sex-workers leaving the industry is thus an important aspect in developing a comprehensive social response to transnational prostitution.

CONCLUSION

Finally, the community needs to acknowledge the reality that, for many women, prostitution is a solution to poverty and a path to independence. While prostitution may present a problem for social commentators, for many women it is simply the way life is. Every effort should therefore be made to support migrant sex-workers in all parts of the world, in their right to work safely, with dignity and to be free from exploitative and oppressive work conditions.

NOTES

1. SQWISI statistics.
2. Discussions with sex-worker organizations.
3. Discussions with Queensland police; 'Fly-in Sex Slaves', *Sunday Mail*, 30 May 1999.
4. To clarify the term 'deceptive coercion', I am referring to cases where women are told they will be working as domestics or waitresses rather than sex-workers. Should such cases occur, every effort should be made to assist the women and penalize those responsible for deprivation of liberty and abuse of human rights.

5. See, for example, the 1997–98 case of extortion and violence against Asian sex-workers by a client impersonating a police officer. He was charged with extortion, armed robbery, sexual assault, violence, and is currently serving five years in protective custody in Brisbane.

REFERENCES

Australian Federal Police (1995) *Briefing Paper on the Movement of South East Asian Women for Prostitution in Australia.*

Bindman, J. and J. Doezema (1997) *Redefining Sex work on the International Agenda* (London: Network of Sex Work Projects).

Brockett, L. and A. Murray (1994) 'Thai Sex Workers in Sydney', in Roberta Perkins et al., *Sex Work and Sex Workers in Australia* (Sydney: University of South Wales Press).

Donovan, B., C. Harcourt et al. (1993) 'Gonorrhea in Asian Prostitution', *Medical Journal of Australia*

Purser, P. (1996) 'Empowerment for International Sex Workers', *National AIDS Bulletin*, 10: 5.

Scarlet Alliance (1998) 'Chapter 9 – Offences Against Humanity – Slavery', Briefing Paper (Canberra: Scarlet Alliance).

FIVE

The Transnational Prostitution of Thai Women to Germany: A Variety of Transnational Labour Migration?

PATAYA RUENKAEW

§ During the last twenty-five years there has been a steady increase in the number of Thai women immigrating to and living in the Federal Republic of Germany. The number of Thai migrant women has risen from 988 in 1975 to 25,529 in 1997 and accounts for 84 per cent of the total number of Thai nationals in Germany. Many of them have immigrated in order to work in prostitution. This transnational prostitution migration is mostly considered as a kind of 'trafficking in women'. According to this point of view, Thai women are passive victims. It does not take into account the migration intentions and aims of the women and has therefore contributed to the invisibility of Thai women as social actors.

Unlike other studies concerning Thai women in Germany, this chapter treats Thai women as social actors capable of accounting for their conduct. It aims to contribute to the development of an analytical framework that provides a space for the understanding of transnational prostitution as a kind of transnational labour migration. Rather than considering transnational prostitution as traffic in women, the migratory process of these women to Germany should be analysed in the context of an international migration system between Thailand, the sending country, and Germany, the receiving one. Hence, this chapter first presents a conceptual framework of the migration system. Based on data from narrative biographical interviews[1] with ten Thai women and information collected through observation and ten years of counselling work with Thai women, mainly in Eastern Westphalia-Lippe, Germany, a discussion of the migratory process of transnational prostitution of Thai women to Germany will be presented.

Almost all the women interviewed live and work in Eastern Westphalia-Lippe, while two have their residence in Hesse and Hamburg. We met all of them, except for the one in Hamburg who was introduced to us by a colleague, during counselling work. The period of their immigration to Germany was used as the criterion for the selection of women to be interviewed. The information about transnational prostitution in different periods of time makes the comparison of causes and factors of such a kind of migration possible. They also enable us to draw a picture of this migratory process.

MIGRATION SYSTEMS: A THEORETICAL FRAMEWORK

The migration system approach was developed in response to the criticism of the two main approaches in migration theory: the neo-classical economic equilibrium approach and the historical structuralist approach. Both these approaches are one-sided in their units and their levels of analysis and hence inadequate when explaining the complexity of contemporary migration (Castles 1994). Thus, this is an attempt to integrate all elements and aspects of the two main strands of migration theories. It examines structures and factors in sending and receiving countries as well as all dimensions of the relations between them.

Patterson has given a general definition of a migration system: 'A migration system, then, is any movement of persons between states, the social, economic, and cultural effects of such movements, and the patterned interactions among such effects' (Patterson 1987: 228). A migration system may comprise a group of countries between which there are movements of population. It comes into existence when places are linked by the flows and counter-flows of people, as well as by economic and political relations between areas (see Boyd 1989: 641). Interactions between societies are created not only by the flows of people but also by the flows of information, services, goods and ideas (Bös 1997). To understand the relations and links within a migration system, one should consider them in a broader political, social, demographic and economic context (Fawcett and Arnold 1987).

According to the migration systems approach, international migration flows should be seen as a result of the interaction between macro- and micro-structures (Castles and Miller 1993: 22–4). The macro-structures refer to large-scale institutional factors such as the political economy of the world market, interstate relationships and also the laws and policy concerning migrants. The micro-structures are the social and informal networks as well as practices developed by migrants and their communities in order to cope with the consequences of migration. These networks bind 'migrants and non-migrants together in a complex web of social roles and interpersonal relationships' and connect them across time and space, which means that migration flows become self-sustaining (Boyd 1989: 639, 641). This involves the establishment of information, support and obligations developed by migrants in the receiving society and friends and relatives in the sending regions.

The transnational prostitution migration of Thai women to Germany involves two countries. Seen as a migration system, the migration of women demonstrates the relations between Thailand and Germany. To explain and understand this female migration it is necessary to analyse the conditions and factors in Thailand and Germany on the structural and individual levels as well as the relations between them, especially the role of social networks that link Thailand and Germany.

TRANSNATIONAL PROSTITUTION MIGRATION OF THAI WOMEN TO GERMANY

The women The Thai women referred to here do not necessarily include all Thai women in Germany. Rather, the study refers to Thai women who have immigrated to Germany and work in prostitution. All names quoted in this article are pseudonyms.

Our findings and those of Yupa et al. (1988) show that the majority of Thai migrant women are poorly educated. Most had completed compulsory education, the elementary level, with four, six or seven years of schooling depending on which of several different school systems was operating in Thailand at the time. Only a few had completed secondary education. In addition, there were a number of migrant women who had had higher education. Like Malinee, they had attended vocational training. Moreover, some women, such as Montira, who have had university training, were also taking part in this migration process.

From the point of view of the last occupation before emigration, two main groups can be distinguished. One consists of women engaged in the sex industry. Most of them were commercial sex-workers serving foreign men. Some of them, such as Sunisa and particularly the women emigrating during the 1990s like Seeda and Som, have experience of doing sex work abroad, mainly in Asian countries such as Hong Kong, Macau and Japan. This includes women working in massage parlours, one sector of the sex service industry. The second group of Thai migrant women earned their income from various professions such as traders, dressmakers, hairdressers, labourers in manufacturing, singers or hotel employees.

Most of them have a rural background and come from the north and north-east of the country. The remaining migrants came from the Central Region and from Bangkok. Only few have their origins in the south. Considering the places of origin of the migrant women, it was found that the proportion of Thai women who migrated to Germany is quite similar to the proportion who migrated to Bangkok, which mainly comprises women from the north and the north-east, followed by those from the Central Region and from the south respectively (see NSO 1991). This is not accidental since most of the Thai migrant women have previously taken part in the rural–urban migration process in Thailand.

At the time of immigration to Germany, the women were aged between twenty and forty years. Most of them were above twenty-eight years, but at the time of their first step in the rural–urban migratory process in Thailand they were much younger, between thirteen and twenty. These figures reveal a long stretch of time between their first movement from their places of origin and their immigration to Germany. The biography of Malin exemplifies this. Malin, an active sex-worker of north-eastern origin, has passed only the compulsory education. At the age of fourteen she had to leave her village in search of a job in the city. Three years later she moved to Bangkok in order to work in a factory. She got married when she was twenty-six years old. After four years of marriage she quit the factory to become a trader. Her husband left her six years later. Malin had to look after four children alone. Hoping to improve her economic situation, which meant the chance to further the education of her children, Malin decided, at the age of forty, to join transnational prostitution in Germany. It can be assumed that these women have experience in adapting to a new environment. In any event, their prior migration experience discredits the idea of innocent country girls being dispatched abroad. Some women might immigrate at the age of twenty like Wimala, but even she was not a naïve rural girl. She left her village for Bangkok after completing secondary school at the age of sixteen. There she stayed with her sister, Sunisa, a sex-worker serving foreign men, who gave her financial support for a dress-making course. During her stay in Bangkok, Wimala also had a foreign boyfriend who would come and spend his whole holiday with her every year.

Patterns of migration The biographies of the women, particularly prior to their immigration to Germany, reveal that the majority of them, all of those who originated in the rural areas and some born in Bangkok, have an internal migration history. The women of Bangkok origin had moved to other provinces for employment. In their younger days these women left their home town somewhere in a rural area, mostly after completing compulsory education. For many of them, such as Sunisa, Suksri, Som, Malika and Marayat, moving to an urban area had allowed them to search for a job in order to support their families and themselves. For the remainder, like Malinee and Montira, it was the only means of access to higher education. After completing higher education or vocational training, another step in migration was undertaken in the search for employment. Realizing that prostitution could bring in a large sum of money in a very short period of time, some labour migrant women such as Sunisa, Seeda and Suksri left their professional work and began a career as sex-workers. Moreover, some of these former internal migrant women had already gained experience as transnational sex-workers in Hong Kong, Macau and Japan. Therefore, one conclusion based on empirical analysis can be drawn, namely that transnational prostitution migration to Germany is the last phase in a long stepwise international migratory process beginning mainly in villages in remote areas, a continuation of internal female migration in Thailand. A similar process was also found in the pattern of marriage migration of Thai women to Germany (see Pataya 1998). As we will show later, there is a strong connection between these two transnational migration flows.

The migratory process of Thai women to Germany includes a variety of internal migration processes. One exception is a small number of women born in Bangkok who have no previous migration history. For the women with rural backgrounds, it is by no means a one-step process, that is from rural poverty directly to Germany, as scholars and activists in Germany usually believe (see, for example, Agisra 1990). Many studies of the issue have no access to empirical data regarding the life histories of the women. Their assertions are usually based on estimates or on conclusions drawn from information on place of birth, neglecting the women's experiences before immigration. Based on their findings, Siriporn et al. (1997: 69) suggest that there is a one-step migration from villages directly to foreign countries. This might be true according to Siriporn et al.'s (1997: 83) definition of one-step migration using the criterion of non-participation in prostitution prior to transnational prostitution migration. If the entire migration histories of the women are taken into account, however, the outcome is unlikely to indicate one-step migration.

The migratory process to Germany can be described as follows:

1. It begins mainly in villages. The women move, usually, after compulsory education to urban areas in a district or provincial capital; some migrate directly to the national capital. They go to search for employment or to attain further education. Many women move directly from villages to become prostitutes in Pattaya.
2. From the district or province, they move on to a bigger city or to Bangkok, looking for better earning opportunities or advanced education.
3. From labour migrant to prostitution: they further migrate to the centres of the sex industry such as Pattaya or Patpong, or to some provinces in the south, and become commercial sex-workers, especially for foreign men. The typical reason for this conduct is the chance of economic advancement in a very short time.
4. The internal labour migrants join transnational prostitution.
5. The last phase is migration to Germany. For women born in Bangkok without migration experience, it is a one-step migratory process.

In summary, there are five routes of transnational prostitution from Thailand to Germany. (1) from labour and educational migration to prostitution in Germany (this is the route taken by Malinee, Malika, Montira, Marayat, Malin and Wimala); (2) from labour migration to prostitution in Thailand, then to immigration for sex-work in Germany (Suksri came to Germany this way); (3) from labour migration to prostitution in Thailand then to work in the sex sector abroad before entering prostitution in Germany; (Sunisa, Som and Seeda followed this path) (4) from village to prostitution, then transnational prostitution to Germany; finally (5), single-step migration from Bangkok to Germany.

These last two routes were not found among the women we interviewed, but Thai women coming for counselling provide evidence of this.

Causes of migration Based on their biographies, the women can be divided into two groups: single mothers and young unmarried women. The single mothers, the majority of Thai migrant women, comprise women who were married or lived with a Thai husband as a de facto couple without a marriage certificate, but who have subsequently divorced, separated or been widowed. They all have children for whom they are the sole breadwinners. This is an important factor in encouraging the women to migrate abroad in the expectation of economic improvement. Malinee, Malika, Montira, Marayat, Malin and Suksri share the experience of this group of women.

Generally, the group of young unmarried women with which some women of the sample, such as Wimala, can be identified, belong to the lower middle class and feel economically deprived. This does not mean that they face severe economic difficulties. Rather that, in their own perception, they see no possibility of achieving social and economic advancement (according to their own criteria) if they stay in Thailand.

Economic incentives are a common factor motivating these two groups to take part in prostitution migration. Thai migrant women immigrate to Germany with the intention of finding employment in order to improve or to stabilize their economic status. Poverty or economic difficulties did not necessarily cause the migration to Germany, because most of the Thai immigrant women belong to the middle class and earn enough for their livelihood. What they want is an opportunity to build an economic future. As an employee in a middle-level firm, Montira's earnings are not that bad, but as she pointed out: 'Of course it was such a good salary that I got. But it is only for the day-to-day cost of living. Nothing left. I wonder how can I pay for the education of my kid.' It is true that some women were in debt and migration serves the purpose of paying it off, but their debts were caused, in the case of Malinee, by the failure of their business or, in the case of Malika, by gambling and not by poverty.

Besides better earnings, one hidden aspiration of these women is the chance to marry a well-off foreigner. Seeda commented: 'My friend who helped me to come here also talked about nice well-to-do men. She said maybe I can get one to marry me. I think why not.' This motive is also found among sex-workers in Pattaya and Patpong who have experience of transnational prostitution (Yupa et al. 1988: 58). They were introduced to this occupation by their predecessors, friends or relatives who worked abroad. Later, they married foreign men and came back to visit home as women of some wealth. From this point of view it can be seen that one factor inspiring the migration of Thai women is social imitation. The economic achievements of previous migrants becomes a desired model for other women.

Moreover, family problems can be an important factor driving women to migrate, particularly those who were married or lived as de facto couples. In the frame of their life history, migration started when a family relationship came to an end. For some women like Malinee, the separation caused psychological troubles. Migration offered an opportunity of escape. She, like many others, was thus spared harassment by her former spouse. For some women, such as Malika and Marayat, migration to Germany demonstrated to the people in their environment, especially their husbands, that they were able to manage by themselves.

On the macro-level, it was found that one important factor pushing Thai women to immigrate to Germany was economic deprivation. This reflects the uneven distribution of economic opportunities that puts poorly educated people, like most Thai women migrating to Germany, at a disadvantage in building an economic existence or in satisfying their consumption demands.

As mentioned before, many Thai migrant women are single mothers with sole responsibility for their children. One question to be raised here is why this burden has to fall only on the shoulders of women. Is not the responsibility of supporting children also a task of the fathers? One explanation for this is the uneven social control over women and men. Control over women seems to be more strictly exercised than over men. Therefore it comes as no surprise to see that remittances from women in Germany meant for their children are continued even when the children live with their fathers.

Despite the social expectation that women take responsibility for their children, there is insufficient support from the state. State policy concerning social and economic welfare and security for single mothers seems to be invisible or non-existent. In practice, the legislation intended to force men to pay maintenance for their children is of little value.

The most decisive factor in making migration possible is the social and kinship networks providing information and support. Empirically, the transnational migration of Thai women to Germany contains a characteristic of chain migration. The pioneer migrant women later function as parts of social networks, maintaining links to their home community, providing information about living and working conditions and on modalities of entrance into the target country. They organize the trip and help at the place of destination, and sometimes even recruit more women. Hence, within these networks, the transnational migration of Thai women becomes self-sustaining.

FEATURES OF TRANSNATIONAL PROSTITUTION OF THAI WOMEN TO GERMANY

The existing data are not sufficient to indicate precisely when transnational prostitution of Thai women to Germany started. In a study by the Women Foundation, it was found that in 1976–77 there were sexworkers from Pattaya and Patpong emigrating to work in prostitution in Europe (Siriporn et al. 1997: 75, 79, 117). As revealed by the figures of the Federal Statistical Office, this period was the beginning of the increase in the number of Thai women in Germany. A report of the Berlin Institute for Comparative Social Research points out that the great increase in the number of Thai women in Berlin, where a huge number of Thai migrant women work in prostitution, started in 1980–81 (BIVS 1988: 32). It was in this period that the women interviewed by us also emigrated to work in Germany. According to these sources it can be assumed that the transnational prostitution of Thai women to Germany started at the end of the 1970s and the beginning of the 1980s. Information from the interviews and the observations show distinctive types and paths of migration which make it possible to distinguish the following two periods.

From the end of the 1970s to 1988 In this period citizens of Thailand did not require visas to enter Germany. They were entitled to stay for three months. Thai women also entered Germany this way. Transnational prostitution of Thai women at this time was periodic. They came and worked for three months, then returned home; or else they left for work in other countries once in a while before returning to work in Germany.

Another way for Thai women to enter the country was to travel on an artist's visa (see Chapter 6 by Prapairat Ratanaloan Mix). Many women travelled to Germany this way in the mid-1980s. While many were encouraged by friends or relatives who had previously been migrant sex-workers abroad, some may have been lured by agents. Many women knew about the nature of work they would have to do, but many others did not. Malinee reported: 'As I decided to come I didn't know exactly what I could do here but it was quite clear which kind of work can bring much money in a short time.' Some women were deceived: Malika and Marayat were told that they would work in a restaurant, but once they were in Germany they had to work as sex-workers. Many women travelling through agencies cannot avoid being taken advantage of.

Facts and figures could be interpreted to indicate that transnational prostitution as such is traffic in women. This might be so if the phenomenon is considered from perspectives other than those of the women themselves. It also depends on one's definition. Whether or not prostitution is traffic in women, it is not within the scope of this chapter to discuss further; there is a sufficient number of studies currently undertaking this task. As to the conditions under which Thai women work, these are well documented elsewhere (see, for example, Siriporn et al. 1997; Prapairat 1999) and therefore it is not necessary to repeat them here. The working conditions of the Thai migrant women interviewed and observed by us do not differ greatly from conditions described in these accounts.

One interesting point we found is that many Thai migrant women who entered Germany in the early years of transnational migration share a similar history. Suksri and some of her friends entering the country in this period had, in their younger days, joined the internal labour migration mostly because of poverty. Hoping for better earnings they later became *mia chaos* (rent wife) for US soldiers during the period of the Vietnam War. After 1975, as the US military bases were withdrawn from Thailand, the women could not, or did not want to, find a job. They migrated to Bangkok and worked in nightclubs, bars or in massage parlours. In these surroundings they were encouraged by friends, migrant sex-workers, to join transnational prostitution in Germany. Here one can see the way in which a career in transnational prostitution might develop.

Since the mid-1980s there have also been women without a background in prostitution searching for economic betterment who have joined the transnational prostitution to Germany. Malinee, Malika and Wimala also belong to this group. Most of them first began as shuttle prostitutes. In order to stay longer than three months they had to search for a German whom they could marry. According to the German law of aliens, they are entitled to obtain residence and work permits only as a spouse of a German or a citizen of the EU states. So many Thai migrant sex-workers married a German for this purpose. Sometimes it was only a 'bogus marriage': the women pay a man to marry them in order to get a marriage certificate but they do not live together as a couple. Malika and Malinee used this method when their visas expired. After a while they found men with whom they really wanted to start a family, so they divorced their hired husbands and married 'real' ones. While some women became full-time housewives after marriage, many still engaged in their profession. At this point transnational migrant sex-workers have become married migrant women.

1989 to the present Since 1 January 1989, Thais entering Germany require visas. The pattern of transnational prostitution of Thai women has changed from shuttle prostitution to migration with visitors' or tourists' visas, from self-arranged to organized migration. For a visa application the woman must have an invitation from a resident in Germany who will take financial responsibility for her. All documents are arranged by friends, relatives or agents. With a visa, women can stay for only three months and are not allowed to work. Like those who migrated in the earlier period, they have to marry a German or someone possessing a residence permit in order to obtain residence and work permits themselves. The arrangements made by friends, relatives or agents therefore sometimes include provision for a marriage candidate. Transnational prostitution is at this point integrated into marriage migration. In other words, transnational prostitution is one form of marriage migration, serving the purpose of working as sex-workers.

By the second period, the women who arrived before 1989 had become part of a social network and even recruiters. Some had their own establishments, usually after receiving a residence permit or after marriage. In this way sex establishments with Thai sex-workers have increased and are no longer concentrated in big cities but are scattered among smaller towns and even smaller villages. The pioneer migrants encourage friends, relatives and women from their place of origin to migrate to Germany, offering them assistance. It is not surprising, therefore, to find a concentration of women from certain Thai villages and districts in a particular area in Germany. Seeda was not the first or only woman from the district where she was born in Udon Thani who came to work in a middle-sized city in Eastern Westphalia-Lippe. The pioneer migrant sex-worker had arrived some years before. She married, obtained a residence permit and opened her own establishment. Seeda told us that some other women from her district in Udon Thani will follow her.

Thai migrant women arriving during these years came from different backgrounds. They comprised sex-workers from Pattaya, Patpong and elsewhere abroad (e.g. Som and Seeda), single mothers (e.g. Montira, Marayat and Malin) and young unattached women (about 20 per cent of women who came for counselling). All share one goal: a search for employment that will guarantee economic betterment. Moreover, we find that during this period Thai men, transsexuals and transvestites, have also joined transnational prostitution to Germany. In the early years these men entered the country using artists' visas to work as cabaret dancers. They became sex-workers later when they realized that they would earn more. Because of the restrictions imposed on artists' visas after 1993, the entry of Thai transsexuals is now organized by other means. The number of people entering Germany on artists' visas has rapidly decreased.

As social networks are maintained and extended by migrants all over Germany, mostly in the west, women are not tied to work in one particular place but can shuttle between cities. They might first work in Berlin, then later move to Stuttgart or Hamburg, then back again to Berlin. After a while they might have an establishment of their own and become recruiters like the pioneer migrant sex-worker from Seeda's home town.

TRANSNATIONAL PROSTITUTION: A VARIETY OF TRANS-NATIONAL LABOUR MIGRATION

In summary, economic deprivation, the dual factors of social expectations and control over women with respect to their responsibility to the family in Thai society, and the transitions in the lives of Thai migrant women on one hand, combined with the attraction of better economic conditions in Germany on the other hand, are factors influencing the emergence of transnational prostitution and marriage migration (see Pataya 1998). Given the restrictions imposed by German immigration law, the only legal way for Thai women to enter Germany is to marry a German. With the status of a spouse of a German citizen they are entitled to obtain residence and work permits that make up the pre-requisites for income earning, their intended aim of migration. Hence, Thai women utilize marriage as a means of immigration to Germany. Marriage migration can thus be defined as a migration concerning or emerging by means of marriage. Given the barriers of immigration policy in the countries of destination, marriage has turned out to be a means of legal immigration coupled with the expectation of social and economic achievement. It follows from our findings that many Thai women migrating by means of marriage to a German share one common intention, i.e. to search for employment in Germany. Because of the constraints of immigration laws, if they want to stay they have to marry regardless of their purpose, which may be to build a new family, to search for higher earnings or to work in prostitution. Migration-cum-marriage should therefore be considered as a variety of transnational labour migration. It is a specifically female form of migration. As our findings and those of others show, this form of migration is used by women rather than men (see also del Rosario 1994; Hugo 1995).

THE OTHER ELEMENT OF THE SYSTEM

Within the framework of a migration system, the causes and factors associated with transnational prostitution in the receiving country, namely Germany, have to be examined. To our knowledge, no empirical study examining such factors exists. In Germany there are some studies of the clients of female sex-workers (e.g. Kleiber and Velten 1994). All we know is that about 35.1 per cent of their respondents (N = 598) have visited foreign sex-workers (Kleiber and Velten 1994: 84). But no distinction between clients visiting native and foreign sex-workers is made. From such studies it is not possible to draw a picture of the character and backgrounds of the clients of foreign sex-workers and their motives in preferring foreign women, which would help us to find causes and factors associated with transnational prostitution to Germany.

In an attempt to draw up an analytical framework on female international migration in the context of social reproduction, Truong (1995) points out the coincidence between changing gender relations at the symbolic and subjective level and the emergence of a new 'corporate' culture as one factor facilitating the growing incorporation of sex-affective services in industrial relations (Truong 1995: 150). The 'corporate' culture requires a high degree and frequency of mobility among executives whose needs must be catered to. New forms of sex-affective services such as massage and even sexual services are also included in basic services. This is why, according to Truong, the sex industry is visible in mega-cities in industrialized nations. She concludes – as do Sassen-Koob (1984), Morokvasic (1983) and Phizacklea (1983) in studies on the international female labour migration from the 'Third World' and the European peripheries to industrialized countries – that the traffic in women and girls for the purpose of prostitution may be seen as one aspect of a transnational transfer of sex-affective labour from low-income areas to high-income areas, to fill gaps which cannot be filled by indigenous labour (Truong 1995: 150). Adapting Truong's hypothesis, transnational prostitution of Thai women to Germany must be seen as cheap reproductive labour required by German society to undertake activities that German women no longer will perform. The figures from the Federal Ministry of Public Health and Hydra e.V. in Berlin cited in *Neues Westfälische* (269, 6 November 1999) reveal that there are about 400,000 women working in prostitution. Most of them chose this job because the income was good. Only 23.5 per cent of the sex-workers are estimated to be foreign women (Kleiber and Velten 1994: 84). This shows that there are enough German women working in this milieu. Hence, the hypothesis is not supported. To explain the causes and factors associated with transnational prostitution in the receiving country we need other analytical frameworks. One alternative is the migration system, an element of which, namely Thailand, has already been analysed. It is now our task to construct a conceptual framework for the study of the character and backgrounds of men who visit Thai sex-workers and also their motives for preferring foreign women. The services offered by both native and migrant sex-workers should also be examined to determine whether there is a gap that requires foreign reproductive female labour. Two important aspects to be taken into account are the interaction between the individual and the structural factors and also the links between the two countries.

CONCLUSION

This chapter has argued that the transnational prostitution of Thai women to Germany can be analysed in the context of a migration system between Thailand and Germany. It has also shown that transnational prostitution has emerged in the form of marriage migration and can be considered as a variety of international labour migration. It is the last phase of a long stepwise transnational migratory process and the continuation of internal female labour migration in Thailand. One aspect of the causes and factors associated with transnational prostitution in Germany – the role of the clients – remains unexamined. Unless studies on clients are conducted, the process of transnational prostitution cannot be completely explained.

NOTE

1. The narrative biographical interviews, a kind of qualitative research method, were carried out for the research project 'Marriage Migration: Towards the Sociology of the Immigration of Thai Women to Germany' conducted by the author, 1994–97 in Thailand and Germany under the direction of Professor Dr Eckhard Dittrich. It was conducted under the auspices of the Faculty of Sociology, University of Bielefeld, Germany, and financed by the German Research Fund (Deutsche Forschungsgemeinschaft). Forty-two women were interviewed. Ten of them had migrated to Germany to work in prostitution. These interviews are utilized as important sources for the analysis in this chapter.

REFERENCES

Agrisra (1990) *Frauenhandel und Prostitutionstourismus. Eine Bestandsaufnahme zu Prostitutionstourismus, Heiratsvermittlung und Menschenhandel mit ausländischen Mädchen und Frauen* (Munich: Trickster).

BIVS (Berliner Institute für Vergleichende Sozialforschung) (ed.) (1988) 'Die Prostitution thailändischer Frauen in Berlin (West). Eine Situationsanalyse zur Problematik der Armutsprostitution und der Heiratsvermittlung ausländischer Frauen. Gutachten für die Senatorin für Jugend und Familie', research project (Berlin).

Bös, Mathias (1997) *Migration als Problem offener Gesellschaften: Globalisierung und sozialer Wandel im Westeuropa und in Nordamerika* (Opladen: Leske und Budrich).

Boyd, Monica (1989) 'Family and Personal Networks in International Migration: Recent Developments and New Agendas', *International Migration Review*, 23: 638–70.

Castles, Stephen (1994) 'Causes and Consequences of Asia's New Migrations', Proceeding of the International Conference on Transnational Migration in the Asia-Pacific: Problems and Prospects, 1–2 December 1994 (Bangkok: Chulalongkorn University).

Castles, Stephen and Mark Miller (1993) *The Age of Migration: International Population Movements in the Modern World* (London: Macmillan).

del Rosario, Virginia O. (1994) 'Lifting the Smoke Screen: Dynamics of Mail-order Bride Migration from the Philippines', unpublished dissertation (Den Haag: Institute of Social Studies).

Fawcett, James T. and Fred Arnold (1987) 'Explaining Diversity: Asian and Pacific Immigration Systems', in J.Fawcett and B. V. Carino (eds), *Pacific Bridges: the New Immigration from Asia and the Pacific Islands* (New York: Center for Migration Studies): 453–73.

Hugo, Graeme J. (1995) 'Migration of Asian Women to Australia', in Department for Economic and Social Information and Policy Analysis Population Division, International Migration Policies and the Status of Female Migrants, Proceedings of the United Nations Expert Group Meeting on International Migration Policies and the Status of Female Migrants, San Miniato, Italy, 28–31 March 1990 (New York: United Nations): 192–220.

Kleiber, Dieterand Doris Velten (1994) *Prostitutionskunden: Eine Untersuchung über soziale und psychologische Charakteristika von Besuchern weiblicher Prostituierter in Zeiten von AIDS* (Baden-Baden: Nomos Verlaggesellschaft).

Kritz, Mary M. and Hania Zlotnik (1992) 'Global Interactions: Migration Systems, Processes and Policies', in Mary M. Kritz et al. (eds), *International Migration Systems: a Global Approach* (Oxford: Clarendon Press).

Morokvasic, Mirjana (1983) 'Women in Migration: Beyond the Reductionist Outlook', in A. Phizacklea (ed.), *One Way Ticket: Migration and Female Labour* (London: Routledge and Kegan Paul): 13–52.

NSO (National Statistics Office) (1991) *Population and Housing Census Bangkok Metropolis 1990* (Bangkok).

Pataya, Ruenkaew (1998) 'Heiratsmigration: Zur Soziologie der Einwanderung thailändischer Frauen in die Bundesrepublik', Research Report, Faculty of Sociology, University of Bielefeld.

Patterson, Orlando (1987) 'The Emerging West Atlantic System: Migration, Culture and Underdevelopment in the United States and the Circum-Caribbean Region', in W. Alonso (ed.), *Population in an Interacting World* (Cambridge, MA: Harvard University Press): 227–62.

Phizacklea, Annie (1983) 'In the Front Line', in A. Phizacklea (ed.), *One Way Ticket: Migration and Female Labour* (London: Routledge and Kegan Paul): 95–112.

Prapairat, Ratanaolan Mix (1999) 'Prostitution Migration: Thai Sex Workers in Germany', Paper presented at the 7th International Conference on Thai Studies, 4–8 July 1999, Amsterdam.

Sassen-Koob, Saskia (1984) 'Notes on the Incorporation of Third World Women into Wage Labour through Immigration and Off-Shore Production', *International Migration Review* (Special Issue on Women and Migration), 18 (4): 1144–67.

Siriporn, Skrobanek, Nataya Boonpakdee and Chutima Jantateero (1997) *Kan Kha Ying: rue witee sang khom thai (Traffic in Women)* (Bangkok: Samnakpimphuying).

Truong, Thanh-Dam (1995) 'Gender, International Migration and Social Reproduction: Implications for Theory, Policy, Research and Networking', in International Peace Research Institute, Meiji Gakuin University (ed.), *International Female Migration and Japan: Networking, Settlement and Human Rights* (Tokyo: International Research Institute): 141–68.

Yupa Wongchai, Lek Sombat, Natthee Chitsawang, Sasipatana Yodpech and Saichit Singhaseni (1988) 'Pat chai tang setakit lae sang khom ti mi pon tor kan pai pra kob a-chip kha pra we ni khong satri thai nai tang pra tes'. Unpublished research report, Faculty of Social Welfare, Thammasart University, Bangkok.

SIX

Four Cases from Hamburg

PRAPAIRAT RATANALOAN MIX

§ This chapter is concerned with the situation of Thai female sex-workers in Germany, particularly Hamburg. It investigates the methods of immigration used, the women's motivations for coming to Germany, their living and working conditions, legal status and relations with other Thai women in similar circumstances. It is based on my many years of experience as a social worker, employed by Amnesty for Women (AfW)[1] as a full-time staff member responsible for assisting Thai women in Hamburg, and more recently as a researcher on the migration of Thai women to Germany.

The views in this chapter deviate from the frequent assumption made by people studying Thai women abroad that these women are always 'victims', i.e. people without power over their destinies, victims of circumstances beyond their control. This view of women as victims has dominated the research on Thai women abroad and contributed to the common perception that these women have been taken advantage of. This perception exists among many researchers, members of organizations that provide assistance to the women and among the general public in the countries to which they migrate. While some Thai women are indeed victims, this chapter assumes that many Thai women make conscious choices about their future and plan their lives carefully in ways that often work to their benefit. These women have significant control over their lives, well-defined life goals, and substantial knowledge of how to achieve those goals.

CASE STUDIES

The information in the following case studies has been collected over a six-year period and is based on interviews, observation and interaction with the women in the course of my day-to-day work for Amnesty for Women. AfW has provided assistance to each of the women for a period of between two to six years. The names of the women have been changed in order to protect their identities.

CASE STUDY I

Name:	Ngamnit
Age:	35
Place of birth:	Central Thailand
Education:	Four years at primary school
Parents and siblings:	Both parents dead; four older sisters, now living in Germany, and one younger brother.
Marital status/children:	One daughter with a Thai ex-husband (the daughter lives with her father in Thailand); now married to a German teacher, with whom she has one son.

Ngamnit said that her family, large by Thai standards, was very poor. Her mother had a small food stall in the market near her home; as her father did not have a regular job, he would often help his wife to cook. All four sisters had to leave school after only four years in order to help their mother. The mother died of cancer when Ngamnit was six years old and she was raised by her sisters. When she had finished four years of primary school, she quit to help out around the house and look after her younger brother when all her sisters were busy with the food stall. Her father died when she was nine. One of her sisters moved out with her boyfriend, leaving the others to run the food stall. Later they found jobs working in a factory. One of her sisters had a Dutch boyfriend who was working as a supervisor at the factory. When his contract ran out, he had to return to the Netherlands, and asked her sister to marry him and go with him. Ngamnit said that her sister was fine in the Netherlands but was unable to send money home as promised because her husband had gone back to university to further his studies. Three years later, a second sister married a Dutch man, a friend of Ngamnit's husband, and moved with him to Saudi Arabia. So at the age of nineteen Ngamnit was left with her unmarried sister and younger brother.

Ngamnit married a Thai Chinese man and moved in with her husband's family as is usual in the Chinese tradition. They had a small grocery store in the market. She did not get along very well with her mother-in-law, especially when she had a baby girl after being married for a year. She said that she was not at all happy with her life. She left her husband's family when her daughter was two years old. She said that she thought of her two sisters who had married European men, and hoped to do the same. Instead of returning home to her sister and brother, she went to Pattaya, hoping to find a job in a restaurant but ended up working in a go-go bar. Ngamnit never told her sisters about her life in Pattaya. She sent money to support her brother's education but while in Pattaya she did not contact her daughter or her husband.

She had a German boyfriend who invited her to go and work in Germany. She told her sisters and went to Germany, hoping to earn enough money during the three-month period to quit her job on her return to Thailand. The boyfriend took her to Frankfurt where she worked in a brothel. He asked her to help him pay for the expenses of the journey and arrangements. She agreed. After two months, the boyfriend suggested that she marry him in order to get a residence permit. Ngamnit said that at first she was not sure, but that she was tempted by the amount of money she earned every day. She knew that she would also have to pay him if she married him, but agreed. They married and moved to Hamburg.

In Hamburg, her husband rented an apartment for her to work with other Thai women. Ngamnit said that she had saved a lot of money to send home for her brother and sisters. She planned to work for another year or so, after which she would go back to Thailand. During this time, she had a regular client to whom she told her story. He said that he wanted to help her and marry her. Her husband threatened to kill her when he found out about the affair, but Ngamnit carried on working for another year and stayed in contact with her German boyfriend. Finally, she told her husband that she wanted a divorce or else she would go to the police. He accepted this in order to avoid problems and also because he still had another two Thai women working for him.

Ngamnit married again. She said that this time it was a real marriage, and that although she does not love her husband very much, he is a nice man. Even though he is not as rich as she expected, at least he has a steady job. He agreed to give her 400 DM every month. Now Ngamnit has a three-year-old son and works as a maid in a hotel. She said she is happy now and never looks back. She sees her daughter every year when she goes back to Thailand. 'She is better off with her own father,' Ngamnit said. All her sisters are now living in Hamburg. Two of them came as sex-workers after their divorces and later married German men. The other two sisters came for marriages which she arranged for them, while her brother still lives and works in Bangkok.

CASE STUDY 2

Name:	Sawittree
Age:	28
Place of birth:	Isarn (north-east Thailand)
Education:	Five years at primary school
Parents and siblings:	Father was a rickshaw driver, mother worked at home; two older brothers, two older and one younger sister.
Marital status/children:	Two sons and one daughter with a Thai ex-husband;[2] now married to a German computer programmer.

Sawittree also comes from a large family. Her mother opened a small food stall at home in order to supplement the father's income as a rickshaw driver. When her two brothers left school, they also became rickshaw drivers. Sawittree had to leave school aged eleven when her two older sisters went to work in Bangkok and her mother wanted her to help out at home. She did not know what kind of work her sisters did, but they sent money home regularly. Her father died two years later. One of her brothers married but continued to stay at home with Sawittree, her younger sister, her other brother and mother. He stopped working and simply waited for his sisters to send money home every month. One of the sisters came home with a German boyfriend and said that she was going to live in Germany with him. She promised to try to find a job and send money home but they did not hear from her for a long time. The other brother decided to go to work in Saudi Arabia, and her mother gave him all the money she had. Sawittree was very upset about this, saying that it was unfair because the money came from her sisters' savings.

Sawittree was sixteen years old when she met her husband, a truck driver, and moved to live with him in a small village nearby. When Sawittree already had three children, her sister came back from Germany and gave her mother some money, saying that she had been unable to send money earlier because she did not work and her husband never gave her any extra money. She was divorced and was now working again. Sawittree told her sister that her husband was hardly ever at home and that, when he was, he would drink and beat up her and the children. Her sister told her that she had been a sex-worker in Bangkok before she went to Germany and because her husband had never supported her financially, she decided to become a sex-worker there too. When the husband got to know about this, he demanded that she quit her job or he would divorce her. She agreed to the divorce and carried on working. She invited Sawittree to come with her and work in Germany, but said that she would have to leave her children with their grandmother. Her sister said, 'You have nothing to lose.' Finally, Sawittree went to Germany on a tourist visa (with the help of her sister's German boyfriend) in 1993.

When she arrived in Berlin and found out exactly what she had to do, she changed her mind, but her sister said that she had to work, otherwise there would be no money for her children at home. Because she had a tourist visa, Sawittree had to work in an apartment brothel, not in a bar like her sister who helped her out financially. Before her visa ran out, her sister said that she could extend it for another three months but that after that she had to go back to Thailand or find someone to marry her. Within six months, Sawittree had managed to save some money and send it home to her mother. She said that it was very hard to do the job, but that once she started to earn money, everything became easier. She did not want to pay anyone to get married, so she decided to stay illegally in Germany.

Sawittree moved to Hamburg and worked with other Thai sex-workers in an apartment brothel. At first there was no trouble from the immigration police. She met a German man who wanted to marry her but her illegal status made it very complicated. Unfortunately, the immigration police arrested her when they raided the apartment building. She was in jail for three weeks before she appeared in court, charged with illegal immigration not prostitution. In court she pleaded not guilty because she was waiting to get married. She was set free but had to pay a fine. She finally married but carried on working, as her husband was unemployed.

Sawittree is no longer working, as her husband found a job. She has not been back to Thailand since she arrived in Germany six years ago. She said she missed her children very much and would like them to join her but she has to wait for legal documents. She intends to ask her other sister to come too, but it will be her sister's decision whether to choose the same path as Sawittree or to find a man to marry her. The sister who brought her to Hamburg is still working in the sex trade.

CASE STUDY 3

Name:	Srithong
Age:	32
Place of birth:	Isarn (north-east Thailand)
Education:	Four years at primary school
Parents and siblings:	Parents have a small food stall in the local market; two younger sisters and one younger brother.
Marital status/children:	Married to a German engineer, with whom she has one daughter.

Srithong's mother inherited land from her parents but did not want to work as a rice farmer, and so rented it out to other farmers. Her mother preferred a small business; her father worked as a bus driver. Srithong said that she had had a wonderful life as a young child. However, her father started to gamble and the family was faced with financial problems. Her father wanted to work in the Middle East, so they mortgaged some of the land to pay for travelling expenses, but he was cheated and never left home. He went back to gambling, mortgaging the rest of the land and the house. The family lost everything and had to move to another province. Srithong had to leave school. Her nightmare began, she said, when she had to start working in a rice field at the age of twelve, earning only 25 Baht per day.

A neighbour invited her to Bangkok to work as a housemaid. She agreed reluctantly since she felt she had no other choice. She worked for a couple who had one young daughter. The husband was a government employee. She had to work every day and earned 1,500 Baht a month, sending most of the money home. After two years, her boss asked if she would like to go to Japan with them because he had been posted there to work for the next four years. She was very excited about going abroad. In Tokyo, Srithong only had to look after the girl, while his wife looked after the household. She was paid only 3,000 Baht per month to work in Japan with the family. Later, she was introduced to a Japanese man by her elderly Japanese neighbour, who thought that she was being treated unfairly with poor working conditions and low wages. Srithong left the Thai family and moved in with her Japanese boyfriend. He was still living with his parents, 300 km south of Tokyo. She thought that Japanese people would be like Thai people because they are also Asian. She was mistaken. His parents hated her because they thought she was a sex-worker like many other Thai women living in Japan.

Srithong tried her best to help out in the household. She said: 'I help them with everything, washing their clothes, ironing and cleaning but they never show me any love.' She tried to tell her boyfriend about this problem but he ignored her. She loved him because in some ways he was a good, responsible man and gave her money to send home every month. Later she found out that he frequented a bar where Thai sex-workers worked. She was very upset. They often fought and she finally left him because he beat her up so badly. She then went to work in the bar but by this time her visa had run out. Later, she was arrested and sent back to Thailand. By that time she had saved a lot of money.

Srithong went home to visit her parents and gave them most of her savings. She then went to Pattaya where she worked in a bar for three months, before being invited by a Thai woman to go and work in Germany. She went to Germany on an artist's visa arranged by the same Thai woman who was married to a German man. She was told that after she started working she would have to repay a large sum of money for the visa, travelling costs and so on. Within six months, Srithong was free of debts. She worked in a bar in a red-light district in Hamburg. The visa lasted three years and could not be extended. Srithong said she wanted to look for another job, but the visa restricted her choices as did her language skills. The visa had nearly run out when she met a German student who came to the bar. On her day off she told him about her problems: the bar owner did not want to employ her any longer because she did not make enough money for the bar, as she often refused clients. The student agreed to marry her in order to help her stay in Germany.

They married, but after graduation her husband found a job in the south of Germany. Srithong lived alone in Hamburg, gave up her job, and joined a two-year course in a textile workshop subsidized by the

German government to help women recovering from drug addiction or wanting to leave the sex trade. Srithong joined her husband in the south of Germany after she had finished the course. It became a real marriage when she became pregnant. Now Srithong is very happy with her life. She said that she no longer sends money to Thailand because she now has her own family. 'They have had enough money from me,' she said. 'I need to have my own life.'

CASE STUDY 4

Name:	Malai
Age:	43
Place of birth:	Isarn (north-east Thailand)
Education:	Two years at primary school
Parents and siblings:	Both parents dead; three older sisters and one younger brother.
Marital status/children:	Two daughters and one son from two Thai ex-husbands; now divorced from a German husband.

Malai's parents died in a road accident when she was four years old. Her sisters raised her. Later, they all moved from Isarn to Bangkok where one of her sisters worked in a factory and the other two opened a small food stall, selling Isarn food. Malai did not go to school until she was nine years old because her sisters had no house registration to show the authorities. She left school after two years because she was embarrassed to be so much older than the other pupils in her class, and started helping her sisters at the food stall. She said that it was not so bad because they could earn enough to rent a small house near Klongthoey, the biggest slum in Bangkok. Two of her older sisters married and moved out, leaving her with her sister and younger brother.

Malai met her first husband when she was seventeen years old. He was a taxi driver and came from the same province. He moved into her house because she wanted to work with her sister. She had one daughter with him and the marriage went well for the first two years. Then one day his first wife came to her house; he was already married and had three children at home in the north-east. Malai was very disappointed and angry and they split up. Then her sister said that she wanted to go back to the north-east and asked her to carry on their small food stall.

Malai agreed and managed the stall with the help of her brother after school and at weekends. Malai met another man who came to eat at the stall every day. They married and he moved into her house and helped her with the stall. Malai became pregnant but continued to work until she went to hospital. She said her husband was very good until she was pregnant with her third child, and then she found out that he had started seeing other women. They fought every day and before she gave birth he took all the money she had saved and disappeared.

Malai said that it was a terrible time for her. Her eldest daughter helped her a lot with the household work and looked after the baby even though she was only six years old. Her sister came back from the north-east after she heard the news. Malai borrowed money to start her business again. One day, she met a neighbour who came to eat at her stall. She looked very rich and wore a thick gold chain. She said that she had just come back from Germany where she worked. She invited Malai to work with her in a Thai restaurant there. She would pay Malai's travelling costs and then Malai would have to pay her back within the first three months in Germany. Her sister warned Malai that going to Germany could be dangerous and that they might force her to work in the sex industry, because she had seen a lot of reports in the newspapers and on TV. Malai said, 'I have to take a risk.' She added that she had had two husbands, slept with them without ever earning any money and still they deceived her. Malai borrowed a large sum of money at a high rate of interest and gave it to her sister to look after her children and carry on the food stall business.

On the way to Germany, her neighbour told her, as she had suspected, that she would work in a bar not a restaurant. Malai worked in a go-go bar in a red-light district of Hamburg. Her neighbour told her that she owed her 8,000 DM for the arrangements but that this amount would be deducted from her salary later. Malai was shocked by the scale of her debts. She started to work after one week. She said that the Thai women she worked with were very friendly and taught her a lot of things. Malai worked for seven months before she was able to pay back all her debts, both in Thailand and Germany. Malai did not want to return to Thailand immediately as she wanted to earn more money for her children. She said that she would never earn as much as she did in the job she was doing then. Malai worked in the go-go bar for two years before one of her regular clients asked her to marry him. She decided to marry him but continued working. She said she needed someone to be with her and look after her, but he did not earn enough to support her family in Thailand. She told him that she would work for another two or three years. She was already thirty-six years old.

Her husband acted as her chauffeur. He would drop her off in the evening and pick her up after work. Later, he gave up his job. Malai said that she was forced to pay for expenses at home and left her job a year later because of this situation. She did not want to work to support him. She found a cleaning job that paid 15 DM per hour. Her husband was very angry about it but he could do nothing. The marriage went downhill. She and her husband went to Thailand, her first visit in three years. She thought of bringing her children back to Germany but her husband did not want them. They often quarrelled about money. Finally, he asked her to leave the apartment because he had fallen in love with another Thai woman whom he met during their holiday. Malai went to stay with a Thai friend. During that time she met her friend's brother-in-law and fell in love with him. She divorced her husband and now has a permanent resident's visa. She stays with her boyfriend and says that she does not have to marry again. She cleans three times a week for a company and cleans a private home as well. She earns enough to get by in Germany. She said she might go back to Thailand but not just yet.

LIVING CONDITIONS (FROM CASE STUDIES AND IN GENERAL)

Ngamnit is now married to her second German husband, with whom she has a son. When she came to Germany the first time with a freelance trafficker, whom she later married, she knew that she was entering the sex trade, but wanted to work for only a few months. She became more deeply involved in the sex trade, initially because her boyfriend asked her to help him out, because it had been expensive to bring her to Germany. Soon she realized that she was able to earn a lot of money through sex work. Later, Ngamnit worked as a maid, earning only 25 per cent of the money she made in the sex trade. Even though she said that her husband is a nice man, she does not love him very much. He has a steady job, and offers security for her and her son. Ngamnit, like many Thai women, initially expected that her German husband would be rich. Although this expectation was not fulfilled, she felt so secure in Germany that she arranged for all her sisters to join her.

Sawittree no longer works in the sex trade. She is currently waiting to be granted legal status and wants to bring her children from Thailand to join her in Germany. Sawittree went to Germany because of family problems, including a husband who abused her physically and psychologically, and related financial problems. When her sister returned to Thailand, she convinced Sawittree that she would be better off leaving her husband because she had nothing to lose. She then decided, on her sister's advice, to leave her children behind and follow her sister to Germany in hopes of a better life. It seems that her sister had not explained everything to her about becoming a sex-worker in Germany, because Sawittree was unable to cope with the work at first. Many Thai sex-workers who live in Germany do not explain the working conditions and other problems faced by Thai sex-workers when they visit Thailand. Instead, they talk about the amount of money they earn and the jewellery they have. Sawittree's life in Germany was not easy, especially when she decided to live as an illegal migrant in order not to pay someone to marry her. I assume that her decision not to marry was made in order to send money home for her children. Even though she tried to avoid being exploited by men, at one stage she had to work in the sex trade to support her boyfriend who was unemployed at the time. Things improved when he found a job, they got married and she became a full-time housewife.

As a child, *Srithong* was not poor, until her father started gambling and led the family into desperate poverty. Leaving for Japan must have been like a dream come true for her, even though the pay and working conditions were very poor by Japanese standards. When she decided to move in with her Japanese boyfriend and his family, she thought that they would accept her like Thai people would have done. However, she was also treated badly by them. Sex work was the only way for her to break her chains, to show her Japanese boyfriend that she could be independent. Although Srithong had already earned a lot of money by the time she returned to Thailand, she wanted to work abroad once again in order to earn more money. Srithong made her own decision to travel, with the assistance of an agency, to work in Germany. Her main motivation for migrating was to earn more money in order to help support her family in Thailand. Now she is settled in Germany and married to a German. She no longer wants to commit herself financially to her family in Thailand. She is satisfied with her life as a housewife and has given up her sex job.

Malai came to Germany for many reasons, including financial difficulties in Thailand, and the dream of a better life. Her two Thai husbands had both deceived her, so she had to take over full financial and parental responsibilities for her children. 'I have to take a risk,' she told her sister, uncertain of her future in Germany. She fell into the hands of a trafficker, and could not refuse to work because of her debts. Malai is now divorced from her German husband and no longer depends on anyone because she has permanent status in Germany. She works as a cleaner and has decided to remain in Germany.

Most of the women in these case studies seem to be satisfied with their situation at this stage of their lives. Some have fulfilled their dreams and have a family and a prosperous life. For some it is like winning the lottery, even if it is not the first prize. Ngamnit, and Srithong, for example, could be considered to have won a major prize. After many problems, Ngamnit feels satisfied with her life and Srithong is happy. Malai, who took a risk in coming to Germany, has managed to pay back all her debts and is able to lead an independent life. Sawittree is also satisfied with her life and is free of obligations. All of them are a vital part of and help to create the Thai community in Germany.

THAI COMMUNITIES IN HAMBURG

Some larger German cities have Thai temples where Thai women can meet and attend religious activities. Recently a Thai temple was established in Hamburg, where Thai monks live and practise religious activities. The temple is attended by Thai migrants including housewives, sex-workers and other workers, students, and so on. There are two other Thai cultural organizations that arrange meetings, language courses, concerts and other celebrations such as Loy Krathong and Songkran. Other activities include teaching German to Thai women and Thai to their children. Asian food shops are also popular places where many Thais gather. Amnesty for Women also plays an important role in the lives of Thai female migrants in Hamburg. Here they can come for counselling, to learn German (from a Thai teacher) and for other courses. Amnesty for Women is also a meeting place for Thai women.

In Hamburg's main red-light district, many Thais work in clubs, bars, Thai restaurants, and Thai karaoke bars. The karaoke bars, especially, are becoming popular places for Thai women who go with their German husbands or friends. Gambling, for example playing cards, is very common among Thai housewives. Many sex-workers go to the casinos to gamble.

Many Thai female sex-workers leave the sex industry and search for other jobs. Like other Thai female migrants in Germany, many have received only primary school education in Thailand and find it difficult to succeed in the German education system. They do not really want to learn German, so many of them give up their German courses after a few months, especially if they get a job. With little knowledge or understanding of the German language, they can find work only in factories, cleaning (in companies, hotels or private houses) or work as a cook or waitress in Thai restaurants. The average wage per hour for such work is 15 DM.

Nearly all Thai women in Germany want their children to have a better education. Many of these children cannot speak Thai because their mothers believe that German is more useful, and many say that they want their children to learn German so that they can learn it from them. It shows that they want to be integrated into German society.

CONCLUSION

The counselling statistics for Thai women from Amnesty for Women from 1993 until 1999 (AfW started to give counselling for Thai women in 1993) show that between sixty and eighty Thai women each year seek help. In 1998 sixty-six Thai women visited the centre for advice and other information. More than 80 per cent of these women were sex-workers in Thailand before going to Germany. Many of them were aware of what was waiting for them in Germany. Most of them had family or health problems or difficulties with legal status.

There are two broad conclusions. First, Thai women migrate to Germany for three main purposes: to marry, for employment and to work in the sex industry. The sex trade in Thailand is so deeply entrenched in Thai society that it has become a form of employment that many women consciously choose. Although the vast majority of Thai people look down on the work, many of them understand the realities of the sex trade, particularly the financial benefits it often provides.

Second, there is a frequent path in life that Thai women in Germany follow. They come to Germany and initially work in the sex trade. After a time (anything from a few weeks to a few years) they marry German men and settle in Germany. After many years some return to Thailand, but many take up residence in Germany, only returning to Thailand for visits.

NOTES

1. Amnesty for Women is an organization based in Hamburg, Germany (it has no connection with Amnesty International). It is a migrant centre that opposes the trafficking of women and forced prostitution. It mainly helps women and trans-sexuals from Southeast Asia (especially Thailand and the Philippines), Latin America and Eastern Europe.

2. Husband: live-in partner, not officially married.

SEVEN

Bodies Across Borders: Prostitution-related Migration from Thailand to Denmark

ANDERS LISBORG[1]

§ For more than two decades, sex tourism has been a well-known and fast-expanding phenomenon. Today, however, interaction between local sex-workers from the 'developing' world and relatively wealthier foreigners is far from limited to sex tourism. The inflow of tourists into countries such as Thailand has to an increasing degree been followed by an outflow of local women. Sex-tourist-receiving countries, as part of the ongoing process of globalization, have become out-migration countries for women who migrate to work in prostitution abroad.

This international prostitution-related migration of women from developing countries to the developed world has, in recent years, been increasing in scope, expanding in geographical dimensions and intensifying in the types of organization involved in it. However, in spite of considerable press interest in the phenomenon, very few empirical field studies of it have been conducted in the receiving countries.

This chapter explores the migration patterns and living conditions of Thai sex-workers in Denmark. Based on months of qualitative research in the Thai prostitution community of Copenhagen, it illuminates the complexity of the issues surrounding prostitution-related migration and provides a glimpse of some of the varieties and realities of the experience of the women involved.

TERMINOLOGY: PROSTITUTION-RELATED MIGRATION

Migrant prostitution is often referred to as 'trafficking in women', a term implying victimization. However, as by most definitions this involves coercion, it does not accurately describe the situation of all

Thai migrant sex-workers in Denmark. From a sociological perspective, this chapter suggests the term 'prostitution-related migration' in order to cover the phenomenon of migrant prostitution in which there are several distinctive characteristics. International prostitution-related migration is thus here defined both as migration for the purpose of prostitution and migration in which the migrants end up in prostitution in the receiving countries without that being their original intention. This definition, broad as it is, makes it possible to view migrant prostitution as a continuum from voluntary prostitution to direct trafficking in women and forced migration.

MIGRANT PROSTITUTION IN EUROPE

Due to the various illegal activities surrounding prostitution-related migration, it is very difficult to get an overall picture of migrant prostitution in a European context. According to the International Organization for Migration (IOM), the number of migrant sex-workers in many countries within the EU is higher than the number of local sex-workers (IOM 1996 from Wijers and Lap Chew 1997; Kempadoo and Doezema 1998). Studies in Holland estimate that 60 per cent of the country's approximately 20,000 sex-workers are foreigners. In Germany, which has been thought to be largest market for Thai sex-workers in Europe, it has been estimated that between 50 and 70 per cent of the sex-workers in the country are foreigners.

In the Scandinavian countries, the number of migrant sex-workers is apparently relatively low compared to the rest of Europe. Denmark and Finland have been mentioned as the two Scandinavian countries most affected by migrant prostitution. Recently it has been estimated that about 2,000 out of approximately 6,000 sex-workers in Denmark are migrants. Furthermore, Denmark is frequently mentioned in the international literature as a transit country for women who end up in prostitution in neighbouring countries such as Germany and Holland (Månsson 1996; Skrobanek 1994; Lisborg 1998; Altrink 1997). However, there has so far been insufficient documented evidence to confirm this or provide further information concerning the actual situation of migrant sex-workers in Denmark.

THAI PROSTITUTION IN DENMARK: AN OVERVIEW

Thai immigration to Denmark is indeed an example of the feminization of international migration. The numbers of Thai immigrants to Denmark have increased rapidly from 529 in 1980, over 1,497 in 1990 and to 4,172 in 1999. The vast majority of these immigrants – 83 per cent – are female. Among immigrants from developing countries to Denmark, the only two groups in which females significantly outnumber males come from Thailand and the Philippines. Looking closer at the age composition of Thai immigrants, there are again interesting gender differences. The majority of females are aged between thirty and thirty-nine years, while in contrast the majority of males are children and teenagers. In most cases these are sons following their migrant mothers. During the same period there has occurred a significant rise in the number of Thai sex-workers in Denmark. Fgure 7.1 below illustrates the detailed counting I did of prostitution advertisements in the Danish newspaper *Ekstra Bladet* (a newspaper specializing in advertisements for commercial sex) referring to Thai women.

It appears that there were very few massage parlours employing Thai sex-workers until the early 1990s. A more than ten-fold increase

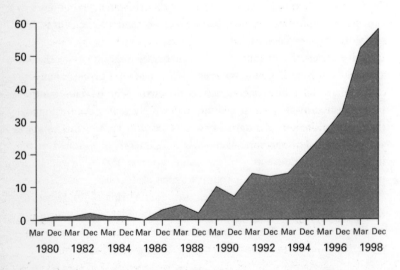

Figure 7.1 Advertisements for massage parlours with Thai sex-workers, 1980–98

occurred in ten years, from four parlours in 1988 to fifty-nine in 1998. The steepness of the curve indicates that this increase is ever more rapid. Each massage parlour employs on average between three and five women, although some individual parlours have been found to employ more than twelve women (including katoeys).[1] This means that the total number of fifty-nine parlours counted in December 1998 would employ approximately 236 Thai sex-workers. Additionally, the expected large number of parlours that did not advertise on the day of counting, and the large number of Thai sex-workers in other forms of prostitution such as call-girls, and nightclub sex-workers, should all be counted in. In summary, it can be estimated that there are somewhere between 700 and 1,000 Thai women in Denmark working in prostitution, and that they therefore might make up as much as 20 per cent of the total number of sex-workers and 50 per cent of the migrant sex-workers in the country.[2]

FIELDWORK METHODOLOGY

The field study was conducted in Copenhagen over a period of five months. Two 'friendly' massage parlours were chosen as the main sources, and were frequently visited informally. Because of the extreme sensitivity and stigma surrounding prostitution-related migration, it was not possible to make use of more formalized pre-structured methods. In order to obtain relatively credible information from the women and agents it was crucial to build up personal relationships and establish basic trust and confidentiality, so a very flexible method based on situation, observation and conversation was applied. Altogether eighteen women were randomly chosen for interview, being workers at one of the parlours visited or connected to the parlours as friends or colleagues. All the names of the women in the study have been changed.

EVERYDAY LIFE AS A THAI SEX-WORKER IN COPENHAGEN

To give an impression of the everyday life of a Thai sex-worker in Copenhagen, three very common characteristics that appeared from the fieldwork should be presented. First it seems to be a full-time job to be a migrant sex-worker; the distinction between work and spare time often becomes blurred. Many of the massage parlours are open twenty-four hours a day and the women spend most of their time there. They typically sit together in groups talking, cooking food, eating and watching TV while waiting for customers. Most of the time is spent in tiny 10–12 square metre living rooms. They are free to go whenever they have something to do outside, as long as one woman stays to answer the telephone and is available to customers. At night, some go home while others sleep at the parlour.

The second characteristic is that the Thai prostitution community has created an ethnic subculture in which the women seek to re-create the everyday life of back home. The women cling together in groups and speak Thai or provincial dialects (predominantly Lao – the dialect of the north-eastern 'Esarn' region). They buy most of their groceries in special Thai import shops, which have mushroomed in Copenhagen, and they eat Thai food – often local specialities from their home provinces. Newspapers, various weekly magazines and TV entertainment are also specially imported from Thailand, and watching videos of Thai talk-shows or soap operas is a main occupation for the women at the parlours.

The third significant characteristic, closely related to the two mentioned above, is that the women are not well integrated into Danish society. Typically, they have only limited contact with Danes, apart from their husbands (if they are married), their customers and a few others who somehow are linked to the prostitution community. Some of the women make an effort to become better integrated and join government-supported language schools, but such efforts seem to have a low priority compared to the work. In general, the women do not understand the Danish welfare system and feel alienated from it. It seem as though they maintain a sceptical attitude towards the authorities, as is common in Thailand where corruption is widespread and where, for example, the police are seen by many people as a kind of Mafia in uniform (see Phongpaichit et al. 1998). However, this sceptical attitude may be well founded. In one case a katoey sex-worker and massage parlour manager used the formal banking system to remit more than DKK 450,000 in one year.[3] The bank became suspicious as the woman officially had no work. The katoey was charged with tax evasion, and ordered to repay a large sum of money. Stories like these spread like bush fires in the migrant prostitution community, and lead to still more cautious and nervous contact with the 'system' and to a preference for relying on informal networks (they are also used to these in Thailand). Several of the women turn to loan sharks who demand very high interest rates and use threats and violence if repayments are late.

A LUCRATIVE BUSINESS

Migrant prostitution is a lucrative business, especially for massage parlour owners and organizers, but also for ordinary sex-workers in comparison both with incomes in their home countries, and with the minimum wage in the receiving country. In the Thai prostitution community in Denmark, the most common distribution of money between the owners of the parlours and the working women is 40 per cent to the owners and 60 per cent to the working women. As the income naturally depends on the demand, the average incomes of ordinary sex-workers vary widely from woman to woman and from parlour to parlour. This makes it difficult to generalize and come up with estimates of overall average incomes. While some women on quiet days made no money at all, on busy days they might have between five and nine customers and make DKK 2–3,000. Based on the interviews, a rough estimate reveals that most of the ordinary Thai sex-workers earn somewhere between DKK 8,000 and 18,000 per month while the most 'successful' minority can earn up to DKK 25,000.

Looking at the massage parlour owners and the organizers of Thai migration prostitution, it is important to debunk the myth that it is always men pulling the strings and making money out of the women. In some cases, Danish or immigrant men are the organizers, but quite often it is other Thai women who own the parlours, occasionally with their Danish husbands. Typically, the women organizers are middle-aged Thais, either still working as sex-workers or retired and now capitalizing on their experiences. Having from three to five employees at a parlour, a manager can make an enormous amount of money. Nonglek, a former owner of two parlours employing ten women altogether, said that at one stage she was making more than DKK 10,000 a day, or around DKK 200,000 a month. Pha, the other manager interviewed, also said that in busy periods she sometimes made up to DKK 200,000 a month as a sex-worker and parlour manager. However, in recent years, there has seemingly been a drop in income because of increased competition from a rising number of parlours. Pha complained that she now on average 'only' makes between DKK 30,000 and 50,000 per month. At one of the parlours where I carried out fieldwork, there were typically no more than one or two customers in the afternoons. I reported this to the forty-seven-year-old Thai manager, Pha, who responded: 'Now it's no good business. You see now how many parlours? Nearly two hundred – before it was better. But now there are too many parlours, because when you get a white card [permanent residence permit] you want to open a parlour. It is not easy to be in business these days.'

Her explanation not only illustrates the actual situation, but also provides an understanding of the rationale of many experienced migrant sex-workers who open their own parlours to increase their income. Pha further illustrated how much busier she was some years ago by saying that, at the time, she had had to use amphetamines regularly in order to keep awake and be able to serve customers at the twenty-four-hour parlour. Today amphetamines are not needed to keep up with the pressure of work.

Often the money seems to be spent almost as quickly as it arrives. For the parlour owners, there are working expenses such as rent, furnishings, various working tools, condoms, costumes and so on. The newspaper advertisements alone cost as much as DKK 3–4,000 a month. For both the owners and the ordinary sex-workers, a large sum of money is typically spent on buying material goods while another large sum is remitted to their families and often spent on building modern houses in their home villages. As also observed by Phongpaichit (1982), female Thai sex-workers consider themselves as earning members of the household and are considered likewise by others. Remittances of between DKK 1,500 and 8,000 each month or as much as 60–80 per cent of their total monthly earnings are common among the ordinary sex-workers. Additionally, huge amounts of money are often spent on gambling. Both the parlour owners and the sex-workers seem eager to try their luck. A former parlour owner and frequent gambler Nonglek said, 'Easy come, easy go', when asked about how she spent her money. Pha, the other manager, said that altogether she had lost DKK 400,000 last year at the Copenhagen Casino and in playing cards with massage parlour manager 'colleagues'.

SOCIAL PROBLEMS AND CIRCUMSTANCES THAT KEEP
THE WOMEN IN PROSTITUTION

There is a range of issues related to sex work generally and the life
of a migrant sex-worker more specifically. First of all the migrant sex-
workers naturally risk all the common health-related complications of
prostitution, such as various sexually transmitted diseases, including
HIV. Violence is another work-related risk factor that occurs in the
migrant prostitution community. Nonglek told of various violent situations, especially with drunken customers, and described how she and
her employees tried to take precautions:

> I had a knife hidden behind the front door, in case anyone tried to make
> trouble. In fact I had a knife hidden in all the corners of the bed,
> because I am a woman. The other working girls there were all bloody
> scared. Quite often we had problems of violence and quite often the
> girls escaped and I had to fight alone. So I would call the police – 112.
> Then they came and helped [because] I have a permanent residence
> permit, and was not scared of them.

Nonglek could call the police in cases of brawls because she had a
permanent residence permit, but she implied that women who do not
have such a permit or who work illegally on a tourist visa generally
would be afraid to contact the police because of the high risk of being
deported. Dao had been raped twice during her three months in the
country as a sex-worker, but as she stayed in Denmark on a temporary
tourist visa, which forbids her to work, she did not dare to call the
police. However, although violence generally can be seen as a real risk
factor, some women say that they almost never have problems with
violent customers. Cases of violence vary and apparently depend on
factors such as the location of the parlour and the number of women
working.

Other and more widespread problems are not solely related to
prostitution but are rather related to the lives of migrant sex-workers
in general. In a report analysing the livelihoods of Thai sex-workers in
Germany and Switzerland, the Thai researcher Sudarat Sereewat concluded:

> They were alienated from the social environment, unable to adjust to

language and other cultural difficulties. To avoid such pains, the women tended to cling to their own group. Monotony and boredom, sometimes despair! No recreation, no way out! No real motivation to learn new things in spite of such original intentions before coming. Therefore many of the women became very unhappy, letting their life drift along day by day with their eyes fixed on one thing: to make money so that they could go home as soon as possible. At the same time they were also alienated from their work. This was due to their sense of moral conscience, guilt and social degradation. This feeling was deeply rooted. They felt that the mark of sin or dark spot had been impressed in their being. (Sereewat 1985: 17)

To a large extent, these social and emotional problems can also be identified among the population of Thai sex-workers in Denmark. The relatively closed Thai migrant prostitution subculture, and the fact that the sex-workers' everyday lives are constructed around the migrant prostitution community, lead to both a real and an emotional state of deadlock.

Apparently, the majority of the women do not like being sex-workers, but seem to accept the situation in an almost fatalistic manner, struggling to get the best out of it. They have dreams and visions of a 'normal', 'better' way of life, but after having been for so long outside commonly accepted social norms, many seem to lose faith in the possibility of change and need help if they are to change their situations. Duan, a twenty-three-year-old sex-worker who had been in Denmark for only a year, explained how she felt about sex work:

> DUAN: I have to work here but I don't like. I think I don't work here long time. I think I want to find the good job. [She then continues talking about how she realizes that she has to educate herself more, and that it is difficult because she has a hard time learning to speak Danish.]
> Q: When you came here at first, did you want to go home or what?
> DUAN: I tried to go home, but I have to work and pay my family. I mean I can go ... but ... my husband ... I have to be patient!

She did not explain further, but she was still an inexperienced newcomer and clearly depressed about her situation. She worked because she felt forced to do so, either indirectly by her relatively poor family background and/or more directly because she owed money. She was therefore not able at that time to leave prostitution. Although, or maybe because of, having been in the prostitution business for almost three decades, Nonglek expressed a similar disgust about sex work. I asked her why she had not stayed in this lucrative business and kept her massage parlours: 'I don't feel like … it's hard for the working girls, OK they make money, but … [sighs] I don't think it's a very good kind of work. I don't think I like it. I did it, because I had to. I didn't like it. I think they just want to make money for their families.'

Pikhun, a still active sex-worker, expressed a similar distaste, and both she and Duan would have left prostitution if they had been offered other jobs. However, a large group of sex-workers seem to have difficulties in adjusting to a more 'ordinary' way of life. First they have crossed a range of psychological boundaries by being compelled to display their bodies for public use in order to make a living, and by having to accept the subsequent low status and social stigmatization. This has hardened the women and has given them the feeling that their lives are already tainted. In other words, some of the women are aware that they have broken society's, and quite often their own, social norms of how a 'good' woman and housewife ought to behave. This situation leads many to despair, and to lose hope that they might lead another kind of life. As a Thai sex-worker in Switzerland put it: 'Now I have become a bad girl [anyway], I want to make good money of it' (Sereewat 1985: 18).

Second, the majority of migrant sex-workers and their families often become dependent on these relatively high earnings. Some families invest in land, new houses or education and thereby become dependent on monthly remittances. Furthermore, a large group of women get into the habit of buying expensive material goods, while others become addicted to gambling; in the two latter cases often as a kind of compensation for a generally depressing situation (see also Archavanitkul and Guest, 1995). However, no matter the individual psychological reasons, a change in attitudes and practices requires a relatively high level of income. The 'addiction' to high levels of income, combined with the above-mentioned feeling of having stepped outside the social norms and the lack of alternatives can all be seen as circumstances which keep a large proportion of migrant women in prostitution, once they have entered.

Still, almost all the women I spoke to hoped to return to Thailand when they felt they had earned enough to secure their future and that of their families. Typically they set goals for themselves, planning to retire after they have made a predetermined sum of money or after they have endured a set number of years (see also Chantavanich et al. 1998). Many women, though, become stuck in prostitution, and what was originally supposed to be a temporary period of stay ends up being much longer or more or less permanent. The result is that a lot of women get 'caught' in a kind of transit, where they are neither here nor there.

Typically the women invest a lot of time and money trying to keep in contact with their families back home. In this way they struggle to maintain their influence and position as mothers, wives or daughters. But a lot of them clearly suffer from homesickness and frustration. The widespread intention of returning, whether it actually happens or not, also explains why so few of the women become integrated into Danish society.

Finally, it is important to emphasize that it is still extremely difficult to generalize about the social difficulties of Thai migrant sex-workers. While an apparently large group of the women faced the hardships described above, others seemed, under the circumstances, to lead quite normal lives as migrant sex-workers and did not consider withdrawing from prostitution. These women were satisfied with their high earnings, and sex work gave them the possibility of increasing their own and their families' livelihoods, power and social status. As one woman expressed it: 'Some tell me that they don't like me because I am a hooker, but who will take care of me? Who? Nobody, I take care of myself and I am content about what I do. It is my body, I take care of my family, and I am proud to do that.' It appears from this that the women are well aware that they are stigmatized by their work, but at the same time to a certain degree they manage to neutralize this, partly by seeing their occupation as a means to survive, and partly by fulfilling other and more important social norms in Thai culture – responsibility for the family and being able to provide for them. This gives them a feeling of pride and self-satisfaction. Nevertheless, irrespective of the women's different experiences and perceptions as migrant sex-workers, these are almost always closely related to the migration method used.

MIGRATION PATTERNS

Prostitution-related migration is organized in a wide range of ways, from well-informed voluntary migration to coercion and human trafficking. Three different ideal types of migration could be identified from the fieldwork.

Type A: Returning with a tourist   The typical woman in this category meets a Danish tourist or expatriate in Thailand, and then returns with him to Denmark. Typically, the woman already works in the sex sector in Bangkok, Pattaya, Phuket, Koh Samui or one of the other famous sex tourism locations in Thailand. It is during their work here that women meet customers who want them to come to Europe. Nonglek, who entered prostitution during the Vietnam War, explained how she met a Danish man while working as a sex-worker in Pattaya in the early 1980s:

> We knew each other for three years. Once a year he came to Thailand and he send money regularly, which I gave to my family. Then suddenly he send me a ticket ... TO DENMARK ... *uuhhii!* [Recalling her excitement with laughter] Where was Denmark?! I told my friend – the owner of the bar that a 'farang' [westerner] had sent me a ticket to Denmark, but she said I should be careful otherwise I would risk being sold like some Thai women in Germany. So I became frightened and refused. But then he phoned and said: don't be frightened, just come. I will pick you up in the airport. I have everything in my house ... If you come you only have to cook for me, you don't have to do nothing and I will buy you a diamond ring. So I decided to try.

Nonglek stayed with the man as a housewife for three years, but the marriage did not work out, and after a divorce she voluntarily entered prostitution again. She started as a waitress in a nightclub in Aalborg, worked her way up, and ended as the owner of two massage parlours in Copenhagen. At the time of the interview she had sold the parlours, retired, married another Danish man – a former customer – and was seemingly enjoying her retirement.

Ore, a former sex-worker from Patpong, and twenty-one-year-old Daeng are two other examples of women who migrated after they had met a Danish tourist in Thailand. Both of them followed a man back to

Denmark and entered on tourist visas, but the men did not want to marry them, which meant that they had to leave the country within three months. They both became involved with the Thai prostitution community, began to work at massage parlours, and tried very hard through the effective social network among Thai migrant sex-workers to get help to arrange pro forma marriages which would secure their stay.

A common characteristic of this type of migration is that even though it might have been a dream for many of the women to have a chance to go abroad, they had not planned their migration in advance. Hence, the destination is random, dependent only upon the country of the man whom they follow. Furthermore, the women did not have any extra expenses, which makes it a cheap way of migrating. However, as the examples of Ore and Daeng show, there is no guarantee that they will be able to stay. If the women are compelled to pay for a pro forma marriage, this kind of migration might in the long term be as costly as any other.

Type B: Migration through transnational social networks This involves women who draw upon social networks in the migration process. Typically, they have relatives or friends in Denmark, or they know someone who knows someone, who can tell them about opportunities abroad and eventually assist in their migration. These transnational social networks both motivate and facilitate the migration. Three of the women I interviewed came through such social networks. Nevertheless, there is a remarkable difference in their migration experiences.

A Thai friend already living in Denmark invited Pha, who arrived in the country in the mid-1980s. She was helped with getting both work and a place to live. She had been in several other countries before and had a lot of friends in Pattaya with experience of foreign countries. This made migration to Denmark for her relatively unproblematic.

Pikhun, another woman who drew upon social networks, went to Denmark for the first time in transit during a flight to another country. She spent some time in Copenhagen airport and wanted to return if she got the chance, which she did three years later:

My sister, not really sister ... but close friend of my mother, went to visit a friend in Aalborg in Denmark, then later she opened a massage parlour, and then she phoned me asking me to come. I bought an

Aeroflot ticket and went. I stayed there for twelve days and went back, but I retuned again. I went to Denmark and came back to Thailand and went to Denmark again about ten times, before I got married here.

Pikhun's narrative actually contains two examples of migration through transnational social networks: both the woman who invited Pikhun, and then Pikhun herself. In this manner, it demonstrates the migration snowball effect, or so-called chain migration, in which women who have already emigrated spread rumours about opportunities in the West, and this leads to further migration.

San, a woman in her early thirties, also used social networks in her migration. Her brother knew a woman who lived in Denmark and who organized pro forma marriages for Thai women who were supposed to go to work in brothels in Germany (see Lisborg 1998). This woman, Jainang, loaned San the money for the air ticket, picked her up at the airport, guaranteed her financially to the immigration authorities for her stay, and arranged accommodation. Furthermore, she promised to find a Danish man who would agree to a pro forma marriage. On the face of it, a woman like Jainang would seem to be a good contact, willing to facilitate the migration in its different phases. But San had absolutely no idea what she would be expected to pay in return for all the 'assistance'. Shortly after San's arrival, Jainang demanded a lot of money. San already knew that she was supposed to become a sex-worker at Jainang's parlour, but she did not know about all the extra costs of staying in the country, and was depressed about her situation.

San migrated using a transnational social network, but her connection was fragile and, unlike Pha and Pikhun in the examples above, she could not rely on mutual trust. In some respects, her network appeared to be more like a commercial enterprise than a social network between friends and relatives trying to help each other. San's example shows that the risks and costs for the migrant of using a social network are not necessarily smaller than those involved in other methods of migration; cost and risk factors are dependent on the quality of the social relations in the network.

Type C: Migration through agents and commercial networks In this category, the women migrate using agents who do the work for financial gain. This group of organizers ranges from single individuals who occasionally profit from bringing a woman to the country, to actual criminal organizations specializing in arranging migration for the purpose of prostitution. The women who migrate through these commercial networks have no social networks abroad they could have drawn upon. Some have not even thought of migration or sex work until agents contact them and lure them with promises of a rich future abroad.

Tang-on was only sixteen when she and her parents were contacted by Sumantha, an older Thai woman who lived in Denmark. Sumantha was originally from the same north-eastern village but had emigrated more than ten years previously, and from her remittances her family had built the largest house in the village. Because of this very visible material success, it was not difficult for Sumantha to convince Tang-on's parents of the advantages if they invested money in their daughter's migration. She promised work as a housekeeper, earning as much as 12,000 THB per month[4] and Tang-on's parents mortgaged their rice fields and paid Sumantha the 50,000 THB she demanded. Tang-on herself did not want to go, but her father persuaded her because he knew and trusted Sumantha. However, traffickers like Sumatha cynically abuse the trust of their former fellow villagers. Instead of finding work as promised, she tried to arrange marriages for the girls she brought by putting contact advertisements in local Danish newspapers. Tang-on landed in Copenhagen with three other girls, also lured by Sumantha. As she was only sixteen years old at the time she was too young to get married, and instead her virginity was sold to two men while Sumantha was watching. She was paid DKK 600 after the rape. Later, she managed to escape with the help of the Danish husband of one the girls she had migrated with.[5] The three other girls did not become involved in prostitution, but they were forced to marry and thereby became victims of trafficking. One of the girls described the first meeting with the man she had been forced to marry:

> I had not even seen a picture of him. Sumantha refused to show me, and said I had to meet him in person. I got frightened. I said I didn't loved him, but she said that if I didn't married him, I had to pay back the money he had given, and then how would my parents survive? (Documentary, 1993)

Traffickers like Sumantha operate by using the power and knowledge they have in both the sending and the receiving countries. They have a dual influence on the continuing migration/trafficking process: in-directly, by having achieved wealth through their own migration and thereby inspiring others; and more directly by promoting migration, becoming agents and traffickers. These small-scale agents seem to be responsible for a large number of the women who come to Denmark through commercial networks.

In the case above, the agent took the initiative and contacted neighbours from her home village in order to get girls she could sell. However, as international migration has become an increasingly popular livelihood-strategy among rural families, many potential migrants simply make contact with agents themselves. As for Dao, the migration process began when she gave birth to a handicapped baby, was abandoned by her husband, and therefore found herself in the middle of a serious economic crisis. Her mother then encouraged her to contact agents in order to go abroad. This demonstrates how the expectations of migration and a life abroad have spread through the media and former migrants to even the most remote areas. Even without having any kind of social network abroad, people wishing to migrate now often know of agents who will be able to facilitate migration. In this way, migration to distant unknown countries has become a livelihood-strategy for most relatively poor rural people.

Twenty-three-year-old Duan also migrated through a commercial agent without having any kind of social network abroad. She had made contact with a trafficker, a Thai man from her home province in the north-eastern region. This man offered her a well-paid job in Denmark. She then, with help from her parents, paid the huge amount of 150,000 THB or about DKK 35,000 for the whole migration package, including the job. On her arrival in Copenhagen a middle-aged Thai woman met her at the airport and told her that she had to marry a Danish man in order to stay. This woman had already made an arrangement with a Danish man, probably through advertisements in the press, and Duan met the man the following day. Not only was she forced to marry a stranger, but she also had to prostitute herself in order to pay her debts. Having been in Denmark for only a year at the time of the interview, and evidently insecure and depressed about her situation, Duan, reti-cently and in a low voice, answered the following questions:

Q: Before your departure to Denmark did you know you were going to work like this? [We are sitting in a massage parlour.]

DUAN: No ... I thought in a Thai restaurant.

Q: So when did you realize it was this kind of work you had to do?

DUAN: Here ... when I came here.

Q: What did you think?

DUAN: Not good ... but I had to pay back the money for come here ... 150,000 THB!

Duan did not really know what had happened to the other women she had travelled with, but she thought they had been married as well, and might have become sex-workers in other parts of the country, under similar circumstances.

THE DIFFERENT MIGRATION PATTERNS COMPARED

As the above three types of migration patterns illustrate, both the ways of prostitution-related migration from Thailand to Denmark, and the migrant women's backgrounds and conditions vary greatly. The women in the two first categories (Type A and Type B) are primarily so-called two- or multi-step migrants. This means that before they migrate abroad they have participated in either internal or international migration. Typically they have migrated from the poor rural areas to end up in the expanding sex sector in the cities. Some have even been sex-workers in other foreign countries before coming to Denmark, and they have an impressive range of contacts to various migrant sex-worker communities throughout the world. One woman interviewed had worked in Thailand, Baghdad, Lebanon, Japan, Malaysia and Israel before settling in Denmark. Thus, these migrants not only have migration experience but also have experience as sex-workers prior to their migration to Denmark. For them the prostitution-related migration to Denmark has just been the last phase of a long stepwise internal and international migratory process with its beginning in the villages in the rural areas (see also Ruenkaew 1999). These groups of migrants, who apparently make up the vast majority of Thai migrant sex-workers in Denmark, are typically strongly autonomous entrepreneurs, who voluntarily have entered prostitution in Denmark and typically they cannot be categorized as victims of trafficking.

However, although the term 'voluntary entry into prostitution' suggests free will, it does not always mean a free choice among the economic alternatives for those women who decide by themselves to enter prostitution (see also Skeldon 2000). Most often these women have entered because of dire economic need within a specific social context. Furthermore, it cannot be ruled out that they may have been victims of internal trafficking when they entered prostitution in Thailand. To state that most of these Type A and B migrants are typically not victims of trafficking is not the same as saying that they have not faced abusive conditions.

The women in the third category (Type C: migration through agents and commercial networks) generally seem more vulnerable and have had harsher migrant experiences. They are mainly one-step migrants, meaning that they migrated more or less directly from their rural home villages or provincial cities, to a destination abroad. As also noted by Ghosh 1999, spectacular improvements in systems of transport and communications, the spread of social networks and above all the rapidly expanding operations of agents and traffickers are now making it possible for many to move abroad directly from provincial areas. Women who migrate through agents and commercial networks can also be recruited while working in the sex sector in the country of origin, and thereby become two/multi-step migrants. But often there will be a higher profit for the traffickers if they recruit the girls directly from provincial areas where the people are relatively poorer and less likely to have access to reliable transnational social networks. In summary, Type C and one-step migrants most often and most evidently are likely to end up as victims of trafficking. However, this does not mean that they, or victims of trafficking in general, are necessarily weak or passive. On the contrary, as noted by Wijers (in Kempadoo and Doezema 1998), a great many of the women who become victims of trafficking end up in this position because they do not want to accept the limitations of their situation; because they are enterprising, courageous and willing to take initiatives to improve their living conditions and those of their families. But somewhere in this process they become trapped.

Looking at the three different migration patterns over time, some interesting characteristics appear. The pattern seems to be that the pioneers of Thai prostitution in Denmark were two- or multi-step migrants with prostitution experience, and that they arrived with a returning tourist (Type A). These first migrants then developed trans-national social networks that motivated and facilitated new migrants (Type B). The last type of migration (Type C) then developed because of an increased awareness of the profit to be made from arranging migration. In other words, it seems that some of the first two types of migrants capitalized on their experiences and knowledge as migrants. They, and their co-operative partners – often their husbands – knew the demand and the supply, had good connections in both the sending and the receiving country, and therefore could easily make considerable amounts of money by entering the business as agents and traffickers. In summary, prostitution-related migration from Thailand to Denmark has changed. At first it was merely more or less random and ad hoc. Today it is also commercially organized and increasingly institutionalized.

CONCLUSION

The research reveals that the increasing migration from Thailand to Denmark is unique and gender-selective, with more than 80 per cent of the migrants being female. A still rising number of these migrants end up in prostitution with various degrees of voluntarism. In less than ten years the number of Thai migrant sex-workers has increased tenfold, and it is estimated that today there are between 700 and 1,000 Thai women in prostitution in Denmark. They thereby make up half of the total number of migrant sex-workers in the country.

The study illustrates how these sex-workers have migrated under various circumstances, and how their differences in living conditions are often related to the migration method used. While some women are coerced into migrating and work in slavery-like conditions, it seems that the majority of the prostitution-related migrants are not victims of trafficking; they are typically opportunity-seeking migrants who use prostitution-related migration as a route to break away from oppressive local conditions. Often they are aware of the implications of their decisions but they still make them relatively independently in the context of their families' economic situations. This need not necessarily imply that, in an ideal world, prostitution would be their chosen occupation. On the contrary, many of the women felt alienated from the work and experienced a range of social problems as migrant sex-workers. However, given the lack of alternatives and motivated by a strong desire to improve their situation and by the spirit of *'pai tai auo dap na'* (prepared to go/act no matter the risk),[6] the women show courage and struggle resolutely to get the best out their situation.

Thai migrant sex-workers share many common characteristics, but are heterogeneous when it comes to migration patterns and living and working conditions, including degrees of voluntarism. It is important that these differences within the group of migrant sex-workers are included in the public debate on the subject and it is crucial to take the point of departure in the migrant sex-workers' self-knowledge and their articulation of needs into account. This, together with an understanding of prostitution-related migration as a continuum in all its complexity, is essential to both future studies and coherent policies.

NOTES

The author's e-mail address is: lisborg@ruc.dk

1. Transvestites or so-called 'lady-boys'. Some strip-bars, massage parlours and call-girl agencies specialize in offering services from katoeys.

2. These research estimates have, since their first publication, been verified from other sources. In July 1999 the Danish police made extensive investigations into prostitution in Copenhagen. They visited 80 (out of approximately 120) parlours in the city. Fifty per cent of the sex-workers turned out to be Thai women. Local Danish sex-workers made up only one-third of the total number of sex-workers in the survey.

3. US$1 = DKK (Danish Kroner) 7.5 (March 2000).

4. US$1 = 37 THB (Thai Bath) (March 2000).

5. Apparently some husbands of mail-order brides are unaware that their new wives did not know that they had to marry before they left their home countries.

6. An old Thai proverb that directly translated means 'Go prepared to die in front of the sword'.

REFERENCES

Altrink, S. (1997) *Stolen Lives – Trading Women into Sex and Slavery* (London: Scarlet Press).

Archavanitkul, K. and P. Guest (1995) 'Migration and the Commercial Sex Sector in Thailand', Research Paper, Institute for Population and Social Research, Mahidol University.

Chantavanich, S. et al. (1998) 'The Migration of Thai Women to Germany – Causes, Living Conditions and Impacts for Thailand and Germany', Paper, Asian Research Center for Migration Chulalongkorn University, Bangkok.

Ghosh, B. (1999) *Huddled Masses and Uncertain Shores – Insights into Irregular Migration* (The Hague/London: Martinus Nijhoff).

IOM (International Organization for Migration) (1999) *Paths of Exploitation – Studies on the Trafficking of Women and Children between Cambodia, Thailand and Vietnam* (Geneva: IOM and CAS).

Kempadoo, K and J. Doezema (eds) (1998) *Global Sex Workers – Rights, Resistance, and Redefinition* (New York and London: Routledge).

Lim, L. L. et al. (1998) *The Sex-sector – The Economic and Social Bases of Prostitution in Southeast Asia* (Geneva: ILO).

Lisborg, A. (1998) 'Koebte Kroppe – om prostitutionsrelateret migration fra Thailand til Danmark', Working Paper 139, Department of Geography Roskilde University, Denmark.

Månsson, S. A. (1996) 'Bordellen "Europa" – om international könshandel, kriminalitet och migration i den europeiska gemenskaben', Working Paper.

Mix, P. R. (1999) 'Prostitution Migration – Thai Female Sex-workers in Germany', Conference Paper, 'Prostitution in a Global Context', Aalborg University, Denmark.

Phongpaichit, P. (1982) *From Peasant Girls to Bangkok Masseuses* (Geneva: ILO).

Phongpaichit, P., S. Piriyarangsan and N. Treerat (1998) *Guns, Girls, Gambling, Ganja – Thailand's Illegal Economy and Public Policy* (Chiang Mai: Silkworm Books).

Ruenkaew, P. (1999) 'Transnational Prostitution of Thai Women to Germany – a variety of Transnational Labour Migration?' Conference Paper, 'Prostitution in a Global Context', Aalborg University, Denmark.

Sereewat, S. (1985) *Prostitution: The Thai–European Connection* (Geneva: World Council of Churches).

Skeldon, R (2000) 'Trafficking – a Perspective from Asia', *International Migration*, Special Issue.

Skrobanek, S. (1994) *The Dairy of Prang* (Bangkok: Women Press).

Skrobanek, S., N. Boonpakdi and C. Janthakeero (1997) *The Traffic in Women – Human Realities of the International Sex Trade* (London: Zed Books).

Wijers, M. and L. Lap-Chew (1997) *Trafficking in Women, Forced Labour and Slavery-like Practices – in Marriage, Domestic Labour and Prostitution* (Utrecht: Foundation against Trafficking in Women).

Wijers, M. (1998) 'Women, Labour, and Migration: the Position of Trafficked Women and Strategies for Support', in K. Kempadoo and J. Doezema (eds), *Global Sex Workers – Rights, Resistance, and Redefinition* (New York and London: Routledge).

EIGHT

Black Prostitutes in Denmark

MARLENE SPANGER

§ The subject of this chapter is African female migrants-who-prostitute in Denmark. Inspired in general by the social constructivist approach, and more specifically by Lorraine Nencel's PhD dissertation on prostitution in Peru, I should like to inquire into the living and working conditions of black migrant women-who-prostitute in the 1990s in Denmark.

I shall present some perspectives that draw on both oral and written sources. I approach this study by focusing on three themes that, in different ways, reveal the living and working conditions of the women and at the same time influence the construction of their identity. All three themes can be seen in an historical and a contemporary perspective:

1. Changing transnational flows to and from Europe.
2. Current Danish policy and discourses underlying public opinion on prostitution.
3. Changing European notions of 'the black woman' since the beginning of this century.

Different perspectives on gender, race and sexuality can be linked to these themes, in which prostitution is the main issue.

Terminology I shall not refer to the women as prostitutes, because the term reflects an identity rather than an act. The women I have spoken to do not recognize themselves as prostitutes but rather as women who occasionally sell sex. Inspired by Lorraine Nencel (1997: 3–4), I find the term 'women-who-prostitute' more precise for my study, because it reflects an act or some discursive practice of the women's lives. The mainstream pejorative term 'prostitute', I shall claim, reflects essentialist thinking.

I also refer to this kind of prostitution as *transnational* rather than the more common term 'foreign' prostitution. 'Foreign' labels the women as 'others' or 'aliens', terms often closely connected to the idea that individuals who are not citizens, or are not a part of the nation-state, have no civil rights. The term 'transnational' prostitution covers this group of women more precisely.

TRANSNATIONAL PROSTITUTION

Denmark is part of transnational prostitution as a recipient country, and over the last ten years the number of transnational female migrants-who-prostitute in Denmark has been growing. Women from the so-called Third World are trafficked or migrate from countries in Africa, Southeast Asia, Latin America and Eastern Europe. They are seeking economic opportunities abroad and the receiving countries are Japan, Australia, North America and countries in Western and Southern Europe (KULU 1996; EU 1996). The number of African women-who-prostitute in Denmark is not known, since they comprise a group that is not very visible, although black women as such are. My estimate is that, in the Copenhagen area, there are about 200 black women-who-prostitute. The existence of coherent groups, with strong social networks, among the African women-who-prostitute is far from certain; women from Thailand and women from the Eastern European countries tend to receive more public attention. This raises interesting issues, for there are fewer black transmigrant women-who-prostitute in Copenhagen in comparison with other cities in Europe, such as London or Paris. As it is a new development within the area of prostitution, it is an issue that creates and reflects new social practices. In the following, the lives of some black women-who-prostitute will be illustrated.

A wide range of sender countries is represented in my oral sources, including women from South Africa, Uganda, Nigeria, Kenya and Madagascar. They are in the age group of twenty-seven to forty-two years. All of them have had children who live with relatives in the sending countries, the receiving countries or in a third country. Some of the women are educated as clerks and one is a teacher, but most have no education at all. The marital status of the women varies: some of them are married to Danish men, some are divorced, two are widows and some have never been married. All in all, the women have different social backgrounds, reflecting a wide and complex group of women. In spite of the complexity, my oral sources show conspicuous migration patterns.

Sarah   Sarah's mobility represents just one of the strategies of migration with prostitution in view, and it can be termed a survival strategy. It relies upon individual and immediate voluntary action. Sarah is very conscious of her ability to choose, and decides for herself when she would like to work. She has legal work and residence permits given to her in the Netherlands that she can use in Denmark because both countries are members of the EU. She is able to steer clear of the Danish tax authorities. Once documents have been acquired, the new internal market in Europe offers new opportunities and a new mobility for transnational women-who-prostitute.

Sarah lives with her husband and child in Amsterdam (both Sarah and her husband came from Ghana). She told me that she has close contacts with her relatives – sisters, brothers and mother – in Ghana and she has taken on economic responsibility for her family, sending remittances back to them. To earn this money she sometimes works as a hostess in a bar in Copenhagen.

Through employment as a hostess, Sarah finds clients who pay her to have sexual intercourse with her. She is very conscious of who she picks up and she emphasized that nobody dictates how many clients she has to have intercourse with.

Sarah does not identify herself as a prostitute. She argues that she is not a professional and that the work is neither stable nor full-time. None of the women I talked to seem to regard themselves as prostitutes, nor do they call themselves sex-workers (Sarah had never heard the term before). Sarah, like all the other women I talked to, describes the way she earns her money as 'that'. The term 'that' might reflect taboos surrounding prostitution or it might indicate that sex is something you do, not something you talk about, even among the women who themselves prostitute.

From her base in Amsterdam, where her husband and daughter live, Sarah migrates for short periods of between one and two months to Copenhagen; she returns to Amsterdam for two or three months and then goes back to Copenhagen again. This mobility pattern – longer-term (permanent) migration from Ghana to Amsterdam and then temporary migration to Copenhagen – gives her different opportunities.

It is easier for Sarah to compartmentalize her life when she lives with her family in Amsterdam and works in Copenhagen. She defines her life in Amsterdam as 'normal', taking care of the household and her child. In contrast, in Copenhagen she works in the strip bar as a hostess and shares a flat with another girl. If she meets businessmen from Amsterdam, she does not tell them that she lives there. As she said: 'They could be my husband's colleagues!'

As a black transnational migrant in Denmark it has been possible to hide her 'real' identity behind a newly constructed double identity, which seems to represent a stereotype of the notion of the black woman. Sarah's case illustrates how black women can be both anonymous and yet very visible, because of the small population of blacks in Denmark. It can be difficult to remain invisible as a social group, though, because prostitution has recently been in the media spotlight and has become a hot political issue in Denmark.

Sarah's husband knows that she works in Copenhagen as a kind of hostess, but she has not told him about the prostitution. This part of her work is easier to hide because she works away from her home base and has a better chance of remaining anonymous. The deliberate choice of working place illustrates that she is hiding from her family, relatives and friends how she earns the money.

The construction of Sarah's life and identity must be understood in relation to the social space (see below) that crosses national borders shaped by her destinations: the locality in Ghana where her relatives live, her home base in Amsterdam and her working life in Copenhagen, where she earns money for her relatives in Ghana. Her transnational life and work reflect a high degree of mobility and a certain degree of independence, expressed in different ways.

Sarah decides for herself who she will have sexual intercourse with. She can choose to work in another bar in another city or in another EU country, because she is not bound economically to the bar in Copenhagen and she has her legal residence and employment permits valid throughout the EU. She is in charge of her prostitution and uses her transnational life as a disguise, allowing her to appear as a housewife in Holland, a dutiful daughter in Ghana and a hostess with a little extra income from prostitution in Denmark.

The network between the destinations can be termed the 'social space' framing Sarah's life; a space which crosses national borders. This kind of mobility reflects new cultural patterns (Basch et al. 1994; Sørensen 1995).

Cathy Cathy comes from Johannesburg in South Africa. She has five children who live in Johannesburg, cared for by her mother. Cathy's first husband died in an accident in a goldmine and her income from school-teaching was not enough to support the family. She emphasizes that she chose to migrate for economic reasons. She worked in London and the USA before going to Denmark, where she had an uncle.

Today Cathy is married again, this time to a Danish man. They have been married for six years and live in Aalborg. According to her, her husband does not know that she prostitutes. She has a cleaning job that she uses as a cover. She has connections with massage parlours in both Copenhagen and Aarhus. She is not dependent on a work schedule – 'they' just call her and then she can decide if she wants to go there or not. Cathy's social network is constructed between Aalborg, Copenhagen, Aarhus and Johannesburg. Her mobility pattern, like Sarah's, involves more than two localities. As in Sarah's case, nobody knows about the prostitution, and it is easier to hide it by working away from her home base.

A third case shows another mobility pattern: Linda is from the Caribbean, she lives in Copenhagen and her children live in London with relatives.

Mobility and the transnational network The transnational network is bound together by contact and communications between the women, their families and their relatives, through remittances, visits, telephone calls and so on. The history of the women can also be expressed in the context of globalization. The time–space compression in communications and transportation makes it possible for them and their families and friends to produce and reproduce a social network connecting several places. Thus economic and social changes make it possible for transmigrants to create coherent life-worlds.

The transnational network challenges the image of a nation-state framed by clear borders, a homogeneous society with one language, one main religion and a common history – ideas underlining the current national discourse in Denmark. By defining the identity of an individual on the basis of a particular territory, transmigrants are labelled as 'foreigners' or 'others', or as second-class citizens, by the receiving country.

The transmigrants' daily activities and social and economic relations, which create social fields across the national borders, call into question the relevance and durability of current mainstream national discourse. It is also important to bear in mind that such mobility also has negative consequences, such as the stigmatization experienced in the receiving country, and a desire on the part of the receiving country to control women's mobility, because of income, work permits and social relations.

THE PROSTITUTION DISCOURSE IN MODERN DANISH HISTORY

The narratives of the life strategies of Sarah and Cathy represent an alienated way of acting according to the discourse of the Danish welfare system. Here, the practice of social agents in relation to legislation plays a central part in the identity of women-who-prostitute in Denmark. During the twentieth century, legislation concerning women-who-prostitute was changed, as was the practice.

The current discourse of Danish public prostitution is connected to the history of the Danish welfare state's policy regarding prostitution. This has been, for many years, contradictory and unclear, creating certain ideas about women-who-prostitute, which have changed over time.

In the following I shall, very briefly, give examples of different views on prostitution, taken from different periods in the twentieth century, that together illustrate that the definition of 'the prostitute' is not an essential or a static phenomenon. The period from 1874 to 1906 can be termed the time of regulation of prostitution (Lützen 1998; Vammen 1989). In this period female prostitution was seen as a problem that was becoming increasingly urgent. On the one hand prostitution was seen as having an important social function, and on the other hand it disturbed public order and involved criminal offenders. Finally, 'prostitutes' were seen as responsible for spreading venereal diseases.

In short, the solution was to legalize prostitution, under certain restrictions. The police were allowed to classify women as prostitutes if they had repeatedly offended legislation regarding prostitution or when they were arrested for having infected a man with a venereal disease.

Such women were obliged to join either public or private brothels. They were not allowed access to certain public places and streets. They were required to have a weekly medical examination. The vice squad were given access to visit the women day and night.

Tinne Vammen (1989) stresses that most of the women-who-prostitute came from the lower social classes. For them prostitution was not a permanent source of income but a way to supplement their main income from their domestic jobs as housekeepers or maids.

During the 1890s abolitionists received wide support and in 1906 public regulation ended and prostitutes (but not their clients) were classified as criminal.

A public way of controlling women At the beginning of the twentieth century, Copenhagen underwent rapid urbanization and modernization. The nightlife of the city expanded and the number of people who migrated from the countryside to the urban areas increased. The number of migrants peaked in the 1930s and 1940s with 60,000 men and 85,000 women migrating to urban areas (Christensen 1995: 45). These social changes influenced female sexual practices and the survival strategies of women in general.

Along with these social changes, the focus of the authorities regarding prostitutes shifted to young women who had moved from the countryside to the urban areas. It was not the 'old established' women in Copenhagen, but the younger women who had migrated there who represented a new and dangerous femininity and sexuality that needed to be controlled. This latter social group of women was regarded by the public authorities as 'the problem'. They were described as 'semi-prostitutes' or 'easy' women, women who had frequent and different sexual partners, young women who visited bars and dance-restaurants. Within the medical discourse of the 1930s and until after the Second World War, these young women were regarded as physically and mentally degenerate (Koch 1996).

A Danish doctor, Tage Kemp, wrote a monograph, *Prostitution: an Investigation of its Causes, Especially with Regard to Hereditary Factors*, in 1936. It was based on case studies of 530 women and purported to explain their loose behaviour. In Kemp's view, it was not a question of whether or not the women were pathologically deviant, but how much. His view was common at that time.

Even in the 1950s, young women who demonstrated a certain sexuality (by a frequent change of lovers or boyfriends) were regarded by the authorities as 'semi-prostitutes', a key problem in prostitution (Hartmann 1949; Jersild 1962; Betænkning 1955). A public report from 1955 – *Public Orders Regarding Combating Prostitution* – emphasized that the motivation underlying prostitution was not economic but, as in Kemp's monograph, pathological. The report also emphasized migration from the countryside to the urban areas as a considerable social reason why women became semi-prostitutes (Betænkning 1955: 31). Female migration thus became connected with uncontrollable sexuality.

Another reason why the sexual behaviour of young women was seen as 'a problem' was that they had intercourse with foreign soldiers. After the Second World War, American service personnel stationed in Germany would visit Copenhagen at weekends and holidays, along with foreign seamen (Jersild 1962: 4–5). Women who had intercourse with these soldiers and seamen were seen as traitors to their country.

Around the 1970s the public view on prostitution changed. Now women-who-prostituted were seen in the context of a socio-psychological discourse. This shift must be understood in the context of Danish society at that time. The feminist movement, which had gender equality as a main issue, played an important role in the understanding of femininity and sexuality.

In 1995, a project about the relationships between women-who-prostitute, social workers and the public social administration was started.[1] It produced six reports on meetings between social workers (the authors of the reports) and women-who-prostitute. All in all, the women-who-prostitute are portrayed in the light of a socio-psychological discourse, as victims, and as women with social and psychological problems.[2] The reports ignored the different kinds of prostitution involved, how long the women had been prostitutes, how often they prostituted, whether they were involved in drug abuse, their backgrounds and so on.

In the reports, all transnational migrants-who-prostitute are described as victimized, unlike those women with a Danish background. In one of the reports it is suggested that the 'weakness' of the transnational female migrant is a function of language problems and it is the authors' impression that 'foreign women' have difficulties setting limits for their customers. All the reports concluded that it was very difficult to get in contact with the 'foreign women'. It is doubtful that the picture of the victimized transnational women-who-prostitute covers all transnational women-who-prostitute.

From the 1960s to the 1980s, Denmark went through a sexual emancipation and a struggle for equal opportunities. This development influenced the wider society in many ways. Even though sexual emancipation and equal opportunity are highly respected issues in Denmark today, prostitution is not legal as it is in the Netherlands.

On the contrary, women-who-prostitute exist in a position that can be described as 'in between' or as 'a gap'. Here, the activities (work) of the women are neither classified as criminal acts nor do they have the status of work. Here, Danish views on equal opportunities and on sexuality and love perhaps play a central role.

THE CONSTRUCTION OF THE BLACK WOMAN'S SEXUALITY

The presence of African female migrants-who-prostitute in Denmark is a recent phenomenon, and Danish perceptions of this social group are based on a distanced relationship to black people. Former European notions and the iconography of black women have become central. The African female migrants-who-prostitute in Denmark are often doubly stigmatized because transnational migrants from the so-called Third World are often labelled as 'others' or 'aliens' by society in the receiving country: and because women-who-prostitute are surrounded by prejudices and myths.

In all forms of stigmatization, racism is a central element – hidden or explicit. Different myths and notions of black women's sexuality can be understood in the light of the history of imperialism and colonialism, which have produced ideologies of race and gender,[3] reflecting a European cultural heritage. Further, the production and reproduction of these ideologies are deeply embedded in the consciousness of many cultures, both in the former colonies and in the former colonial powers.

The icon of the black woman has been changed and reproduced in different discourses during the last century.[4] It is not necessarily the visualized icon itself – as a commercial, a photograph or a painting – that reflects the racist or sexist attitudes to black women, but the meaning ascribed to the icon of the black woman, which may be understood in the context of time and space.

I have found it difficult to find any specific sources that reflect a clear notion of the black woman and her sexuality in Denmark today. One way to try to pin down the notion(s) of black women in society would be to interview their male clients about their expectations and perceptions of this group of women.

That the women advertise themselves in newspapers and magazines using such terms as: 'exotic', 'mulatto babe' or 'chocolate-brown' may be understood in relation to certain historical discourses. Here I shall give only two examples from the Danish context, which may be considered as part of a wider European heritage. With these two examples I would like to show how the icon of the black human being in general is framed and expressed in a certain discourse and how the icon of the black woman in particular is expressed in another. These two discourses existed at the same time in Denmark and came to the fore in the inter-war period.

Jonathan Leunbach In 1920s a Danish doctor, Jonathan Leunbach (1884–1955), became famous for his radical views on the termination of pregnancy, which was illegal at that time, and for his views on sexuality which he linked to his political views. In 1925 he wrote a small pamphlet about eugenics. It was Leunbach's conviction that Negroes belonged to an inferior race and should therefore be prevented from mixing with white people. It was his hope that socialism and eugenics together could save the white race (Koch 1996: 46–7).

The doctor's conviction was not unusual at that time in Denmark or in Europe and the USA. But the race perspective, as presented in his pamphlet, was not as common in Denmark as in America. The Danish population was at that time relatively racially homogeneous, and tension between different social groups was not so great. Therefore, the ideas and views of the colonial powers on race were not so well known in Denmark. At that time a majority of Danes had probably never seen a black person, so the arrival of a visiting black American dancer in 1928 caused upheaval in the Danish media.

Josephine Baker (1906–1975) lived in Paris. Her appearance in the *Revue Nègre* in 1925, wearing only a skirt made of bananas, made her internationally famous (Nederveen 1994: 142). She visited Denmark for the first time with the show in 1928. A debate was started in the newspapers even before the opening night. Many articles reflected racist opinions and her performance was accused of being pornographic.[5] There were also more positive articles written at that time. One writer and artist, Poul Henningsen – an exponent of Culture Radicalism – reflected the idea of the black woman as 'natural' and as a kind of 'noble savage', unspoiled by civilization. He wrote that her black skin was like clothes, so even if she did not wear any garments she was not naked. For the Culture Radicalists, not only the body but also the rhythm and music (jazz) and art of black people were unspoiled and natural; they were closer to authentic human beings. The Culture Radicalists' views were positive – a strategy of emancipation (Thing 1996: 14, 208–9). By contrast, the Eugenicists[6] considered black people to be degenerate by virtue of their race. Thus 'uncivilized' became an ambiguous term at the beginning of the twentieth century.

Although Josephine Baker was primarily remembered as 'the black woman with the banana skirt', she was very politically aware and campaigned for human rights after the Second World War (Rose 1991: 212–15). She spoke on race equality at public events several times in Denmark (Hammerich 1977: 506–7; and the newspaper *Aktuelt*, 6 June 1963).

The Danish narrative of the black woman is based on relatively few statements and ideas. These can be linked historically to theories of race, such as those expounded by Leunbach in his pamphlet, where 'Negroes' were seen as inferior.

Josephine Baker was one of the few sources for Danish notions of the sexuality of the black woman. Her performance, though, reflected an ambiguity. On the one hand she was condemned in 1928 even before the opening of her show; on the other hand, many reviewers did not find her show erotic at all, even seeing it as silly. It confused most of the audience that she played with the picture of virginity and sin of the Black Venus – the male European fantasies of the black woman.

HOW IS TRANSNATIONAL PROSTITUTION LINKED TO GENDER, RACE AND SEXUALITY?

The newspaper *Weekendavisen* (12–20 May 1999) published an interview with a student who had made a study of Danish clients and prostitution. By interviewing male clients he discovered that they refer to women from Thailand as bearers of a 'real' or 'natural' womanhood. Furthermore, the study points out that when the clients visit Danish women-who-prostitute, being able to talk to them is a central argument for visiting this group. This example illustrates that different stereotypes of women-who-prostitute exist, building on different images of race and femininity. The idea of gender equality – which was a main issue for the Danish feminist movement – and the idea of the separation of love and sex are important aspects in the construction of the notion of white Danish femininity, which at the same time contrasts and challenges notions of 'the other' women's femininity and sexuality.

The idea of the white Danish woman-who-prostitutes as a kind of confidential partner with communications skills, implies a degree of equality between the client and the sex-worker, and ascribes to the women dignity and equality. In contrast, Thai women's bodies are emphasized, and the erotic services and acts performed for their clients are described in essentialist terms.[7]

Without any documentation, it is my conviction that it is not enough to distinguish between the notion of the white woman and the notion of the coloured woman, but it is also important to distinguish between different ethnic backgrounds; for example, to distinguish between the notion of the Thai woman and the black woman. Notions that surround women-who-prostitute also surround women in general, although they are much more visible in prostitution. These notions are incorporated in our everyday language and understanding, reflecting a hidden and very deeply embedded racism in society.

Concerning the European stereotypes of the transnational coloured woman, it is my thesis that the stereotypes must be seen as ambiguous. On the one hand they reflect elements of racism and sexism; on the other hand, the stereotypes can be useful when the woman-who-prostitutes needs to emphasize her sexuality. She is thus able to hide her real identity behind the stereotype. In this respect stereotypes can be used as a kind of strategy in the way she earns her money. This concealment is easier if she is able to operate in different social spaces too. From that perspective, the women can be seen as acting individuals, with agency, and not only as victims of the system.

CONCLUSIONS

The narratives of Sarah and Cathy illustrate how gender, race and sexuality can be linked to mobility, to Danish notions of black women and the cultural meeting with the Danish welfare discourse through their life strategies – prostitution. The first theme in the list on page 121 has shown how the women, through their mobility, can remain anonymous to the Danish authorities and how they hide the way they earn their money from family and friends through their compartmentalized way of living. This mobility on a European level is a result of the EU's economic and political integration.

The second theme. In the inter-war period, ideas about female migrants (mobility) and the then prevalent notions of promiscuity were linked. In different ways the Danish authorities have tried to control prostitution in relation to modern globalization. Their focus on foreign seamen and Danish women-who-prostitute illustrates this. Today, in the context of the Danish welfare state, mobility is also understood as something that should be controlled. In the light of the Danish public view on women-who-prostitute, transnational women-who-migrate represent the opposite: they are women who do not wish to become a part of the Danish welfare system. Further, the survival strategies of women reflect independent action in contrast to the Danish public construction of a 'prostitute', which reduces women to marginalized social subjects by labelling them as socio-psychological cases – an identity that reflects a victimizing of women-who-prostitute. This identity can also be described as a stereotyped picture, which in general covers all transnational female migrants-who-prostitute. These notions are a hangover from former times.

The third theme. A variety of 'pictures' of black women serve to make African female migrants-who-prostitute in Denmark anonymous. The first picture is of a woman who has been victimized by sexual exploitation. The second picture is of a sexualized woman with a more 'natural' and 'wild' sexuality. Both pictures alienate women. They are static stereotypes that are constructed by and are a result of certain cultures, and which reduce the women to sexual objects.

Through the encounter with Danish public institutions, the African female migrants-who-prostitute are viewed as an anonymous social group by virtue of their gender and appearance.

NOTES

1. The name of the project was SLUSE-PROJEKTET. It was worked out in co-operation with six communities, a public guidance centre for women-who-prostitute (Pro-Linien) and an EU organization (EUROPAP Denmark).

2. One of the reports classifies the women into three groups: (1) foreigners; (2) Danish women who are seen as strong; and (3) Danish women who are seen as weak. The conclusion is that all women, strong or weak, in the end will be affected by their work and acquire some social and psychological problems such as: being incapable of combining sex and love or of showing emotions; being isolated; being emotionally amputated because they are used to distinguish between soul and body in their work.

3. Nederveen 1994; one of Nederveen's main theses.

4. Gilman 1985; Gilman focuses on two discourses – painting and medicine – which reflect notions of black women's sexuality in the nineteenth century.

5. Newspapers: *National Tidende*, 13 and 21 June 1928; *Aftenbladet*, 13 June 1928; *Ekstra Bladet*, 16 June 1928.

6. Lene Koch (1996) has pointed out that eugenic ideas were not limited to a certain group, but widely represented among different social groups such as politicians, scientists, social workers and writers at that time in Denmark.

7. A notion about Thai women which has been seen before. See Det danske center for menneskerettigheder (1989).

REFERENCES

Primary sources

Betænkning; Afgivet af Det af indenrigsministeriet nedsatte udvalg ang. Revision af lov nr. 81 af 30. marts 1906 om modarbejdelse af offentlig usædelighed og venerisk smitte; J. H. A/S universitets-bogtrykkeri København 1946.

Betænkning om foranstaltninger til bekæmpelse af prostitution: afgivet af Udvalget til overvejelse af foranstaltninger overfor prostituerede kvinder og ændring af de gældende bestemmelser til modarbejdelse af prostitution; bind nr. 139, København 1955.

Bredmose, Georg V. (1938) 'Psychiatriske undersøgelser af prostituerede kvinder i København', *Juristen* 20: 293–9.

Det danske center for menneskerettigheder (1998) 'Rapport om udtalelse om erhvervsmæssig formidling (annoncering m.v.) af kontakter til udenlandske kvinder'.

Formidlingscenteret Storkøbenhavn (1998) *Prostitution i Danmark i 1990'erne – en statusopgørelse over prostitutionsområdet*, unpublished paper.

Hartmann, Grethe (1949) *Bolig og Bordeller* (Rosenkilde and Bagger).

Jacobsen, Jytte et al. (1996) *Rapport for 'SLUSE-PROJEKTET' i Aarhus kommune 1996*.

Jacobsen, Thune (1937) 'Prostitutionen som politimæssig og socialt problem. Forhandlingerne på Dansk Kriminalistforenings otte og tyvende årsmøde den 15. nov. 1937', *De Nordiska Kriminalistföreningarnas Årsbok*.

Jersild, Jens (1962) 'Løsagtige kvinder', *Rapport til Kriminalforsorgsudvalget*, 2, unpublished paper.

Kemp, Tage (1936) *Prostitution, an Investigation of Its Causes* (Levin and Munksgaard).

Konsulentkompagniet og Formidlingscenteret Storkøbenhavn (1998) *Indendørs prostitution i Danmark – en evaluering af et forsøgsprojekt med socialt arbejde for prostituerede i 6 kommuner*, unpublished paper.

Kriminalforsorgsudvalgets betænkning om prostitution (1973) *Udvalgets 4. betænkning*, 678.

Mainz, Hanne (1996) *'SLUSE-PROJEKTET' i Herning og Ikast*, unpublished paper.

Mortensson, Gunnar og Vestergaard, Emma (1961) 'Psykiatriske undersøgelser af unge prostituerede kvinder', *Nordisk tidsskrift for Kriminalvidenskab*.

Nielsen, Vibeke (1996) *Rapport om Sluse-projektet i Odense*, unpublished paper.

Stoustrup, Else (1996) *Sluse-projektet i Horsens*, unpublished paper.

Bills and laws concerning prostitution and pimping

Lovforsalg nr. L 43, første behandling : Forslag til lov om ændring af straffeloven.

Lovforslag nr. L 43, tredje behandling; 60. møde, Torsdag den 4.marts 1999 kl. 10.00.

Beslutningsforslag nr. B 110 (1998–1999) 'Foreslag til folketingsbeslutning om bekæmpelse af organiseret udnyttelse af udenlandske kvinder til prostitution', Folketinget.

Notat om straffelovens bestemmelser om prostitution, rufferi og alfonseri m.v. d. 19. okt. 1993; L.A. 1993-20002–115.

Books and articles

Appadurai, Arjun (1993) 'Patriotism and its Future', *Public Culture*, 5: 411–29.

Basch, Linda et al. (1994) *Nations Unbound. Transnational Projects, Postcolonial Predicaments, and Deterritorialized Nation-States* (London and New York: Gordon and Breach).

Bechmann, Torben et. al. (1990) *Prostitution i Danmark* (Copenhagen: Socialforskningsinstituttet).

Bjørnholk, Janne (1994) 'Daphne-syndromet – Om følger af et liv i prostitution', Sydjysk Universitetscenter, *Socialområdet*, 18.

Burmeister, Tereza (1996) '"Mae preta" og "neguinha" – etniske dimensioner i konstruktionen af kvindeligheden i det koloniale Brasilien', *Kvinde, køn og forskning*, 4 (5).

Christensen, Hilda Rømer (1995) *Mellem backfische og pæne piger* (Copenhagen: Museum Tusculanums Forlag).

Elgan, Elisabeth (1997) 'Prostitutionen vålnad – om sexualitet och ekonomisk ojämlikhet', in I. Hagman (ed.), *Mot halva magten* (Stockholm: SOU), p. 33.

EU (1996) *EU Conference on Trafficking in Women For Sexual Exploitation*, unpublished papers.

Gilman, Sander L. (1985) 'Black Bodies, White Bodies: Toward an Iconography of

Female Sexuality in Late Nineteenth-Century Art, Medicine, and Literature', *Critical Inquiry*, 12 (1).

Grant, Joan (ed.) (1996) *Women, Migration and Empire* (Stoke on Trent: Trentham Books).

Gravers, Mikael (1989) 'Den ædle dansker i "Orientens" spejl. Billeder fra det danske eventyr i Siam omkring 1900', in O. Høiris (ed.), *Dansk mental geografi* (Aarhus: Aarhus Universitetsforlag).

Hammerich, Poul (1987) *Lysmageren – En krønike om Poul Henningsen* (Copenhagen: Gyldendal).

Hannerz, Ulf (1993) 'Hvilken Globale Kultur', *Samtiden* 4.

Kemp, Tage (1936) *Prostitution. An Investigation of its Causes* (Copenhagen: Levin and Munksgaard).

Kirkebæk, Birgit (1993) *Da de åndsvage blev farlige* (Copenhagen: Forlaget Socpol).

Koch, Ida (1987) *Prostitution – Om truede unge og socialt arbejde* (Copenhagen: Munskgaard).

Koch, Lene (1996) *Racehygiejne. Danmark 1920–56* (Copenhagen: Gyldendal).

KULU (1996) 'Kvinder én gros -om handel med kvinder', *KULU*, 15.

Lützen, Karin (1998) *Byen tæmmes. Kernefamilie, sociale reformerog velgørenhed i 1800 tallets København* (Copenhagen: Hans Reitzels).

Mannion, Patoommat P. (1999) *Ethnic Minorities Thai Women in Copenhagen and Frederiksberg*, Projektrapport fra Hiv-Danmark, unpublished paper.

Nederveen, Jan (1994) *Hvidt på sort, Illustrede fordomme* (Copenhagen: Mellemfolkeligt Samvirke).

Nencel, Lorraine (1997) 'Casting Identities – Gendered Enclosures', unpublished PhD dissertation.

Pheterson, Gail (1996) *The Prostitution Prism* (Amsterdam: Amsterdam University Press).

Rose, Phyllis (1991) *Jazz Cleopatra; Josephine Baker in her Time* (New York: Vintage).

Scott, Sue and Stevi Jackson (1996) *Feminism and Sexuality – a Reader* (Edinburgh: Edinburgh University Press).

Sørensen, Ninna Nyberg (1995) 'Telling Migrants Apart: The Experience of Migrancy among Dominican Locals and Transnationals', unpublished PhD thesis, Institute for Anthropology, Copenhagen University.

Spivak, Gayatri C. (1992) 'Woman in Difference: Mahasweta Devi's "Douloti the Bountiful"', in A. Parker (ed.), *Nationalisms and Sexualities* (London: Routledge).

Stoklund, Bjarne (ed.) (1999) *Kulturens nationalisering – et etnologisk perspektiv på det nationale* (Copenhagen: Museum Tusculanums forlag).

Thing, Morten (1996) 'Negre, børn og orgasme – Overvejelser omkring kulturradikale frigørelsesstrategier', *Nordisk Sexologi*, 1996: 14: 207–15.

Thorbek, Susanne (1997) 'Human Rights and Bodies: Sex, Race, Sexuality', unpublished paper for the Researcher Training Course.

Vammen, Tinne (1989) *Rent og urent. Hovedstadens piger og fruer 1880–1920* (Copenhagen: Gyldendal).

PART THREE

Critical Reflections

A Portrait of the Lady: the Portrayal of Thailand and Its Prostitutes in the International Media

CHITRAPORN VANASPONG

THE PORTRAYAL OF THAILAND: PROSTITUTION ...

Thailand was often perceived by western media as a country plagued by sex-abuse (Bunyaphusit 1997).

Everybody knows how people think about Thailand, and what is best for the country. I have no need to spell out how my country is perceived; I would rather show a few examples of how Thailand has been covered by the media in recent decades.

A 1993 paper on the sexual exploitation of children in tourism and international travel published in London by K. Ireland claims that the 1987 'Visit Thailand Year' was promoted with the slogan, 'The one fruit of Thailand more delicious than durian – its young women'.

Thailand is known worldwide as a land of sex tourism. In 1993,the Thai government reproached the London-based publisher of the *Longman Dictionary of English Language and Culture* for describing Bangkok as a city 'famous for its temple ... and where there are a lot of prostitutes', an entry that would 'project a negative image of Thailand ... [and] erode the good moral standards of Thais'. Although the definition of Bangkok related to prostitution was withdrawn from the dictionary, the image had already been circulated. For example, on 2 August 1998, the *Sunday Times* in the USA published as its headline: 'Romania Seen as Thailand of Europe for Paedophiles'. The whole, written by Alison Mutler (AP), was about how Romania has become a destination for paedophiles because of the large number of homeless children looking for comfort, the widespread poverty and a perception that law enforcement officials are corrupt or deal leniently with foreigners.

More recently, a local edition of *Esquire* (1999) said that the 1997 financial crisis resulted in about 170,000 Britons visiting Pattaya the following year to enjoy its cheap sex, drugs and fake designer goods: 'Young British men go to Thailand in their thousands to get what they can't at home – endless sex with as many beautiful women as they can manage.'

Prostitution has become a fundamental part of Thailand's international image and draws in millions of dollars and western clients every year. Thailand's sex trade is sold to westerners through the news media, travel guides and on the streets. Tourists and expatriate men are inundated with information about where to buy women, cheap gems and Thai silk. It becomes part of the shopping trip.

The popular emphasis has also been on the 'innocents' of this industry: young children and only slightly older virgins, sold by desperately poor parents to the brothel keepers of Bangkok and Pattaya, lured to the cities by the false promises of employment in the service sector by pimps and procurers. .

... AND ITS PROSTITUTES

Along with the general image of the country, Thai sex-workers also play a big part in the story. They appear as 'women who are so passive, beautiful, innocent and poor', according to foreign tourists, and they are viewed by their customers as sex objects and commodities: 'They are all woman'; 'They know how to give a man what he wants'; 'She cannot do enough for me. When I go into the bathroom in the morning, I find the toothpaste already squeezed on to the brush – that's what I call caring'.

Such phrases are quoted in many popular media as well as academic reports. In this version of woman as nurturer and as sensual Oriental they are considered as sexist and racist stereotypes (Seabrook 1997). Moreover, to justify their act of having sex with the women, sex-tourists would claim that 'the woman feels very grateful [to her client or short-term partner] that he is helping her family getting tractors, drinking water, mosquito nets etc.', or:

they are prostitutes and we feel sorry for them. They are very poor but we love 'em. I feel sorry for them because they have to resort to what they do. I think that it's best that we do go with them because what we give them ... it helps them, it's not so wrong. The oldest girls come to Thailand, they try to get a job and this is all they can really get because they haven't got an education. So to break the vicious cycle they send the money home to get an education for the younger ones, which is good, because eventually there won't be this, they won't need to do this. (O'Rourke 1991)

Interestingly, such images of the passive, innocent women of Thailand have been sustained and reinforced in the international media for the last two or three decades. An article published in an Israeli newspaper on 11 June 1999 provide a good example. Entitled 'We're here just for the sex' (*Ha'aretz* magazine) it is about organized sex tours in Thailand offered by Israeli entrepreneurs. Ben, a marketing expert who set up such a tour, is quoted as saying: 'As soon as you get off the plane, you see that everything there is based on sex, that this nation really knows how to serve you. The whole trip was one giant orgasm.'

And the women of Thailand are exactly as they were described over ten years ago:

My friend told me about massages and other special treatments, not just sex. For instance, a man or a woman gets into a bathtub with a girl or two, and for two to four hours – and you pay hardly anything for this ... There's terrible poverty there, and sex is the major national product. My friend told me about how the women there are unlike the prostitutes in the rest of the world. To them, you're not just another one in a long series of clients. You're more like their date. You're the king. They walk hand-in-hand with you, go shopping with you. It's another world. It's not just an hour or hour and a half. It's more like a one-day marriage.

WHY ARE THESE IMAGES CONSTRUCTED AND REINFORCED?

Most major cities have red-light districts, but why are they not advertised for the tourist trade? Why single out Thailand when prostitution flourishes all over? Why has the image of Thais and other Asian prostitutes not changed for more than twenty years? These are questions that are asked most frequently in Thailand. And to answer these questions, I will just bluntly say: because we are women, because we are prostitutes, and because we are citizens of a Third World country. Combining these three, the prostitutes of Thailand are the best bad-news-makers for the international media.

Prostitutes as very bad girls As you may already be aware, both prostitution and prostitutes are seen as a cancer in society, both in reality and in the media. It is too complicated for the media to bother educating the public to appreciate the difference between condemning prostitutes and condemning prostitution. Negative attitudes towards sex-workers are everywhere:

> Because to be a 'whore' is to be the lowest type of person, subhuman even, men use that word when they really want to be nasty, when 'bitch' won't suffice, when probably sexuality has nothing to do with the anger; but 'whore' and 'slut' really pack a wallop for most women. While men who use women as vessels into which they project their sexuality are just 'lonely' or 'desperate'. (DePasquale n.d.)

The portrayal of women in the media Images of women in the media are, in general, not very satisfactory. There are a few images of women as policy-makers, or as powerful people in one field or another, but they are very few. According to a recent paper for the ESCAP Meeting in Bangkok on 'Women and Media', women's visibility in the news is often in relation to sensational stories of rape, sexual harassment and domestic and other forms of violence.

The core message that women are victims or prone to abuse has been more pronounced than any condemnation of men's continued violation of women's rights. Such a portrayal has served only to reinforce rather than challenge men's oppression of women. In this sense, freedom of expression has become a licence for the continued negative portrayal and representations of women in print, broadcast and film (Economic and Social Commission for Asia and the Pacific 1999).

Journalistic value: what is news? My work at ECPAT (End Child Prostitution, Child Pornography, and Trafficking of Children for Sexual Purposes) includes dealing with journalists' inquiries and interviews. A reporter rang and asked me to confirm some statistics about prostitution and child prostitution in Thailand. The statement that she wanted me to comment on was 'Thailand has 2 million prostitutes and 800,000 of them are underage.'

I told her that, first, such statistics do not exist. Since prostitution is not totally legal, it operates partly underground and no researcher is able to count exactly how many prostitutes there are. Second, according to many studies undertaken in Thailand, the most reliable figure should be 200,000, not 2 million. And, out of this number, child prostitutes would total only between 30,000 and 40,000. Furthermore, these are all estimates.'That is very low,' she almost screamed at me. Disappointed, she hung up the phone.

Responding to media inquiries over a period of time, I came to know what foreign journalists generally look for, what constitutes the major ingredients they need to make news and how they cook those ingredients up. In short, to make a good story about prostitution in Thailand, the worse the situation is the better, the younger the child is the better, and the more irresponsible the government is the better for their coverage.

The media's interest in the issue of prostitution only reflects how the international media perceive 'what is news' in general. That is, information that is timely, of magnitude, or that has human interest qualities or that excites the emotions is frequently the basis for many of the stories which are transmitted in international information flows (Bunyaphusit 1997).

'FIRST WORLD' REPORTERS, THE 'FIRST WORLD' INTEREST, AND NEWS ABOUT THE 'THIRD WORLD'

Not only the 'news' value alone, but the fact that those media are representatives of 'First World' nations also plays a major role in how the 'developing countries' are portrayed in the international media.

As Chaowalit Bunyaphusit's study *Coverage of ASEAN Countries in the International Newsmagazines*, March 1997, shows, most of the information about the South was gathered by correspondents from the North. In this sense, Thailand, a 'Third World' country, and its prostitution problem are not only 'a piece of news' that people read about and forget the next morning; they are also 'facts' that people in the West want to hear, believe in and read about. Reporters, subeditors and editors play a big role in confirming such facts for their readers. As Walter Lippman has said, in reality the role of the media, in general, should extend beyond showing a passing interest in events. The important duty of the press is to do 'What every sovereign citizen is supposed to do but has not the time or interest to do for himself – that is, to gather information, pick up what is important, digest it thoroughly and without passion or prejudice relate it to the problems of the day.'

We may believe that western interest in news about the Third World reflects concern about our problems and a desire to help, as many activists in the Third World hope. Many times, the media report tragedies or disasters that happen in the South because these affect their own citizens. One example is when the Australian media reported widely on the issue of sex tourism and the spread of AIDS in Thailand, for it affects their own interests. As Lenore Mandorson said: 'For countries such as Australia, in recognition of this fact, the primary issue has been an unsurprising self-interested concern that nationals might become infected with HIV by Thai prostitutes, and that would then spread infection at home' (Mandorson n.d.).

It is a Third World problem As well as journalists from all over the world, academics from various fields are also attracted by the fascinatingly controversial phenomenon of Thailand and its prostitution. They were among the first, even before the journalists, to bring the issue of prostitution in Thailand on to the international agenda.

Examining the question of why Thailand is singled out when prostitution flourishes all over, Julia O'Connell has an explanation:

Any analysis of sex tourism which fails to consider its economics is doomed to provide only a partial explanation of the phenomenon, for without the obscene disparity in average per capita incomes between the countries which host sex tourists and those which supply them, sex tourism would be a marginal activity of a very different character.

Feminists, socialists and policy makers may not all be entirely happy about the tourists who visit Amsterdam in order to buy sexual services from local people, for example, but because the power relations and economics involved here are of a very different order from those involved in sex tourism in underdeveloped countries, it does not excite the same moral and political repugnance. (O'Connell and Taylor 1994).

Sustaining the tourist market The portraits of Thailand included in many films that depict the Patpong sex shows as well as other 'out-of-the-ordinary' acts that include opium smoking, eating baked snake, tattoos, and riding *tuk-tuk* (trishaws) are symbols of 'weird' Thailand. The images in this kind of material are fantastic and partly 'imaginary exotic', a means of marketing a product. The marketing of a destination through sex is part of the promotion scheme. The tourist can step outside his own culture; unconstrained/temporarily un-enculturated. He is able to act in ways unimagined or barely imagined at home.

In reality, the promotion of Thailand as a sex haven has occurred with official complicity and with wider political support. During the 1960s many politicians were reported to argue that a larger sexual service industry would result in increased tourism, with attendant economic advantages. The image created a vicious circle: the media and travel literature influence the western view, this creates more demand for information about Thailand's prostitution, and encourages the media and travel literature to play it up that much more (Combe 1990).

IMPACT OF THE IMAGE

Although the problem of prostitution really does exist in Thailand, the presentation of Thailand, its sex industry, and its prostitutes is likely to be exaggerated, particularly by the popular media, due to the factors mentioned earlier. Additionally, such media images are always simplified, and various aspects of the whole picture are excluded. As a result, it leads to the generalization of the image. In other words, all Thai women are seen as prostitutes.

For example, a Thai woman who lives in Norway confessed in a Danish newspaper: 'I am frequently asked the question whether I come from Pattaya where people become prostitutes. That hurt my feeling, and I got both angry and upset' (*Dagbladet*, 18 January 1998). This attitude, though it is not universal, is also reflected at the level of national policy in many countries. For example, a Hong Kong newspaper reported in March 1999 that every Thai woman arriving for the first time in Hong Kong international airport was asked by immigration officers if she was involved in prostitution (*The Nation*, 18 June 1999).

However, the reaction of Thai women who face such an insulting greeting does little to help the image problem that they are facing.

'Where are you from?' asked a German man.

'Thailand,' a female friend of mine replied. She is a journalist and had gone to Germany to attend a conference on media and human rights.

'Thailand! I know Patpong.'

'I also know Hitler!'

As do other Thai women, she feels angry every time Thailand, our home country, is identified by foreigners as a sex tourism centre, and nowhere beyond Patpong, Pattaya, and sex tourist destinations is known to them. Some Thai women express their anger directly to the person who reiterates this stereotyped image of Thailand, some fall silent and some have enough patience to defend themselves. However, most of the time, the anger of respectable Thai women points directly to those who are considered whores.

Let me give an example. The *Aftenposten*, a Norwegian newspaper, on 11 August 1999 published a letter from the Royal Thai Embassy that claimed to 'express the feeling of Thai people in Norway'. This letter was sent to the newspaper after it had previously been published on 23 July 1999 in an article about how residents in the neighbourhood of Oslo felt harassed by a massage parlour operated by a Thai national in one of its municipalities.

The letter stated:

> The Embassy was asked by Thai people to inform you that we feel upset about the behaviour of these Thais. They damage the dignity of the majority of Thai people who make a living by doing a proper job. Most Thais feel that the Thais who do this embarrassing job do not represent Thai women as a whole. Besides, they are never welcomed by Thai people in Norway, because their behaviour is so annoying and damages the image of Thai women and the country.

On the other hand, Thai sex-workers can also answer back. When asked by a reporter about how they feel when educated Thai women complain about how offended they are when they travel abroad and are mistaken for sex-workers, one of them said:

> If women who claim to be educated can't prove themselves (to im-migration officers and other foreigners) that they are not prostitutes, then why did they bother going to the university in the first place? They should simply tell people that they are not sex workers. But, come to

think of it, what's wrong with being a sex worker anyway? (Rajana-
phruk 1999)

The hostility between 'respectable' women and 'whores' is not a
new phenomenon in Thai society (and also in other societies). Actually,
the word 'hostility' is too blunt to describe the complicated relationship
between these two groups of women. It may be best to quote Ann
Danaiya Usher's article 'After the Forest: AIDS as Ecological Collapse
in Thailand':

> As a respectable woman, she despises her morally inferior sister, and yet
> she is taught to believe she 'needs' the prostitute to protect her virginity
> and to absorb her man's 'negative sexual behaviour'. Her view of the
> prostitute oscillates between scorn and pity. Either the sex worker is a
> poor helpless child, tricked into a life of sin, or she is easy and weak-
> willed, an essentially immoral being from whom the respectable woman
> should keep a healthy distance. (Usher 1994)

There has been an effort to create solidarity between all women
through women advocates. However, the presentation of Thailand as a
sex destination, and Thai women as prostitutes in the international
media reinforced the hostility between women from different groups in
society, and this has affected the development of the women's movement
as a whole.

THE GOVERNMENT'S RESPONSE

The controversial *Newsweek* article 'Beyond Sex and Golf' (12 July
1999) is just another example of how the international media keep on
reinforcing the stereotyped image of Thailand as a sex paradise. The
headline for its cover story was based on a quote from an unnamed
western diplomat in Bangkok: '*Thailand has two comparative advantages.
Sex and golf courses.*' However, the overall content of the article focused
on the present state of the Kingdom's economy and where it is actually
heading after weathering two years of turbulence. 'Thailand could well
become little more than a slick, foreign-dominated export-processing
zone that will fall farther behind its aggressive neighbors. It may be
remembered not for its economic prowess but for the live sex acts of
Bangkok's Patpong district,' *Newsweek* stated.

Whenever the foreign media publish reports on the sex industry in the Kingdom, the government is usually quick to react with denials, criticism and threats of blacklisting. In the *Newsweek* case, Prime Minister Chuan Leekpai of Thailand commented: 'People just focus on these small things.' Deputy Finance Minister Pisit Lee-artham also reacted, saying: 'We admit that we have a lot of weak points which must be corrected but to point out only these two issues [sex and golf] is not completely correct' (*The Nation*, 7 October 1999). Akapol Sorasu-chart, a government spokesman, was the one responsible for taking action: 'I will send a letter on behalf of the Thai government to the publication that the criticism had been based on exaggerated facts and thus has caused a lot of damage to the country's reputation.'

As always, the government response to the problem focused on the country's image and how to reconstruct a 'good image' of Thailand, Thai women and the Thai people as a whole. That is why, when it came to the response to the *Newsweek* case, Prime Minister Chuan said that the national humiliation caused by the story should spur on the government's media relations officers to work harder: 'We need effective communication to prevent misunderstandings, such as in the case of *Newsweek*. Thailand has a lot of good things going for it that require your ability to provide the public with the right information.'

In 1997 the government planned to use the Internet to improve international understanding of Thailand's economic, political and social situation. Kanala Khantaprab, a deputy government spokesperson, admitted that some of the negative reports about Thailand were true, but added that their contents, such as the economic situation and problems of prostitution, were often exaggerated (*The Nation*, 28 June 1997).

Wanchai Roujanavong, however, pointed out some of the difficulties facing the government in their task of reconstructing the image of Thailand. One was the fact that the Ministry of Foreign Affairs, though in charge of the country's image problem, was not responsible for solving it. If no action is taken against prostitution by governmental agencies, the statements by the Ministry of Foreign Affairs will lose all credibility (Wanchai 1997). Wanchai also suggested that the best way to solve the image problem was as follows: 'It is not easy to clarify this problem because prostitution does exist. The first thing to do is to accept that prostitution is existing, and explain how Thailand has been trying to solve the problem.'

THE POWER OF INTERNATIONAL MEDIA: ONLY THE POSITIVE SIDE?

I would now like to discuss the positive side of the international media. Communication technology and information processing are believed to play an important role in informing and educating huge numbers of people. Hence they help to raise living standards. A few of the very large mass media companies affect not only their own citizens but also citizens all over the world.

On the positive side, there is the global media's potential for raising awareness about issues and developments that affect nations and peoples as well as for bridging cultural and political differences through shared information and dialogue. People have witnessed how various actors have been brought together on their screens to debate an issue from different perspectives. People have watched positive images, portrayals and representations of women by gender-sensitive reporters and artists who present alternatives and challenge the sexist and stereotyped norms prevalent in the media. To a certain extent, the globalized media have allowed for greater sensitivity and action on violations of women's rights in contexts outside their own. These, however, remain exceptions to the dominant sexist and stereotyped material disseminated to a global audience.

The globalized media have facilitated the export of cultural models and their codes, perceptions and prejudices, including gender, cultural and ethnic stereotypes that are produced and controlled by a few trans-national corporations. Moreover, the images and messages often stand in stark contrast to local values and norms and lack social reality and relevance.

Most importantly, the international media are always seen as an important tool for raising awareness among the public, to put pressure on the government, or even to pressure the international community to take action.

As Alvin Toffler said in *The Third Wave* (1981), the mass media have become a giant loudspeaker. And their power is used across regional, ethnic, tribal and linguistic lines to standardize the images available to a society. Toffler also repeated the idea in *Power Shift* (1990): 'the use of media outside a country to influence political decisions inside it is also becoming more common'.

Many NGOs, activists and international organizations give priority to working with media in the hope that newspaper headlines will urge their governments to seek solutions to problems. But does it really work that way? Or is it just an excuse that the media deploy to justify their 'right' to get the information they want by any means, even though it might affect the privacy or safety of a woman? This question becomes more acute in that the concept of 'investigative journalism' has become increasingly popular among media in the western world.

BEHIND THE SCENES

Investigative journalism and life stories of young prostitutes   On 29 April 1999, blue flyers were inserted in newspapers throughout Britain posing the question: '*Is Thai sex slavery coming to Britain?*' The flyers were advertising Channel 4's Dispatches, 'The Sex Slave Trade' broadcast that evening. The programme is an undercover investigation into the vicious trade in Thai women to the sex industry in Britain, where they have been beaten, locked up and forced to service up to 700 men for the price of their ticket and UK visa. The programme turned out to be a courageous piece of investigative journalism. Before travelling to Thailand the year before, Lee Sorrell, the producer/reporter, had created a website advertising an escort business and presenting himself as a bar owner in London. He then went to Thailand pretending to look for Thai women to work as service girls in his London bar. He contacted local and foreign traffickers as well as women who were rescued from the forced sex trade, filming them all with a secret camera. Not surprisingly, Channel 4 says it is immensely proud of the programme, 'which led directly to eight girls being saved from slavery in East London'.

However, in Bangkok, many people felt frightened and fearful following the broadcast. The two underage girls who had been lured into the sex industry from remote north-eastern Thailand were interviewed with their faces and voices clearly visible on the programme. Andrew Drummond, a British journalist based in Bangkok, who played a major role in assisting the production of the programme, said:

> Producers of this kind of investigation are always torn in two directions. They owe a duty to those they interview not to leave them vulnerable to revenge attacks by those pimps who were out to exploit

them. This usually means hiding their identity by filming them with their back to the camera or in silhouette and by disguising their voices. But at the same time, producers know that programmes are much more compelling if people are interviewed face to face and names, locations and other details are given. (Drummond 1999)

As stated on the programme, the story ended happily. Women were rescued, and Channel 4 sent information to the Bangkok police about what it had uncovered. In reality, all this information was sent after the programme had been broadcast, which was too late as all the pimps will almost certainly have vanished. As a result, the investigation in Thailand has gone belly-up. The traffickers remain at liberty, seeking revenge. The real tragedy of this programme is that while some girls may have been saved from the clutches of pimps in the UK, there are other girls in Thailand who will, for a long while to come, remain fearful of the beating they may get from those who sought to exploit them.

This case reflects clearly the problems that investigative journalism faces in producing results. The need to sell the programme does not allow the information it contains to reach the police before the programme goes on the air. Instead, the media have a problem justifying their invasion of the very personal life of a prostitute.

Welcome to the internet world And then comes the Internet. Communication in the computer era is even more exciting than in the era of the global village. The number of Internet users is growing fast. According to NUA Ltd, there are roughly 120 million Internet users worldwide and these are distributed broadly as follows:

USA and Canada	70 million
Europe	23 million
Asia/Pacific	17.25 million
South America	7 million
Africa	1 million
Middle East	0.75 million

It is also estimated that by 2001 there will be approximately 200 million users worldwide, of whom roughly 40 million will be US households. For Thailand, KSC Internet expects to promote 1 million Internet users by the year 2000.

The promotion of prostitution through sex tours on the Internet expands men's access to women as sexual commodities. The Internet is the fastest growing and most unregulated communication network in the world. It is a rapid-publishing medium that can reach its readership anywhere within minutes. These factors make it a thriving site for the global trafficking in women, leading to an escalation of the global sex trade. And yet the entrance and growth of the sex industry on the Internet is both symptom and evidence of the harm that is being done to women (Hughes n.d.).

Men exchange information on where to find prostitutes and describe how they can be used. After their trips, men write reports on how much they paid for women and children and give pornographic descriptions of what they did to them. New technology has enabled an online merger of pornography and prostitution, with video-conferencing bringing live sex shows to the Internet. The Internet now becomes a medium for the abuse of women and is accessible to everyone; there are no ethical codes prohibiting violence and obscenity such as exist in the print media. This rapid-publishing electronic medium has enabled men to pimp and exploit individual women. Men can go out at night, buy a woman, and post the details on a newsgroup. By morning, anyone with an Internet connection can read about it. Given enough information, they can find the same woman (Hughes 1999).

At the same time, the age-old images of Thailand and its prostitutes are consistently sustained and reinforced. As Donna M. Hughes states in her article:

> The most voluminous coverage is on Bangkok, Thailand. The men give information on everything from currency exchange rates to how to run a bar tab. The names, addresses and phone number for 150 hotels where men feel comfortable are listed. All the city sections and their sexual specialities are listed and described. Does the man want a massage? Discos? Escort services? A lady house? Japanese club? A short-time hotel? A blow job bar? (Hughes 1999)

The posting of this kind of information reveals that men are using the Internet as a source of information for where and how to find women and children for prostitution. Men describe taking a computer printout of hotels, bar addresses and phone numbers with them on their trips, or describe how they used Internet search engines to locate sex tours: 'This three-day trip happened in June 1995. On the flight I read all the information I had printed out from the World Sex Guide – I had a lot of expectations of the City of Angels [Bangkok].'

The fact is that the Internet is like a private medium where everyone can become a reporter, including sex tourists. As a result, the language that is used and the accuracy of the information are more difficult to monitor and control than they are in the professional print media or news agencies.

A LOOK AT THE NEWS PRESENTATION IN THE MEDIA: A CONCLUSION

Thailand is, in fact, conspicuous by its presence in the popular media, but audiences are told the same story over and over again. There are distortions, over-simplifications, de-contextualizing of human lives and a wilful ignorance of the many factors that shape human choices.

That these women have little education, few qualifications and even fewer job prospects explains some of the local, national and international reasons for the existence of the sex industry. Yet both the officials and the media refuse to see these facts as causes, and instead impose more hardships by a crackdown on individuals and families. They further ignore the fact that hardships also exist within the sex industry, and invariably avoid the conclusion that the lack of local jobs supplies cheap labour for sweatshops as well as the sex industry.

Few journalists question why poverty is so extreme and pervasive; no theory is offered to explain why this industry is so lucrative; no attention is given to the demand side of the equation. All we get is the same journalistic sleight-of-hand highlighting human misery, a trick that fools the eye and makes it unable to see the real machinery of the act. Missing from the picture are issues such as environmental destruction, international planning, the creation of an unskilled labour force for international use, and those aspects of the sex industry – as either erotic institution or labour process – not related to AIDS or child prostitution.

Many voices have not been heard. As Oi Ing, a Thai sex-worker who responded to pictures of sex-workers appearing in *Esquire* magazine as well as an article on sex tourism in Thailand, said: 'I'd like to ask the photographer if he asked for the women's permission before he took and published those photos. Sex is natural but when you take someone else's sex life and publicize it then it's no longer natural. I think that's a violation of human rights' (*The Nation*, 25 August 1999).

Images of Thailand and its women only reflect the attitudes and selection process of the international media when portraying Third World countries. 'News' does not necessarily tell us what is going on.

Belief in the power of the media to make the world a better place needs to be challenged. As in the case of prostitution in Thailand, the media reports fail to stimulate society to solve its problems. Instead, they affect the image of the country and its women and lead to discrimination in various ways.

All stakeholders, including governmental agencies and NGOs, may need to readjust their strategies and policies to deal with the international media. This does not entail refusing to co-operate with the media or allowing only 'good news' to be reported. But more comprehensive knowledge about the effects of international media reporting about Third World countries will be of help. At the same time, we must accept that prostitution does exist in Thailand, it is a source of the country's revenue and it is well known among the people of Thailand, whether the international media report on it or not.

Despite all the international reporting on prostitution in Thailand, there has never been a clear message from the Thai government about its policy on prostitution. Is it seen as a source of national income so that it has to exist, or should it be banned? There is only silence. For how long will the Thai public tolerate the farce of its government falling back on national dignity as a means of avoiding the real issues of the flesh trade?

REFERENCES

Bunyaphusit, Chaowalit (1997) 'Coverage of ASEAN Countries in the International Newsmagazines', Dissertation, University of Pune, India.

Combe, Victoria (1990) 'Buying Sex in a Different Currency', *The Nation*, 2 July 1990.

DePasquale, Katherine M. (n.d.) 'The Effects of Prostitution'. www.feminista.com/vln5/depasquale.html

Drummond, Andrew (1999) 'How Dispatches Abused My Trust', *The Times*, 14 May 1999.

Economic and Social Commission for Asia and the Pacific (1999) 'The State of

Women and Media in Asia: an Overview', paper presented at the High-level Intergovernmental Meeting to Review Regional Implementation of the Beijing Platform for Action, Bangkok, 26–29 October.

Hughes, Donna M. (n.d.) 'Sex Tours via the Internet'. www.feminista.com/vln7/hughes.html

— (1999) 'The Internet and Global Prostitution', *Women in Action*, 1 (Manila: Isis Women's Resource Centre).

Mandorson, Leonore (n.d.) 'The Pursuit of Pleasure & the Sale of Sex'. www.hsph.harvard.edu/Organisations...net/sasia/repro2/pursuit_of_pleasure.html

O'Connell Davidson, Julia and Jacqueline Sanchez Taylor (1994) *Sex Tourism: 'Thailand'* (Bangkok: ECPAT International).

O'Rourke, D. (writer and director) (1991) *The Good Woman of Bangkok* (O'Rourke and Associates Filmarkers in association with the Australian Film Commission and Channel 4) (82 mins).

Seabrook, Jeremy (1997) 'North–South Relations: the Sex Industry'. www.captive.org/Information/Generalinfo/Seabrook_Jan_1997_htm

Toffler, Alvin (1981) *The Third Wave* (London: Pan Books).

— (1990) *Power Shift: Knowledge, Wealth, and Violence at the Edge of the 21st Century* (New York: Bantam Books).

Usher, Ann Danaiya (1994) 'After the Forest: AIDS as Ecological Collapse in Thailand', in Vandana Shiva (ed.), *Close to Home* (Philadelphia: New Society Publishers).

Wanchai, Roujanavang (1997) *Prostitution Problem in Thailand* (in Thai) (Bangkok: Office of the Attorney General).

TEN

'Il y a 50.000 prostituées marocaines de luxe dans la côte espagnole': A Necessary Myth

ANA LOPEZ LINDSTROM

§ In the course of my PhD research on 'Gender relations in Morocco and in the Spanish Migration', I conducted two years of fieldwork among Moroccan women and men in Spain and Morocco. I became interested in Moroccan prostitution when the testimony of different women made me aware of the importance of the idea of Moroccan women as prostitutes in Spain. My first contact with the subject came during an encounter with a woman from Fez who lives and works in Madrid. She told me that another woman approached her in Malaga, where she used to live, and asked where she worked and how much she earned per month. When my informant told her that she was a domestic servant and made 35,000 pts (about 210 euros) per month, the other woman laughed at her and explained that she made that sum every night, as a prostitute. When I talked about this with a colleague she told me a very similar story. On another occasion, this time in Rabat, Morocco, the former director of a women's magazine told me and some other researchers that a person from an embassy (she did not specify which) had told her that on the Spanish coast there were more than 50,000 Moroccan luxury prostitutes. When we expressed our surprise, she hesitated and said that there were maybe 5,000, but that she was positive that the phenomenon existed.

Another time in Tangier, I told a Moroccan immigrant who lived in the Netherlands that I was studying the lives of Moroccan women in Spain. He said that women who left the country to work in Spain were in danger of being kidnapped and that he knew of a few cases. Ángeles Ramírez, who did her PhD research on Moroccan women in Spain, was told in an interview with a lawyer from Tangier that he had seen many

Spanish pornographic films with Moroccan women. Other men and women in Morocco and in Spain have similar stories. I wondered why there were so many Moroccan prostitutes according to the Moroccan people I knew and so few according to personal observations and the mass media in Spain. I decided to do some research into the extent of Moroccan prostitution in Madrid, where I am conducting my PhD fieldwork.

I began by consulting the literature on the subject, visiting organizations that work with prostitutes and asking my informants for their opinions. The only empirical data I had when I started were some, apparently Moroccan, prostitutes I had seen in a central square in Madrid.

I found very little literature on prostitution in general and none at all about Moroccan prostitution in Spain. I did not get much information from the organizations either: they talked about women who were originally from Sub-Saharan Africa, Eastern Europe or Latin America; they had no contact with Moroccan women or they knew of very few. The head of a nationwide non-governmental organization which, among other activities, works with prostitutes told me that there were fewer than a dozen Moroccan women on the streets and she described them as middle-aged (from forty to sixty), illiterate, very secretive and with a poor command of Spanish. Some of them, she said, had a Spanish identity card and worked in central Madrid. They had been there for between ten and fifteen years and their clients were middle-aged Spanish men. They dressed in a particular manner, that is, they were well-covered. Algerian prostitutes were younger, more open and had a better knowledge of Spanish.

Another association working with prostitutes drew a similar picture, but most organizations and associations, and even governmental institutions, had no data on the subject. News reports occasionally focus on clandestine clubs where foreign women are forced to practise prostitution and are not allowed to leave. They are mistreated and coerced by the threat of violence and the confiscation of their passports. Among these reports there is no mention of Moroccan women.

According to all these data from different sources, there is only a small number of Moroccan prostitutes, probably fewer than twenty. This is not to say that there are no Moroccan prostitutes in Spain. Informants, social workers and researchers said that these women *might* be working in clubs, where no research has been undertaken. Besides, I concentrated my research on Madrid, and it is possible that there is a concentration of Moroccan prostitutes in other areas of Spain. The Malaga area has a high concentration of people originally from the Gulf states, especially from Saudi Arabia and Kuwait, whose economic situation is such that they are known for having domestic servants whom they bring from Morocco. The fact is that the proportion of Moroccan women workers in Malaga is very high.[1] It could be hypothesized that the demand for sex-workers is also determined nationally or by religion, and this would explain the higher rate of Moroccan prostitutes in the area. I have also been told by several Moroccan men who have worked in the eastern provinces of Spain (Almería and Murcia especially) that, among this group, there were Moroccan sex-workers. This could be an example of how Moroccan women fulfil a specific demand for prostitution.

This chapter argues not so much that there are no prostitutes of Moroccan origin in Spain, but that the number of them is considerably lower than is apparently believed in Morocco and among Moroccans in Spain. Available data are scarce but what there are contradict the idea of a massive influx.

The fact that the discourse on female Moroccan prostitution in Spain and the actual data were so far apart made me consider the possible reasons for this discrepancy. Is it true that there are many Moroccan prostitutes in Spain? And if so, where are they? Or, if it is a myth, why do Moroccan men and women in Morocco and in Spain encourage this idea?

My hypothesis is that it is a myth as to numbers, and that the myth is necessary both at the point of origin and in the context of migration. In the context of origin, it is part of a discourse that aims to control female mobility. In Spain, women use the myth in order to ease the stigma of having migrated alone to work and thus for having challenged the Moroccan gender system.

To this effect, the chapter will first describe the context where the myth is shaped (Morocco), and define what is understood in Morocco by prostitution and female sexuality. The assumption is that any concept is shaped in a particular context. The Spanish context will also be briefly described in order to explain the immigration of Moroccan women to Spain and their strategies of adaptation. There will also be a discussion of the erotic image of the 'other' in order to understand other ways of categorizing the phenomenon.

THE CONCEPT AND ITS CONTEXT: PROSTITUTION IN MOROCCO

Any definition of a concept is conditioned by the context in which it is conceived. Every culture classifies different practices as suitable or unsuitable, moral or immoral, and as healthy or unhealthy (Weeks 1998). Definitions of prostitution are made in a context of particular ideas about sex and gender relations (Shrage 1994).

Are there any national variables that make Moroccan prostitutes a specific phenomenon? It is interesting to study a society where a concept of prostitution has been shaped, in this case Morocco, and to compare the role it plays there and in Spain, where it is considered differently. It can be said that in Spain the difference between prostitution and other sexual encounters is the fact that money is involved. In Morocco, the economic exchange is not as important as the fact that the sexual encounter takes place outside marriage. In this respect it is revealing to note that most Arabic words for prostitute or prostitution also mean fornication and adultery:

- *Bga'*: prostitution (*baga* means to desire, to seek)
- *'ahara*: adultery, fornication, whoredom, prostitution
- *Fayira*: adulteress, whore, harlot; *fayir* (m.): libertine, adulterer, liar, shameless
- *Fahisha*: harlot, whore, prostitute; *fahish* (m.): monstrous, abominable, repugnant, shameless; *fawahish* (pl.): monstrosity, adultery, fornication, whoredom; from the same root, *mufhisha*: harlot, whore
- *Saqitat* (pl.): fallen woman, harlot; *saqit* (m.): fallen man, vile, mean
- *Qahba*: whore, harlot, prostitute
- *Zaniya*: whore, harlot, adulteress

As can be observed, most of these terms have a negative connotation. They are considered evil activities, and prostitution, fornication and adultery are almost always lumped together. It should be said that fornication and infidelity are considered the worst of sins (Bousquet 1990) and censured (Ben Jelloun 1997). Any illicit activity, that is any female activity outside the family and the house, is censured. One way of curtailing female mobility is to question their decency.

In Morocco, sexual segregation makes men's and women's worlds two separate domains and relations between the sexes are usually based on ignorance, distrust and fear. Sexual segregation is also space segregation, the street and public places being the male domain and the house the female domain. Gender relations are unequal because women always depend on men, a lack of equality contradicted by the Moroccan constitution, which states that all Moroccans are equal, regardless of their sex (Al Ahnaf 1994). Nevertheless, the *Moudawana*, a personal status code that regulates marriage, divorce and inheritance, grants different rights and duties to men and women. From the personal *Moudawana* it is understood that women are minors all their lives: depending first on their fathers and then on their husbands, brothers or sons. This legal and de facto inequality is justified and legitimized by several discourses, the most common one being the religious discourse (Saltzman 1992; Haeri 1989). Another is the biological discourse: if men and women are different physically, it is natural for them to have different duties and places in society (Haeri 1989). These discourses are used to explain and to legitimize unequal practices.

Inequality is also present in the field of sexuality where it is understood that women and men have different sexualities. Women's lives are determined by their sexuality: they are *bint*[2] (girl, daughter and, by extension, virgin) until they marry and become *mra'* (woman, wife and, therefore, not virgin). It is understood that women's sexuality is active and disturbing for men, who must control it. Women are accused of causing *fitna* (to question faith; temptation, disturbance, civil war) in men and in society. On the one hand women are vulnerable, minors all their lives and in need of protection. On the other hand they are sexually powerful and dangerous. Women's sexuality is, thus, always 'protected' and therefore their mobility is controlled. Women are relegated to the physical sphere of the house and to the conceptual sphere of marriage. All activities outside the house or outside the family (marriage) are considered to be outside the realm of 'proper' female space and behaviour. The family serves to create political and social marginals (see Jacques Donzelot's elaboration on Foucault's concept of marginality, in Guy 1991: 4).

The social group that produces independent female emigration is *grosso modo*, the lower-middle urban class. In this group, any woman departing from her 'natural' environment, the house, without a decent goal (visiting an acquaintance or neighbour, on small errands) runs the risk of being considered indecent. The structural economic crisis that

Morocco has undergone since independence (1956) has been particularly hard on Moroccan youth (Bennani-Chraïbi 1994) who find it difficult to conform to the social sexual roles. The age of marriage has been delayed as it is more difficult for men to maintain a job and therefore a family. The desirable and ideal role for a woman is to wait at home for a marriage proposal. Working outside the house is unacceptable. The 'natural' breadwinner is the husband and so the woman who goes out to work questions both the role of the woman as daughter, wife and mother and the role of the man as the natural supporter of the family. Furthermore, the jobs that are available to them at their educational level are low-skilled, poorly paid and considered indecent because they either involve going out and being in contact with men outside the family (factories) or they are identified with a much lower social class (domestic service). More qualified jobs without a stigma are not available.

Women who can no longer expect marriage to support them are not prepared or educated for 'modern' life, or for jobs that might offer them economic and social independence (Ramírez 1998). Their families of origin are also unable to support them for life and cannot afford to provide them with goods such as jewellery and dresses that would position them in the marriage market or would serve as an insurance for the future (Rosander 1991).

As we can see, in this social group, women's options are very limited. In the contradiction between the ideal (the wife and mother) and the reality (economic crisis, unemployment and lack of alternatives), emigration is an option, and emigration to Spain is, at least, an audacious act. The fact that a woman not only leaves the house but also her country to live and work in another country known for its moral laxity in sexual matters is considered a dual transgression. First, such women will live outside the reach of social and family control. Second, these women are questioning the Moroccan sexual roles of man as breadwinner and woman as mother, wife and housewife.

In the process of female emigration to Spain, women's mobility is controlled by the threat – real but exaggerated – of being kidnapped by a network that trades in women and forced to prostitute themselves; at the very least, they run the risk of being suspected of leading an indecent life abroad. Thus, the idea of thousands of Moroccan women being prostitutes in Spain should be framed in this context of female emigration and the social control of women's mobility.

MOROCCAN FEMALE MIGRANT WORKERS

What about Moroccan women who live and work in Spain? It should be understood that this analysis is concerned only with women who emigrate with the intention of working and who emigrate without their husband or father. Spain is a host country for young, single, divorced and widowed women who emigrate to work, usually in domestic service (see below). This makes Spain a host country specifically for Moroccan women workers, unlike other European host countries for foreign workers (Ramírez 1998).

Spain attracts many Moroccan women who enter the labour market bacause of its demand for domestic servants. It is understood – from the state immigration quotas and by employers – that domestic service is carried out by women. The increasing prosperity of Spanish society has caused a rise in the number of females who have access to employment and education. This has left gaps in certain sectors of the labour market – the 'caring' and 'female' sectors (domestic service, prostitution, care of children and elderly people) – that are characterized by low educational level requirements and bad working conditions. Many of these jobs were formerly carried out by Spanish women in the home, but now they have higher expectations in terms of wages and working conditions, such jobs have become unattractive for indigenous women. Neither the state nor the family assumes these tasks, so foreign women are filling the gap. (See Del Oso 1998 for an analysis of changes in Spanish society in relation to foreign domestic service; and Herranz 1998.)

It is interesting to examine the similarities between prostitution and domestic service. Both have changed in Spain over the last twenty-five years (Sequeiros Tizón 1989). In the 1980s, fewer and fewer local women worked as prostitutes; virtually all indigenous sex-workers were also drug addicts. In the 1990s, foreign women started practising prostitution in Spain in larger numbers (Carmen Meneses, personal communication; Comas 1991). Whether as cause or effect, Spanish men's tastes have also changed and more exotic erotica is a new attraction (Shrage 1994; Sequeiros 1989).

Women who come to Spain to work, usually as domestic servants, are likely to be categorized as prostitutes because they leave their homes and are not controlled by men. But, paradoxically, they also take part in the construction and development of the myth. These migrant women are aware of their transgression, that their decency is being questioned and that their role in their country of origin is a delicate one, so they use the myth of prostitution to distinguish between the 'real' transgressors and the 'honest' workers. They say, I could be working in the streets, making much more money than I do by working in a house but I choose to work hard and make decent money. They show that even though they have come alone and they are doing things that are not expected of women – working, supporting themselves and their families, being autonomous – they are actually doing a 'typical female job' (household chores) in a sexually segregated (female) domain (the house), surrounded by women, children and elderly people. Moroccan women exaggerate their chastity in order to stress the differences between them and the 'evil' women. 'The open doors proclaim the chastity of closed doors' (Guy 1991: 154).

The discourse on prostitution serves the purpose of highlighting their efforts to stay decent in an indecent atmosphere and it also stresses the differences between different transgressions. The analogy between physical and moral outsiderness is very strong in Morocco. As can be noticed in the euphemism 'mra dez-zanqa' (woman of the street), the street is considered a male space and women who are outside their 'natural' space, that is the house, are not women properly speaking. Being outside the physical and moral limits they are therefore outsiders. Emigrant women are outsiders and prostitutes are outsiders too. Ergo emigrant women are prostitutes. What emigrant women try to achieve with the help of the myth is the end of this analogy. There have been other historical moments when this myth has been used for the same purposes in a different context. Moments of new female mobility and the incorporation of women into the labour market occurred at the beginning of the century in Buenos Aires. 'A society where working women were the exception and thus, female labour outside the house was identified as sexual commerce' (Guy 1991: 46).

THE EROTIC 'OTHER'

So far it has been argued that the myth of Moroccan prostitution in Spain serves the purpose, in Morocco, of controlling and liberating emigrant women outside the country. But another question arises about the use of the erotic image in order to categorize the other. Moroccan women use it in an effort to put themselves on the same level of female attractiveness as the Spaniards, while maintaining a superior moral level. The Spaniards, on the other hand, use the myth to prove the under-development of Moroccans.

First of all, it is interesting to notice how what is right or wrong is measured differently when talking about different societies. Moroccans consider western women's practices differently from Moroccan women's practices. Western women are known to be sexually active, and therefore accessible, while Moroccan or Muslim women are either decent or prostitutes.[3] So a Muslim woman who laughs too much, smokes, talks with men to whom she is not related, goes out of the house often, has – or is suspected of having – sexual relations outside or before marriage, is considered to be a prostitute. As said above, sexual encounters outside marriage (*zina'*: fornication, adultery, whoredom) are severely repressed (Ben Jelloun 1997; Bousquet 1990). Western women's sexual practices are 'excused' because in their culture they are not considered to be wrong, but even though they are not considered prostitutes they are treated as 'easy' women and are often harassed (Reed 1992; Ben Jelloun 1997). It is common among Moroccan men to think that if a woman has had more than one sexual partner she will be available to anyone.

In the eyes of Muslim men, western men have a different sexual image. Muslims consider westerners to be 'feminine; their white soft skin and polite urban behaviour make them less virile' (Schmitt 1992b: 20). The different shades of skin colour and geographical origins con-dition male sexual potency; the whiter a man is, the less sexual power he will have; the further north a man comes from, the less of a man he will be; black Africans are the most potent. Moroccan men tend to think that the sexually active western woman travels to 'darker' countries looking for that sexual strength she cannot find back home.

It is also interesting to see the power game that develops in mixed sexual relations. If a western man has sexual relations with a Muslim man or woman it is considered to be exploiting the Third World. But when a Muslim man has a sexual encounter with a western man or woman, it is 'well deserved revenge for suffered injustice and … an expression of physical and moral superiority over a decaying West' (Schmitt 1992b: 125). Defining superiority and inferiority by means of sexuality is what the lawyer from Tangier was trying to do when he placed Moroccan women in Spanish porno movies. The decadent West is responsible for making porno movies (evil) and for forcing Moroccan (ergo decent) women to take part in them because their natural beauty makes them attractive to Spanish men. Otherwise, why would they import them if they have enough Spanish women? Because marriage and relations between a Muslim woman and a non-Muslim man are *haram* (prohibited, sinful), the only space of possible contact is that of prostitution, which is anyway *haram*. Also, when talking about large numbers of Moroccan prostitutes, what can be read between the lines is a specific demand for Moroccan prostitutes because of something that they have that cannot be found in Spain. The 50,000 Moroccan prostitutes rumoured to work on the south coast of Spain were not regular prostitutes; it was stressed that they were luxury prostitutes, that is to say that Moroccan women are luxury women even when they are prostitutes. This kind of myth also serves as a means of constructing or strengthening national feelings by downplaying the 'other'.

What about the erotic image Spaniards have of Moroccan men and women? The erotic image of the Moor in Spain does not include an erotic view of Moorish woman (Eloy Martín Corrales, personal communication); it is concentrated on young men (Schmitt 1992b; Weeks 1992). On the contrary, the image of the female Moor has been used historically as a means of measuring the grade of (under-) development of a culture, in this case, the Moroccan culture (Dieste 1997). In the Spanish imagination, the image of an erotic Arab is an orientalized image of attractive women in contexts such as the harem. It is interesting to look at the leisure sections in Spanish newspapers advertising sexual services. What is considered attractive to Spanish men includes different tones of dark skin (mulatto, Caribbean), oriental (Japanese), Nordic (Swedish, Norwegians, Russians, blondes with blue or green eyes), or Spanish women from Extremadura, the Canary Islands, Madrid or Catalonia) but never Arab women. Sexual images are not applied to women of Moroccan origin who are seen as victims of men who are known to be sexually aggressive (Ben Jelloun 1997).

CONCLUSION: THE MYTH OF MOROCCAN PROSTITUTION IN SPAIN

All myths serve the interests of the particular group that creates and encourages them. In this case, the myth of Moroccan prostitution in

Spain is useful for Moroccan society with its gender system and for Moroccan women who live and work in Spain.

In Morocco, discourses such as the prostitution myth are intended to prevent female mobility by threatening women either with the stigma of being categorized as sexually deviant or of being captured by slave-trading networks. In Spain, Moroccan women use the same discourse, among others, to legitimize 'honest' emigration. It is interesting that discourses used to legitimize these women's 'transgressions' usually have to do with gender and are opposed to women's liberation. Migrant women claim that they work to support their families, that they do female work in female environments and that they avoid being in the streets. The main aim of these explanations is to prove that these women are decent and thus improve integration with the Moroccan communities in Spain and in Morocco.

As was said above, these discourses are common in such situations of new female mobility and integration into the labour market. At the end of the nineteenth century in Buenos Aires there was a similar myth about the trade in white women. It was said that many European women were tricked by promises of marriage or a job and were taken to Buenos Aires where they were forced to become sex-workers.

> In fact, verifiable cases of white slavery were infrequent, but they did involve a system of forced recruitment by lovers, fiancés, husbands and professional procurers. European prostitutes in Buenos Aires, for the most part, came from poverty stricken families and worked out of despair. Marginalised by the Industrial Revolution, they saw immigration to a new land or a new continent as the key to survival. (Guy 1995)

In conclusion, the existence of Moroccan prostitutes, mythical or not, serves various purposes:

1. To control female mobility by threatening women liable to emigrate and their families with the social stigma of the slave trade.
2. To distinguish between 'decent' women who transgress and 'real prostitutes', and thus defend the reputations of Moroccan female immigrants.
3. To prove that Moroccan women are attractive to European men (otherwise they would not be so much in demand).

This mythical image of the Moroccan woman is used to prove that the West (Spain in this case) is responsible for moral decay and not Muslims (Moroccans), and therefore to prove that Muslims are morally superior to westerners (Ben Jelloun 1997; Schmitt 1992c). At the same time Moroccan women's respectability is not questioned because they are the victims and therefore bear no responsibility. In the first years of the twentieth century, European moral reformers branded Buenos Aires as the scapegoat, responsible for all the evil that happened to female nationals in foreign countries: 'rather than recognize their own complicity, Europeans perceived the roots of the problem to be inherent female vulnerability and the immorality of host societies' (Guy 1991: 12).

This over-representation of Moroccan prostitutes serves many purposes and is encouraged by different social groups. It is another example of how nations and ideologies use women for their own goals and how women themselves adapt these imposed images to suit their own interest.

NOTES

I wish to thank Dr Ángeles Ramírez, member of the Taller de Estudios Internacionales Mediterráneos, for her continuous support and useful advice in the preparation of this chapter and throughout my PhD research.

1. If we compare the three provinces with the highest number of Moroccan women – Barcelona, Madrid and Malaga – we find that in Barcelona female immigrants are older and live mostly with their families while in Madrid and Malaga the women are younger, more autonomous (they work) and originate from the western coast of Morroco (Rabat, Casablanca, Sale). Malaga is the first province where women started coming alone to work and it is the province with the highest rate of widowers and divorcees (Ramírez 1998; López et al. 1996).

2. All translations of Moroccan words are taken from R. Harrell, *A Dictionary of Moroccan Arabic* (Washington: Georgetown University Press, 1966). For the classical Arabic words, H. Wehr, *A Dictionary of Modern Written Arabic* (Beirut: Librairie du Liban, 1980).

3. When categorizing groups of people it is common to identify Spanish, Christian and westerner versus Moroccan and Muslim as the same people. In Morocco and in Spain there is a tendency to consider the 'other' as a homogeneous entity that lumps together religions (Islam or Christianity), language (Arabic) and geography (East or West). I therefore use them indistinctly when I describe images of a wider population than the strictly Spanish or Moroccan.

REFERENCES

Al Ahnaf, M. (1994) 'Maroc: Le Code du statut personnel', *Monde Arabe. Maghreb-Machrek*, 145, July–September: 3–19.

Anderson, Bridget (1996) *Living and Working Conditions of Overseas Domestic Workers in the EU* (Utrecht: STV/GAATW).

Ben Jelloun, T. (1997) *La Plus Haute des Solitudes* (1977) (Saint-Amand: Editions du Seuil).

Bennani-Chraïbi, M. (1994) *Soumis et rebelles des jeunes au Maroc* (Paris: CNRS).

Bousquet, G.-H. (1990) *L'Etique Sexuelle de l'Islam* (1966) (Paris: Desclée de Browner).

Chafi, M. (1996) *Code du statut personnel annoté* (Marrakesh: Imprimerie Walili).

Comas, Amparo (1991) *La prostitución femenina en Madrid* (Madrid: Dirección General de la Mujer, Comunidad de Madrid).

Del Oso, L. (1998) *La migración hacia España de mujeres jefas de hogar* (Madrid: Instituto de la Mujer).

Dieste, J. L. M. (1997) *El 'Moro' entre los Primitivos. El caso del Protectorado español en Marruecos* (Barcelona: La Caixa).

Guy, Donna J. (1991) *Sex and Danger in Buenos Aires: Prostitution, Family and Nation in Argentina* (Lincoln and London: University of Nevada Press).

Haeri, Shahla (1989) *Law of Desire. Temporary Marriage in Iran* (London: I.B.Tauris).

Herranz, Y. (1998) 'Servicio doméstico y feminización de la inmigración en Madrid', *Ofrim Suplementos*, December: 65–83.

López, B., A. Planet and A. Ramírez (eds) (1996) *Atlas de la Inmigración Magrebí en España* (Madrid: Eds de la Universidad Autónoma de Madrid y la Dirección General de Migraciones).

Maher, V. (1974) *Women and Property in Morocco* (Cambridge: Cambridge University Press).

Naamane-Guessous, S. (1997) *Au-delà de toute pudeur* (Casablanca: Editions Eddif).

Ramírez, A. (1998) *Mujeres Marroquíes en España* (Madrid: Agencia Española de Cooperación Internacional).

Reed, D. (1992) 'The Persian Boy Today', in A. Schmitt and J. Sofer (eds), *Sexuality and Eroticism among Males in Moslem Societies* (New York: Hayworth Press), pp. 61–6.

Rosander, E. (1991) *Women in a Borderland. Managing Muslim Identity where Morocco Meets Spain* (Estocolmo, Stockholm Studies in Social Anthropology).

Saltzman, J. (1992) *Equidad y Género* (Madrid: Ed. Cátedra).

Schmitt, A. (1992a) 'Preface' in A. Schmitt and J. Sofer (eds), *Sexuality and Eroticism among Males in Moslem Societies* (New York: Hayworth Press), pp. xiii–xv.

— (1992b) 'Different Approaches to Male–Male Sexuality – Eroticism from Morocco to Uzbekistan', in A. Schmitt and J. Sofer (eds), *Sexuality and Eroticism among Males in Moslem Societies* (New York: Hayworth Press), pp. 1–24.

— (1992c) 'Sexual Meetings of East and West. Western Tourism and Muslim Immigrant Communities', in A. Schmitt and J. Sofer (eds), *Sexuality and Eroticism among Males in Moslem Societies* (New York: Hayworth Press) pp. 125–30.

Sebti, Fadela (1997) *Vivre Musulmane au Maroc* (Casablanca: Editions Le Fennec).

Sequeiros Tizón (ed.) (1989) *Estudio sobre a prostitución no sur de Galicia* (Vigo: Universidad de Vigo e Xunta de Galicia).

Serhane, A. (1995) *L'Amour Circoncis* (Casablanca: Editions Eddif).

Shrage, L. (1994) *Moral Dilemmas of Feminism. Prostitution, Adultery and Abortion* (New York: Routledge).

Weeks, J. (1998) *Sexualidad* (Mexico, Barcelona and Buenos Aires: Paidos; 1st edn London: Routledge, 1986).

— (1992) 'Foreword', in A. Schmitt and J. Sofer (eds), *Sexuality and Eroticism among Males in Moslem Societies* (New York: Hayworth Press).

Wijers, Marjan and Lin Lap-Chew (1997) *Trafficking in Woman, Forced Labour and Slavery-like Practices in Marriage, Domestic Labour and Prostitution* (Letrecht, Bangkok: Global Alliance Against Traffic in Women).

PART FOUR

New Policies on Prostitution

ELEVEN

Migrant Sex-workers in Canada

NOULMOOK SUTDHIBHASILP

§ In Canada, prostitution is one of the few areas of consensual sexual activity that is still subject to legal control and punitive measures under criminal laws (Allain 1996). Taking the view that sexual matters are always contested political issues and sites of socially constructed power relations (Brock 1998), I decided to approach the issue of migrant sex-workers[1] in Canada, the major theme of this chapter, by exploring it from a number of perspectives. These include the imposition of criminal sanctions on prostitution, current immigration policies and attitudes that further victimize migrant sex-workers, and the way the media and police action co-create public fears of 'organized crime' and their involvement in the 'sex trafficking ring'. Each of these reinforces the others in the field of power relations and it is their overall effect on migrant sex-workers living in Canada that is explored here.

I have made, whenever possible, parallel comparisons between human rights violations of migrant sex-workers and of other workers. It is an attempt to desensationalize the disproportionate concentration on the abuse and exploitation of migrant prostitutes as well as move beyond a universalistic moralizing position with regard to sex work. Further, it also suggests that sex-workers share similar concerns about abuses in labour migration with other migrant workers.

SETTING THE CONTEXT

Though prostitution is legal in Canada, the Criminal Code criminalizes the activities of prostitutes and their associates. The punitive measures imposed on prostitute-related activities are based on the assumption that prostitution is deemed a threat to public order or is offensive to public decency. The criminal law prohibits solicitation, the places where prostitution takes place, and other related activities such as being in or operating a common bawdy house,[2] procuring and living off the profits of prostitution, and committing 'indecent acts' in a public place or in the presence of one or more people. Advocates and supporters of sex-workers and human rights contest that these criminal charges deprive sex-workers of their basic human rights. From this perspective, the United Nations' Human Rights Treaties guaranteeing the right to free choice of work and to just and favourable work conditions are clearly violated with the placing of criminal laws as legal obstacles to engagement in sex work (Bindman 1997). The lack of human rights protection for sex-workers in general renders anyone in the sex trade vulnerable to exploitation. These conditions preclude the application of existing labour laws to employer–employee relationships, thus increasing the opportunity for harassment and extortion by the police and other authorities. Therefore any sex-worker in Canada, whether working independently or in an establishment, can face discrimination, exploitation and violence in almost every aspect of her life as such workers rarely enjoy full rights as citizens and as workers.

Immigration policy related to migrant sex-workers In principle, because prostitution per se is not a criminal offence in Canada, sex-workers cannot be found inadmissible under the Immigration Act and immigration officials cannot refuse entry or issue a removal order solely on the basis that a person is alleged to have or admittedly engaged in prostitution (Federal Government 1996).[3] In practice, due to the social stigma attached to sex work, a sex-worker who wishes to enter Canada as a visitor is unlikely to receive an entry visa or be admitted at the port of entry if she reveals to immigration officials that she is a 'prostitute'. Because the Immigration Act does not empower an officer to refuse admittance to sex-workers, such arbitrary behaviour is discriminatory as it is a discretionary decision acted upon by an individual towards the prostitute's status. In this regard, immigration officials are often aided by the use of profiling, which requires the stereotyping of certain groups of people, to judge whether or not a person is admissible.

Because sex work has never been officially recognized in Canada as 'work', there is no work authorization issued to sex-workers for temporary employment as guest workers in Canada. It is also unlikely that migrant sex-workers are able to migrate easily to Canada and become permanent residents. Canada's overall immigration policies, which are more open to highly skilled and adaptable independent immigrants at the top end of the socio-economic scale, than to those who work in the low-status, undervalued female labour sectors (such as domestic work, prostitution and invisible labour in marriage), are another obstacle faced by migrant sex-workers who wish to immigrate legally. This policy bias in fact supersedes the application of human rights charters when it concerns women in the informal sectors of reproductive work. The 1992 Live-In Caregiver Program (LCP),[4] designed to bring in domestic workers to provide care for children, the elderly or the disabled in private households, is a prime example. The point system used to recruit these highly skilled migrants gives greater merit to those who possess higher education, official language proficiency, and professional skills in these areas, which are in demand in the Canadian labour market. This immigration system makes it virtually impossible for migrant sex-workers, most of whom are from a less well-off socio-economic background, to immigrate legally.

When there are no legal means for migrant sex-workers[5] to work in Canada or to immigrate, many women turn to third parties for assistance to facilitate their migration. Migrant sex-workers from Thailand, for example, normally enter Canada with false travel documents prepared by third parties. Others travel with their own passports and legitimate visa or come from countries where an entry visa is not usually required. Making false and misleading statements in connection with the admission or application of admission of any person, overstaying their visa, or working without work authorization are considered offences under the Canadian Immigration Act. These policies, which are dominated by concerns over border control, deprive migrant sex-workers of the right to work legitimately and to immigrate to Canada

When the police, usually consisting of the RCMP (Federal Police), local police forces and immigration officials, raid a workplace used by migrant sex-workers, they are typically charged with prostitution-related offences. They are then held in custody for a criminal bail hearing. If a justice of the peace grants bail and they have both the money and someone ready to bail them out, they will, technically speaking, be released on bail. However, due to the fact that many migrant sex-workers lack identity documents, they are often further detained by the immigration authorities.[6] Although the Immigration Act does not limit the duration of detention, there are implicit restrictions on its length (Immigration and Refugee Board 1998). In practice, long-term detention happens to migrant sex-workers and asylum seekers[7] alike when immigration authorities cannot ascertain the identity of the persons in custody. In one incident, a sex-worker from Myanmar who used a Thai passport to travel to Canada was arrested by the police in 1994 and was detained for over a year and a half because she was unable to provide the adjudicators with proof of her Myanmar citizenship.[8] She tried to acquire identity documents from the Myanmar Embassy a few times but the embassy refused to co-operate. She could not return to Myanmar as the country is run by a military government which represses its citizens and imposes punitive measures on those who leave the country without government permission. The policy of detaining those who arrive without valid documents further penalizes migrants and asylum seekers and contributes to the public view of them as criminals (UNHCR 2001).

International instruments At the international level, Canada has recently signed two UN protocols: 'The Protocol Against the Smuggling of Migrants by Land, Air and Sea', and 'The Protocol to Prevent, Suppress and Punish Trafficking in Persons'. These two protocols are specifically intended to be used under the auspices of the 2000 UN Convention Against Transnational Organized Crime. Canada is particularly interested in the smuggling protocol and defines the smuggling of people solely as a criminal activity that will not be tolerated. Measures such as strengthening border controls, increasing information-sharing between police in countries of origin and countries of destination, and minimizing the effectiveness of certain resources used by smugglers, such as fraudulent passports, are priorities for the Canadian government (Galloway 2000). Government measures are geared towards closing borders and increasing penalties for those who facilitate migration. Measures introduced in the Bill C11, the new Immigration and Refugee Protection Act, which increases fines of up to Can. $1 million and life imprisonment for people smugglers and traffickers (Citizenship and Immigration Canada 2001a), however, will only exacerbate the already vulnerable situation of migrant workers and asylum seekers. When agents face increased risk due to higher penalties when caught, this has a direct impact on migrants as it can increase the travel fees they have to pay (Ghosh 1998) and adds to the risks of travel.

The trafficking protocol, which focuses on the extreme abuses (the use of force, coercion and deception) that can occur at the point of entry prior to migration, as well as on forced labour and slavery-like conditions in the workplace in countries of destination, is unable to protect the rights of voluntary, undocumented migrant women in the sex trade. This is because it neglects to acknowledge the needs and problems of those exploited workers who are typical of the majority of sex-workers and other workers in general (Bindman 1997). Many migrant sex-workers who agree to migrate (without force or coercion at the point of entry and/or no outright deception) but find themselves in exploitative work conditions similar to those in other informal labour sectors (but not in slavery-like conditions) are not protected under such international standards.

Often, trafficking is equated with irregular migration for sex work or with prostitution (Leigh and Wijers, 1998). In Canada, Asian migrant sex-workers are frequently labelled victims of 'sex trafficking', whether or not the women's situations involve trafficking or labour exploitation. In many instances, anti-trafficking sentiments are used to prosecute and further victimize any migrants lacking documentation. In 1999, for example, Canada used the power of detention to respond to the irregular arrival by boat of people from China, despite the fact that they were commonly described as victims who were unwittingly brought over by traffickers (Canadian Council for Refugees 2000). Adults and children were detained in normal jail facilities and immigration holding centres on the assumption that these persons would disappear into the hands of their presumed traffickers if released. Ironically, the very policy that was supposed to protect those 'victims' of trafficking was in fact used to punish them.[9]

MIGRANT SEX-WORKERS IN TORONTO

The majority of migrant women working in Toronto's sex industry come from countries in the South. They are primarily from Southeast and East Asia, and South America. Others are from countries experiencing abrupt political, economic and social restructuring such as the former Eastern European countries. Many of them, like other migrant workers, leave their home countries because of violations of their economic and social rights.[10] Others may seek greater income and a higher standard of living. For many, migration is a calculated and conscious financial decision to improve their situation in spite of the risks involved.

Migrant sex-workers enter Canada through both regular and irregular channels. As indicated earlier, a small number of migrant women enter Canada with legitimate employment visas to work as exotic dancers in strip clubs. Some women from visa-exempt countries enter Canada as visitors and find themselves employed in informal labour sectors including the sex trade. Some immigrant women find themselves facing economic and immigration dilemmas when their family/spousal sponsorships break down or their refugee claims are rejected. They may decide to work in the sex trade where formal legal documents are not required.

Many women travel to Canada to work in the sex trade through irregular channels with the help of professional agents or personal contacts who arrange for necessary travel documents, transportation and jobs upon arrival. Most of the women in this group pay steep fees of between Can. $15,000 and $45,000 for such arrangements and have to work for employers in the sex trade to repay this debt[11] before they are able to earn income of their own. In formal interviews with thirteen Thai migrant sex-workers in the two research studies[12] and informal talks with twenty-one Thai migrant and former sex-workers, the general consensus was that the verbal debt contract was honoured and respected. However, three of these women[13] did state that they were charged higher fees than initially negotiated and another woman said that her employer was inconsistent in calculating the amount of money she earned and that was to be applied towards her debt.

It should be noted that other migrant women workers often have their labour rights violated when they enter Canada, even with legitimate work visas and contracts. In Winnipeg, thirty-nine women from the Ukraine were brought over to work in the garment industry by a local recruiter. They indicated that the recruiter exaggerated the wages they would receive in Canada, overcharged them for accommodation and provided them with work permits that did not make them eligible for government health coverage. The allegations were similar to a case involving thirty-seven Thai women who were recruited by an immigration consultant earlier that year (Guttormson 2000). The principal difference between the women who worked under work authorization and formal contract and those migrant sex-workers who were undocumented and worked in a criminalized, informal work sector, was that the former had the right to seek recourse and redress.

There was no evidence that any of the Thai women were forced or coerced (abduction, coercion, threat of violence, and/or the misuse of authority) or deceived (the provision of false information) by their agents in Thailand into migrating. However, some women reported that motivational techniques, such as emphasizing only the positive aspects of living and working in Canada, were employed by third parties. The hard-sell technique is commonly used by employment agents to recruit migrant workers. The fact that first-time travelling migrant workers are probably unaware of some of the risks and problems they might encounter upon arrival is another factor contributing to the lack of full disclosure at the point of departure. Some have different expectations about work and living conditions. A Thai woman who worked in the sex trade in an Asian country thought that work and living conditions in Canada would be no different from those she previously experienced in another country.

As mentioned earlier, most migrant sex-workers either overstayed their visas or worked without employment authorization. As a result, they became undocumented, which not only made them vulnerable to arrest by the police and immigration services but, once placed in the legal system, their loss of certain rights exacerbated their vulnerability. Their undocumented status also limited their access to public health and social services for fear of being reported to the authorities, and this was further exacerbated by language and cultural barriers.

Employers of Thai migrant sex-workers normally keep their passports (forged or genuine) until the debt repayment period is over. Some, however, reported that their agents took the forged passports back to Thailand. Keeping the workers' passports is one way for employers to ensure that the Thai migrant sex-workers would work until the debt was fully repaid. Having no access to their travel documents poses at least two problems. First, it hinders them from using public health services where identification documents are normally required. Second, as previously indicated, it results in lengthy detentions by Immigration Canada when they are unable to provide proof of their identity.

The labour standards for, and welfare of, the migrant sex-workers vary from place to place, depending on the 'good will' of employers.

Some employers maintained acceptable work standards but one or two (of the five or six known) employers did not. In terms of work conditions, the Thai sex-workers appeared to be most vulnerable during the two- to five-month debt payment period. It is the period in which employers can exercise a large degree of discretionary control over the women's labour. Although in most cases, the employers would use pressuring tactics on the women who still had outstanding debts, there was no report of physical abuse. Because most women wanted to relieve themselves of this debt as soon as possible, many compromised their occupational health and safety by working long hours[14] (fourteen to twenty hours a day) without adequate rest and by occasionally serving clients who did not want to use condoms. Without the support of labour rights or codes, the women had to rely on their own ability to assert their boundaries, and in most cases had little bargaining power to negotiate work conditions with employers.

After the debt repayment period was over, the Thai women were able to work with other employers. Some decided to stay with the same employers if the work conditions were adequate or if they did not know other potential employers. Others switched to other establishments or worked part-time between two different employers. Their income after the debt payment period was comparable to what local sex-workers received in similar establishments. The women would normally receive Can. $80 or $90 out of $120 per client; employers would keep the rest.

Due to limited support networks, language barriers and incurred debts, Thai migrant sex-workers work are employed in venues such as massage parlours and rarely work independently. In such establishments they are adversely and directly affected by the bawdy house and procuring laws. They can be charged with being inmates of a common bawdy house while their employers can be charged with procuring and keeping a common bawdy house. In other words, such criminal laws have a discriminatory impact on sex-workers and their professional associates. These criminal laws only penalize them without dealing with migrant workers' work conditions. The disruption to work that the raids create caused the Thai migrant sex-workers to become very worried about their financial situation, since many of them are single mothers and the sole supporters of their families in Thailand.

Project Orphan: stirring public panic with media reports of sex traf-

ficking and Asian organized crime in Toronto The Canadian public debate on and concern with prostitution was, until recently, mainly limited to street prostitution, (alleged) nuisances and hazards associated with street prostitution, and child prostitutes (Federal-Provincial-Territorial Working Group on Prostitution 1995). The issue of migrant sex-workers has never attained a high public profile, nor was it construed as a 'social problem' until recently. During the past few years, most police raids in Toronto have primarily targeted massage parlours, apartment-style establishments, strip clubs and bars where migrant sex-workers were employed. On 10 September 1997, Canadian law enforcement and immigration officials arrested twenty-two Thai and Malaysian women on prostitution-related charges in an operation code named Project Orphan (Burnett 1997). Project Trade, a second mass raid of Asian massage parlours, was carried out in December 1998. The raid was part of the fourteen-month operation in which a total of ninety-five people, mostly Thai women, were arrested on charges related to prostitution (Lamberti 1998c). In 1999–2000, Project Almonzo, a series of on-going raids of migrant exotic dancers in strip clubs and bars, was conducted. The police brought 650 criminal charges against club owners and exotic dancers in Toronto (Jaminez and Bell 2000).

According to the police's news release on Project Orphan: '[T]he focus of this investigation was not prostitution per se, but that women were being exploited and bought and sold for the purposes of prostitution' (Combined Forces Special Enforcement Unit 1997). In Project Trade, Captain Doug Heaton, RCMP officer, stated that, '[i]t's not just whorehouses … It's a bigger problem than that. It's international traffic of people. It's a global problem' (Lamberti 1998a: 46–7). The *Toronto Sun* reported: '"We're not saviours … We're smashing an organized crime syndicate," said Det. Peter Yuen of 52 Division's Asian-crime unit. "For the girls, being in jail makes coming to Canada a wasted trip"' (Lamberti 1998b: 4).

Project Orphan has often been cited as marking the turning point where Canada changed from being a country of transit to a country of destination for the Asian sex trafficking rings. In fact, sex-workers from Asian countries had been migrating for quite some time prior to Project Orphan. One piece of evidence for this is a news report on Asian massage parlour raids. Between 1989 and 1991, several such raids occurred but remained low profile. Asian women from Hong Kong,

Malaysia, Singapore and Thailand were 'imported, recruited, brought to Canada' with the help of third parties (Lamberti 1989, 1991; Stancu 1989; Wong and Pron 1990). Surprisingly, the news coverage did not regard this movement of migrant sex-workers as 'sex trafficking' or a 'sex slave ring' in spite of police reports documenting threats of violence in the recruitment process and the work conditions (Stancu 1989). The police only alleged that some bawdy houses were run by members of the 'Big Circle Boys' gang from Hong Kong and that those men who were arrested had ties with the Asian underworld throughout North America (Wong and Pron 1990, Lamberti 1991).

It seems that the purpose of large-scale raids such as Project Orphan and Project Trade is to allow the police to send a message to the public about the connection between the movement of migrant sex-workers and serious organized crime activities that need to be tackled. Their large-scale Asian bawdy house raids and considerable budget were thus justified on the grounds of battling against organized crime involving sex trafficking.

In the official Canadian context, organized crime is defined as: 'economically motivated illicit activity undertaken by any group, association or other body consisting of two or more individuals, whether formally or informally organized, where the negative impact of said activity could be considered significant from an economic, social, violence generation, health and safety and/or environmental perspective' (Public Works and Government Services of Canada 1998). According to this broad definition, virtually any party of two or more who help to organize and facilitate the transport of migrant workers can be considered an organized crime group.[15] The definition also suggests that something becomes an organized crime activity when it causes significant negative impact on the public. However, in each raid mentioned above, the police did not seem to offer any substantial evidence that the 'sex trafficking activity' of the so-called organized crime groups had created any notable threat to the public. Their only claim was that the women had been traded, indentured and worked as prostitutes in slavery-like conditions. My speculation is that there is a tendency for this broad definition of organized crime to be exploited in order to accommodate and serve the police's agenda, creating the perception that the transnational migration of sex-workers is a 'social problem' related to organized crime groups who operate global sex trafficking rings.

It has been pointed out that, in policing prostitutes, '[t]he power of the police is accomplished as much through an alignment of police interests with the media and residents' organizations, as through the provision of a legal mandate to act through the federal state' (Brock 1998: 10). In other words, the police and the media work together to create 'news' on the transnational migration of sex-workers, framing it within the broader context of 'organized crime activity'. Reporters from local newspapers were informed ahead of time about the raids and so were able to be present at the arrest sites and police stations where the women were brought in (Multicultural History Society of Ontario 2000). Coincidentally, two weeks before Project Trade was launched in early December 1998, a Canadian Broadcasting Corporation's (CBC) Television Witness Program[16] aired *Thai Girls*, a documentary about two Thai women who came to Canada to work in the sex trade. The only source of 'prostitution experts' the filmmaker sought to consult and put in her documentary was a police officer from the 52 Division's Asian crime unit. The content of the documentary emphasized the stereotypical 'Life' of Thai sex-workers and all references regarding organized crime involvement came from the so-called 'expert'. Another interesting coincidence occurred two to three weeks before the trial of a Thai massage parlour owner and another person arrested in Project Trade, when CITY TV channel ran a five-day documentary series (29 January to 2 February 2001) entitled *Human Cargo*. One of the first segments of this series was about Thai sex-workers in Toronto. The same police officer was interviewed for his expert opinion in the documentary. He again emphasized the connection between 'organized crime' and Thai women in the sex trade. Later, the trial itself became the news on TV and in the newspapers and the same police officer gave an interview to the media about the case.

THE PORTRAYAL OF ASIAN SEX-WORKERS IN THE CANADIAN MEDIA

Since September 1997, 'sex slaves' has become a popular term bandied about freely by the police and the media to describe the migrant sex-workers who were arrested. Media reports about Project Orphan sensationalized the raids and the facts about the women's lives. They were described as victims of unscrupulous pimps, agents, recruiters and others involved in a well-organized international crime syndicate who took advantage of their situation of poverty at home and their illegal status in Canada, forcing the women to work for next to nothing while the 'pimps' and others stood to earn thousands of dollars. Some articles provided details on how the women travelled to Canada, their income, the 'factory-like' conditions in which they worked, who profited from the women and how much money was involved. The subtext of the news articles was that sex slavery was an insidious 'Third World' problem threatening the perceived 'law and order' and moral conventions of mainstream Canada.

Later newspaper articles related to Project Orphan seemed to acknowledge that the women were not victims of sexual servitude, conceding that they chose to come to Canada to work in the sex trade. However, they were still regarded as victims forced by desperate circumstances and poverty. They were sold by their families into sex slavery to pay for debts back home. Some articles suggested that the women knew what they were getting into but were painted a rosy picture of working conditions in Canada that failed to materialize.

In general, an unquestioned moral judgement ran throughout the articles. As a result, the women were seen as being worthy of sympathy and understanding only as long as they were portrayed as victims, either as victims forced into sexual servitude or as victims of circumstance and desperation (i.e. poverty at home). This view also seemed to be used to justify to the public the efforts and resources put into the police raids, which were meant to rescue the women from sexual slavery and organized crime syndicates. However, soon after the September 1997 raid, the police did concede that the women were not happy with being 'rescued' (Mandel 1997), and only much later did they suggest that the raids were in fact undertaken to discourage other women from coming to Canada; that, in effect, there would be consequences if they came.

What was missing from all the earlier news reports was an adequate explanation of the apparent contradiction: why had the women been arrested, charged, detained, sentenced and deported when they were being depicted as victims of organized crime? None of the articles mentioned that it is the criminalization of the sex trade, as well as repressive moral conventions that serve only to regulate women's sexual labour and their relations to their bodies, and restrictive immigration policies that do not recognize those whose economic and social rights were violated in their home countries, and global economic forces that contribute to their actual victimization.

Although many of the articles focused on both the work conditions of the women and the fact that they had to provide sexual services without seeing any pay for at least three months, none of the articles regarded the issue in terms of the violations of labour rights. Nor did any of the articles ask whether the women's rights as guaranteed by the UN Human Rights Code had been violated by the enforcement, legal or immigration systems. In all, none of the articles raised questions as to whether the presently biased criminal laws outlawing sex work and immigration policies contributed to encouraging the conditions that allowed for the exploitation of the women.

TREATMENT OF THE WOMEN BY THE STATE

At least since 1989, regardless of whether Asian migrant sex-workers were considered to be sex slaves, victims of organized crime or prostitutes per se by the police and the media, they have been consistently treated as criminal offenders and illegal migrants. They were typically arrested, charged with prostitution-related offences, dragged through a long criminal court process, detained and finally deported.

All the women who were arrested in Project Orphan were charged with being found in and managing a bawdy house, the latter being an indictable offence. At the court hearing in February 1998, the crown prosecutor dropped the second charge. The women received conditional discharges and had to report to their probation officers every month for a year. The probation conditions were such that they were not allowed to work in or go anywhere near any massage parlour or associate with other offenders.

For Thai migrant sex-workers who were arrested in Project Trade, the charges of being inmates in a common bawdy house were dropped on the condition that they were required to participate in a five-day rehabilitation training[17] with Street Light Program. This was originally designed to assist local sex-workers who were arrested to get off the street and out of the profession. This group of women was detained anywhere from several months to over a year in a criminal jail.

Some women, in spite of being arrested, went back to work in the sex trade, not because they were forced to by pimps or madams as many believed, but because, like many other migrant workers, they wanted to fulfil their migration dream to work and send money home, to save some money for themselves, or to save and start their own small businesses later.

From the two studies mentioned earlier and informal talks with the Thai migrant women, it soon became clear that it is in fact the state that is the principal violator of migrant sex-workers' human rights, especially in the area of legal rights and the right to due process. For example:

- Thirteen Thai migrant sex-workers arrested in Project Orphan reported that they were strip-searched by the police at the police station while the door was left open. According to Kara Gillies of the Toronto's Migrant Sex Workers' Advocacy Group, strip-searches were often intentionally used improperly in order to humiliate both migrant and local sex-workers and to make the experience of their 'arrest' as unpleasant as possible.
- After being released on bail, the women arrested in Project Orphan were interviewed by the police through an interpreter about their personal and occupational backgrounds, and how and why they travelled to Canada. They were misled by the interpreter who insisted that the interviews were for Statistics Canada and had nothing to do with the court case. In fact, the statements they made and signed could have been used in court if the matter had gone to trial.
- While staying at a temporary shelter, and before having had an opportunity to consult with legal counsel, five women from Project Orphan were threatened by phone by the interpreter, and pressured by the RCMP and Thai Embassy representatives to plead guilty.
- The criminal bail ($1,000–$5,000 cash) and immigration deposit money ($2,000–$5,000 cash) imposed on the women arrested in Project Trade, most of whom had no or limited support network in Canada, resulted in their continued detention in West Detention Center, a medium-security jail in Toronto for a period of time ranging from one to fourteen months.
- A sex-worker from Myanmar who had no proof of her identity and nationality was detained by Immigration Canada for more than eighteen months.
- Thai sex-workers who were detained at the West Detention Center reported that they felt they were discriminated against when receiving

treatment (i.e. when asking for medical assistance, they had to wait longer) in comparison to others because 'We are not Canadians'.

- Bail conditions that prohibited them from engaging in sex work further placed them in a vulnerable position. The lack of support from government authorities coupled with their undocumented status and language barriers hindered them in their efforts to find alternative work while awaiting trial.

CONCLUSION

Migrant women who work in the sex industry are highly stigmatized because of their occupation, and marginalized because of the language barrier and their undocumented status in Canada. In addition, on a global scale, regressive and repressive immigration and prostitution laws in countries of destination account for the principal elements in the exploitation of migrant women. These policies serve to push the international sex trade further underground and increase women's reliance on potentially abusive individuals and organizations, including those representing the states.

For many Canadians, it was inconceivable that women from the South would consciously decide to migrate and join the international sex trade. In one way or another, these women must have been seen as trapped and victimized. As a result, Asian sex-workers were constructed as 'sex slaves' rather than as workers, and the campaign by the police to rescue them was depicted as a glorious battle against organized crime. The portrayal of migrants as being a part of organized criminal activity can lead to the expression of xenophobic sentiments in the larger community and can fuel racial prejudices.

In order to ensure that the human rights of migrant sex-workers are respected and protected by authorities and agencies, it is imperative that strategies be developed to assist migrants to travel, live and work legitimately. These measures should be based on the stated needs of migrants and avoid developing policies that work against their interests. These formulations should work towards moving away from those that rationalize and entrench the social control and criminalization of both sex-workers and migrant women.

NOTES

1. 'Sex-workers' is the term used to describe those women, men and transsexual persons who work in the sex industry as prostitutes, exotic dancers, sex telephone operators, pornographic actors and others. In this article, 'sex-workers' refers only to female prostitutes who form the majority of migrant sex-workers. According to the International Labour Organization, migrant workers are persons who are economically active in a country of which they are not nationals, asylum-seekers or refugees.

2. A place where one or more prostitutes regularly work or where 'indecent acts' are performed.

3. However, according to the government's immigration policy, if a person has been convicted on prostitution-related charges, that person will be deemed inadmissible under section 19 of the Immigration Act, and therefore either refused entry into Canada or enforcement action will be taken.

4. The LCP requires a mandatory two-year 'living-in' with their employers before domestic workers can apply to become permanent residents. It is discriminatory because the two-year requirement is essentially a probationary period for permanent residency which is not required for other persons with skills in short supply. The 'live-in' requirement as well as the informal, isolated environment of the private home makes domestic workers more vulnerable to long working hours, low pay, and physical and sexual abuse. In addition, the points system which is used to evaluate a domestic worker who applies for permanent residence does not credit domestic work with any value, despite the fact that these skills are valuable and in demand in Canada (Clark 2000).

5. The only group of women in the sex industry that can enter Canada legally is exotic dancers. Immigration Regulation R20(5)(e)(iii) allows for the issuance of temporary employment authorizations to foreign exotic dancers under the auspices of performing artists. Approximately 1,000 work permits were issued annually for exotic dancers (Federal Government 1996). However, in mid-1998, the government proposed more rigorous management of exotic dancers' work authorization applications than other occupations by requiring visa applicants to be interviewed by Canadian visa officers and to show proof of a work history as dancers with photographs and portfolio, before granting a six-month work visa (Godfrey 1998). The strict rule applied only to foreign exotic dancers. It was the government's intent to 'recognize the well-documented situations of abuse and criminality associated with workers entering Canada as exotic dancers' (Citizenship and Immigration Canada 1998).

6. Current grounds for detention are: failure to establish identity; constituting a danger to the public; being unlikely to appear for future immigration proceedings or removal (Citizenship and Immigration Canada 2001b).

7. According to the Canadian Council for Refugees (2000), many asylum seekers, unable to obtain legitimate travel documents from repressive governments in their own countries for fear of persecution, use the services of third parties to facilitate their migration. The smuggling process, as it is called by state authorities,

often involves the use of false travel and identity documents, and sometimes deceptive and dangerous means of travel.

8. The average length of detention for persons held in jail or correctional facilities is eighteen days, and eight days for those held in immigration holding centres (Citizenship and Immigration Canada 1999).

9. Furthermore, the new Bill C11 gives more power to immigration officials to detain those who arrive in Canada through irregular channels on the grounds that 'smuggled' migrants will be kept from fleeing and protected from those who would 'enslave' them for passage debts (Editor 2001).

10. The global restructuring of the economy has had adverse effects on the economies of and women from countries in the South. It fosters the emergence of a work structure in which women find themselves occupying low-status and low-paying jobs that make surviving difficult. This universal gender-bias division of labour has created impoverishment and a feminization of poverty. The current trend is that the majority of women who migrate to other countries do so as principal wage earners rather than as accompanying family members. As the industrialized economies become more service-oriented, the jobs that are available to migrants in destination countries are increasingly in the reproductive sector, be it domestic work, sex work, or the invisible work that occurs in marriage. The sex industry helps absorb many migrant women workers and create substantial income for them.

11. Some literature refers to the excessive fees and resulting debts set by contacts/ agents and employers as 'debt bondage'. According to the 1956 Supplementary Convention on the Abolition of Slavery, the Slave Trade, and Institutions and Practices Similar to Slavery, the Supplementary Convention does not prohibit a person to pay her debt by working for those who gave loans. However, debt bondage is prohibited when the precise terms of the repayment (i.e. length or amount of loans) have not been specified or the person who gave the loan can potentially add unspecified interest or other costs to the loan, or when work done by the debtor is not assessed reasonably at least in comparison to the rates paid for in other similar work (Anti-Slavery International 1995). The majority of Thai migrant workers' experiences in Toronto clearly did not meet the conditions of debt bondage.

12. Two research studies which I also happened to be involved in as a principal researcher are 'Trafficking in Women including Thai Migrant Sex Workers in Canada' (Multicultural History Society of Ontario 2000) and 'Migrant Workers in the Metro Toronto Area and Issues Related to Trafficking in Women' (Global Alliance Against Traffic in Women, Canada, 2001). Both studies were sponsored by the Status of Women and were conducted between 1998 and 2000. My informal talks with Thai migrant and former sex-workers happened at the same time that I volunteered as a crisis intervention worker for the Toronto Network Against Trafficking in Women, an ad hoc community-based group in Toronto established to assist Thai women arrested in Project Orphan in 1997.

13. Two weeks after starting work in Canada, two women decided to leave the job after an unsuccessful attempt to renegotiate their contract which had been violated by their employer.

14. During the debt repayment period, the women said some employers did not want them to go out on their own unless accompanied by someone the employers trusted. Others were not so strict. However, due to long working hours during the debt repayment period and being new to Canada, the women reported that they did not have much free time to leave the workplace which, in many cases, was also their living quarters.

15. From the statements of the Thai sex-workers, travel arrangements and all necessary documents required for border crossing were arranged by small-scale operations involving a few individuals who had connections with corrupt immigration officers, 'helpful' travel agents, those who could supply forged documents, and establishment owners in Canada. The agents in Thailand may have known someone 'influential', be it a politician, or high-ranking police or government officer, to whom they could refer or ask for assistance when problems arose.

16. A popular documentary show on current social issues broadcast regularly on CBC.

17. One Thai woman stated that the programme was too short and if they really wanted to help her get a new job other than sex work, they needed to do more than offer her a five-day training course and expect her to find a job on her own.

REFERENCES

Allain, Jane (1996) *Prostitution* (Ottawa: Research Branch, Library of Parliament, 17 September).

Anti-Slavery International (1995) 'Contemporary forms of slavery requiring action by governments: Examples of a large-scale and persisting problems in the 1990s'. http://www.antislavery.org/types.htm

Bindman, Jo (1997) 'Redefining prostitution as sex work on the international agenda'. http://www.walnet.org/csis/papers/redefining.html

Brock, Deborah R. (1998) *Making Work, Making Trouble: Prostitution as a Social Problem* (Toronto: University of Toronto Press).

Burnett, Thane (1997) 'Suspect madam to get the boot', *Toronto Sun*, 13 September: 4.

Canadian Council for Refugees (2000) 'Migrant smuggling and trafficking in persons'. http/www.web.net/~ccr/traffick

Citizenship and Immigration Canada (1998) 'Exotic dancers'. http://www.cic.gc.ca/manuals/english/om%2/Dweb/1998/ip/ip98-07.html

— (1999) 'Enforcement fact sheet'. http://www.cic.gc.ca/english/pub/03detention-e.html

— (2001a) 'Immigration and refugee protection act introduced'. http://www.cic.gc.ca/english/press/01/0103-pre.html

— (2001b) 'Background #4: Detention provisions clarified'. http://www.cic.gc.ca/press/01/0103/bg4.html

Clark, Tom (2000) 'Migrant workers in Canada'. htttp://www.december18.net/ paper4Canada.htm

Combined Forces Special Enforcement Unit (1997) 'News Release: Project Orphan'. http//www.dcsnet.com/cfseu/orphanfs.htm

Editor (2001) 'Fed press new immigration law', *Guelph Mercury*, 14 June: A5.

Federal Government (1996) *Canada's Paper for EU Conference on Trafficking in Women for Sexual Exploitation* (Ottawa: Federal Government).

Federal-Provincial Territorial Working Group on Prostitution (1995) *Dealing with Prostitution in Canada: a Consultation Paper* (Ottawa: Federal-Provincial Territorial Working Group on Prostitution, March).

Galloway, Gloria (2000) 'Canada signs UN agreements to prevent crime and people smuggling'. http//www.friends-partners/stop-traffic/1999/1446.html

Ghosh, Bimal (1998) *Huddled Masses and Uncertain Shores* (The Hague: Kluwer Law International).

Global Alliance Against Traffic in Women (Canada) (2001) *Migrant Workers in Toronto and Issues Related to Trafficking in Women* (Victoria: Global Alliance Against Traffic in Women [Canada]).

Godfrey, Tom (1998) 'Police applaud stripper blitz', *Toronto Sun*, 25 June: 5.

Guttormson, Kim (2000) 'Immigrant worker recruitment investigated', *Winnepeg Press*, 29 June: A1.

Immigration and Refugee Board (1998) *Guidelines on Detention Issued by the Chairperson Persuant to Section 65(4) of the Immigration Act* (Ottawa: Immigration and Refugee Board).

Jaminez, Marina and Stewart Bell (2000) '650 charges in Canadian sex slave trade', *National Post*, 4 April: 1.

Lamberti, Rob (1989) 'Bawdy house raided: women imported from Malaysia', *Toronto Sun*, 17 November: 32.

— (1991) 'Police smash hooker outfit', *Toronto Sun*, 20 December: 53.

— (1998a) 'Sex slaves: Fodder for flesh factories', *Toronto Sun*, 10 May: 46–7.

— (1998b) 'Sex slave raids', *Toronto Sun*, 3 December: 1, 4.

— (1998c) 'Teen sex slave: My life of shame', *Toronto Sun*, 6 December: 32–3.

Leigh, Carol and Marjan Wijers (1998) 'Statement on trafficking, stigmatisation and strategies for alliance prepared for the transnational trafficking seminar on trafficking in women in Budapest, Hungary'. http:bayswan.org/alliance

Mandel, Michele (1997) '"Slaves" didn't ask to be free', *Toronto Sun*, 14 September: 5.

Multicultural History Society of Ontario (2000) *Trafficking in Women Including Thai Migrant Sex-workers in Canada* (Toronto: Multicultural History Society of Ontario).

Pron, Nick (1990) 'Bawdy house owner "peddled humans", gets 3 years in jail', *Toronto Star*, 4 January: A9.

Public Works and Government Services of Canada (1998) 'Organized crime impact study prepared by Samuel D. Porteous'. http://www.sgc. gc.ca/Epubl/Pol/e/1998orgcrime/e1998orgcrim.htm#Toc 427745369

Stancu, Henry (1989) 'Police arrest 12 in bawdy-house raid', *Toronto Star*, 6 October: A10.

UNHCR (2001) Global Consultations on International Protection, 'NGO background on the asylum and migration interface'. http://www. december18.net/ UNHCFconsulationsNGO.htm

Wong, Tony and Nick Pron (1990) 'Impoverished Asian women recruited for metro brothels', *Toronto Star*, 4 February: A1.

TWELVE

A Business Like Any Other? Managing the Sex Industry in the Netherlands

MARIEKE VAN DOORNINCK

§ In the Netherlands, as in most other countries, prostitution as such is legal, but all forms of exploitation are forbidden. This was regulated by law in 1911. At the beginning of the twentieth century, the abolitionists took the view that closing down the houses of sin and prosecuting pimps would stop the trafficking in women. However, before long, this idea was soon proved to be wrong. It appeared that the police were not able to uphold the law and, as a result, prostitution was tolerated as long as public order was not disturbed and as long as it was restricted to certain locations. Initially, the business was still hidden and on a small scale, but after the sexual revolution and the economic prosperity of the 1970s, prostitutes' workplaces became visible on a large scale, even when run illegally by a third party.

Today, in most of the bigger cities of the Netherlands, women in city centre shop windows offer sexual services for cash. There are also brothels in business and shopping areas and in respectable neighbourhoods. They are advertised in newspapers in graphic terms; escort services take full-page advertisements in the yellow pages. Local councils designate areas for streetwalkers outside the town centre, where drug-using women and transsexuals solicit men in cars.

POLITICAL PRAGMATISM

This is an example of the Dutch tradition of tolerance. Political pragmatism makes it possible to see the sex industry as just another social phenomenon. A number of 'private' activities that take place in public or semi-public locations are officially tolerated as long as they do not interfere with public order. So if prostitution is not disrupting ordinary life in a residential area, the brothel, shop window or sex club will be allowed to exist openly.

The practice of tolerance is official policy, it is not just an individual policeman or civil servant turning a blind eye. The rationale is that prosecution will produce more problems than it solves. This is called the 'opportunity' principle and it is put into practice in areas such as prostitution, euthanasia and soft drugs. Tolerance is based on pragmatism and, perhaps, indifference: as long as you do not bother others, or interfere in their daily lives, you can do what you like. This is the 'not in my back yard principle'. The moral attitude of Dutch people, however, is not much different from that of people in other countries in the European Union: prostitution is not considered proper or acceptable behaviour and sex-workers face the same condemnation and stigma.

Street prostitution policies Although not in the penal code, street prostitution is prohibited under city ordinances all over the Netherlands. Until the 1970s, streetwalking was more or less condoned in red-light areas as long as public order was not disturbed. In the 1970s and 1980s more and more heroin-addicted women started to walk the streets in order to earn the large amounts of money needed to pay for their habit. These women were not professionals and their presence on the streets caused problems: drug dealers and boyfriends came along; used needles and condoms littered the ground. All this drastically changed the character of the area.

For the sake of public order, the police regularly arrested working women. The courts fined them, so they had to put in overtime or spend time in jail. Time and again, this practice was criticized as counterproductive and many police officers, especially from the vice squad, were unhappy about it. At the time one could not help but conclude that these police actions were not so much prompted by the desire to get the women off the streets but rather were intended to show residents that the city was doing its best to get rid of the problem.

This repression also caused a lot of tension on the streets. The women felt hounded and insecure, and took less care to select their clients – even getting into cars with more than one man. It is well documented that during periods of frequent police raids, women are robbed, raped and assaulted more often, and social and health workers have a harder time finding and helping them. The police force was not altogether happy with their difficult and unsatisfying task. The uniformed officers saw no results from their work and inexperienced young officers sometimes lost their patience with the vehemently protesting women. They were criticized by their plainclothes colleagues from the vice squad who preferred to maintain good relations with the women, because their primary task was to solve rape and assault cases. This internal conflict exacerbated the frustration felt by the police who believed they were being forced to clean up the mess left by incompetent and half-hearted politicians.

Streetwalking zones Since the early 1980s, one by one, Dutch cities have changed their policies. Nearly all now have an official zone where women are allowed to solicit and work, their numbers varying from some eighty women a day in Amsterdam to twenty in smaller locations.

How can these zones be described in general terms? The model consists of a street or an area where inconvenience to residents is minimal and where a reasonable degree of safety for prostitutes can be organized. Business takes place in the evening and at night, depending on the local situation, 365 days a year. The zone contains a shelter which operates the same opening hours. Here the women can have a break, drink a cup of coffee, eat something, exchange information, talk to the staff and buy or get condoms for free. On some nights a medical doctor can be consulted about sexually transmitted diseases (STDs) and on general health issues. Medical examinations for STDs are voluntary; compulsory check-ups would only chase away the most vulnerable women hiding from the authorities. Inside or near the zone there is an area with a fenced-off space for parked cars where the women go with their clients. In this way, all activity is concentrated in a relatively safe environment.

POLICIES TOWARDS SEX CLUBS, WINDOW BROTHELS AND PRIVATE HOUSES

The system of tolerance of brothels and private houses has worked satisfactorily for a long time. As long as the sex clubs or window brothels were not causing too much trouble, the city councils could ignore the sex industry. Club owners could practically do as they pleased, as long as public order was respected. As their (illegal) businesses did not officially exist, strict compliance with the rules that apply to every other business operation was not really necessary.

When the sex industry expanded in the 1980s, local administrators began to realize that their towns accommodated large economic activities over which they had very little control. The structure of prostitution had become so complex that its regulation badly needed more precise instruments, but existing laws had very little to offer. The idea of legalizing the exploitation of voluntary prostitution in order to regulate the sex industry became more or less acceptable in certain circles in the 1980s.

The public debate lasted for over ten years. In actual practice, legalization would not make a major change in the way Dutch society handles prostitution. It would, in effect, formalize the existing system of tolerance. But bridging the gap between Dutch society and the prostitution scene was a tedious process; both sides were reluctant to accept the idea of a legal sex industry.

THE CHANGE OF LEGISLATION

The first attempt to change the law in 1993 failed on moral grounds. In 1997 another proposal to legalize brothels was presented by the former Minister of Justice. The Bill was accepted by Parliament in February 1999 and by the Senate in October 1999. The new law came into effect in 2000 and the Dutch Penal Code no longer treats organizing the prostitution of an adult female or male person as a crime, provided this is done with the consent of the prostitute. If a woman regards prostitution as the best way to earn a living, she has the same rights as any other worker. Any form of forced prostitution, pimping or trafficking remains in the Penal Code, with a maximum penalty of six years' imprisonment. In short, the exploitation of voluntary prostitution is now legalized; the exploitation of involuntary prostitution is punished more severely.

The Ministry of Justice formulated six major aims with this proposal:

1. To control and regulate the exploitation of prostitution.
2. To improve the prosecution of involuntary exploitation.
3. The protection of minors.
4. The protection of the position of prostitutes.

5. To combat the criminal affairs related to prostitution.
6. To combat the presence of illegal aliens in prostitution.

Local prostitution policies In the new situation, prostitution policies became a matter for the local city council only. In other words, the city administration is fully responsible for its own policy on prostitution. This means that cities are free to choose their own way of dealing with it, although a complete ban is not possible. Prostitution is managed by a system of licences. Several municipal services are responsible for checking the conditions of the licence under which prostitution is allowed to operate. One category of these conditions deals with city planning: for instance, no brothels are permitted near schools or churches. Another deals with the conditions of the building, of safety and sanitary measures. A third deals with the type of management: no forced drinking, no unsafe sex, no minors and no illegal workers. The owner must not have a criminal record. If an owner does not meet these requirements, his brothel will eventually be closed under city ordinance, which is a much easier and more effective procedure than having to prosecute him for pimping.

This all sounds very promising: a sex industry which is completely regulated, prostitution regarded as a normal profession and prostitutes considered as sex-workers with the same rights and duties as any other worker. But will it work out that way? What are the opportunities and what are the difficulties that the new Dutch prostitution policy will face?

OPPORTUNITIES AND DIFFICULTIES

First of all, the fifteen years of preparation that it took to change the law has been useful. Both civil servants and sex club owners have had abundant time to get used to the idea of doing business with each other. Some brothel owners, who foresaw the changes, organized themselves into the Association of Sex Club Owners and together decided to submit themselves to the new regulations.

On the other hand, officials in the major cities started to think about the prostitution business in their own towns. Both sides have had sufficient opportunity to reflect upon the new situation and to make the necessary preparations.

An important positive effect is that the prostitution sector will become more open. Inspectors will visit the brothels on a regular basis; critical conditions can be detected earlier.

Regulation also allows a distinction to be made between the good guys and the bad guys among brothel owners. Those who have a brothel to make a quick profit or as a cover for criminal activities, will no longer be part of the legal sex industry as they will not meet the requirements for a licence. Those who want to be regarded as ordinary businessmen will invest in their property and obey the rules in exchange for having a legal business.

On the whole, the sex industry will become more professional. Those owners and sex-workers who avoid paying taxes, who do not or cannot conform to the rules, will find it difficult to survive. To choose to work in the sex industry will be to make a business decision.

Illegal circuit? The new prostitution policies also face some major difficulties. The Netherlands is trying to regulate an industry which has attained its current dimensions precisely by operating as an informal and non-regulated business. For a lot of people, a regulated official sex industry will be less attractive. Will they disappear, will they find another sphere of activity or will they set up an illegal circuit? We must bear in mind that a very profitable business has been taken away from criminals. And not only criminals, but also owners of small brothels who cannot afford to make the investment needed for improvements. Will they be willing to leave voluntarily the business they have worked in for so many years?

At present, many migrant women from outside the European Union work in the Dutch sex industry. Although they do not have work permits and therefore no legal status, their presence has been tolerated for many years. Now, though, their position is worse than that of their European colleagues. Sometimes they are victims of trafficking or they face extradition or they suffer from slave-like exploitation. Under the new legalization a brothel owner will lose his licence if he employs illegal migrants. As with most EU countries, the Netherlands is excluding non-EU sex-workers because borders are closed to all migrants. The struggle against trafficking in women is another reason for excluding illegal migrants from sex work. The problem is that these women first came to the Netherlands to make money. What will they do if they are not allowed to work in legal brothels? Will they return home, will they go to another country or will they go underground and work in an illegal brothel that operates outside the rules?

There are dangers, on the one hand, in having a perfectly regulated sex industry under the control of the municipality. On the other hand, there are dangers in an underground illegal sex business which cannot be scrutinized. It may become a refuge for criminals and a place where illegal women work under even worse conditions.

The position of sex-workers It is not only the migrant sex-worker whose position is at stake. One of the goals of legalization is to improve the position of sex-workers in several respects. The requirements concerning safety, hygiene and sex-workers' rights to self-determination, which the brothel owner has to meet in order to get a licence, will improve their working conditions. The fact that sex work is considered labour and sex-workers will have the same rights and duties as any other worker will improve their position in society. Insurance companies and banks are no longer allowed to discriminate against sex-workers. These factors will have an empowering effect on women who have become used to the idea that they have no rights at all, and that society looks down on them. With the change in the law, the government is saying in a way that it does care about the social and legal position of sex-workers and that their working conditions should meet the same standards as those required in any other kind of labour.

Clean sheets and fire safety instructions, however, are not enough. Neither national nor local governments seem to have a clue as to what else has to be done. More important, as the date of the change in the law approaches, the government has tried to renege on its promises. Local politicians as well as most government institutions now claim that they are not authorized to interfere in relations between employers and employees so there is nothing they can do. Because sex work will be considered as labour in the future, sex-workers are supposed to stand up for their rights like any other employee. The problem is that most labour has a history of nearly a century of emancipation. Large and influential labour unions defend the rights of their members, but the emancipation of sex-workers has just started. In most cases working conditions are still bad and relations between employers and employees are far from equal. As long as the position of sex-workers *vis-à-vis* brothel owners and society at large is not strong enough for them to stand up for their rights, it must be the government's responsibility to create opportunities and conditions in which sex-workers are able to struggle for emancipation. The most important step is for the government to acknowledge its responsibility in this process. If it does not, it would appear that legalizing brothels is only a tool to defend public order and to regulate and control the sex business instead of improving it.

CONCLUSION

On the whole, I support the plans for the legalization of the sex industry. They present opportunities to regulate the business; to make it more professional; to eliminate criminal activities within the sex sector; to improve the working conditions of the prostitutes.

There are some dangers, though. Dutch policy is entering completely new territory. It is not possible to follow examples from other countries on how to regulate an informal sex industry. The new policies have been designed on a theoretical premise, and it is uncertain how they will work out in real life. It is therefore important to monitor the effects of the new policy on the sex industry, how it reacts, and to note any developments that were not foreseen. The policy must be flexible enough to change if a situation requires a different approach.

Finally, the time has come to practise what has been preached for so many years. I do hope it will work out the way it was planned and, perhaps, one day Dutch prostitution policies will offer a shining example to others.

THIRTEEN

Sweden's Law on Prostitution: Feminism, Drugs and the Foreign Threat

ARTHUR GOULD

§ In the 1960s, foreign visitors to Sweden often referred to the pragmatism which characterized the country's approach to moral issues – in particular in attitudes towards pre-marital sex and sex education. It would be difficult today to reach to the same conclusion. It is the Dutch who are seen as liberal and pragmatic on a range of issues such as euthanasia, drugs and prostitution. The Swedish authorities and public opinion, by contrast, are firmly behind a prohibitionist approach. Drug use and the buying of sexual services are seen as unacceptable activities, incompatible with the traditions and values of Swedish society. In 1993 the pursuit of a drug-free society resulted in a law which made the consumption of drugs an imprisonable offence. In 1998, a similar law was passed concerning the purchase of a prostitute's services. This chapter will begin by describing the passage of the *Sexköpslag* (the sex-buying law) and then examine the two main forces behind the reform – the ideology of the Swedish women's movement and public concern about migrant prostitution. It will then show how the association of prostitution with coercion and drugs strengthened the prohibitionist case. The concluding discussion will draw on the concept of *banal nationalism* to explain the significance of Sweden's new law.

The sources for the information on which this chapter is based are official reports and newspaper articles collated routinely over a number of years. On a visit to Stockholm, in which a library search revealed further newspaper and journal articles, interviews were carried out with women representing each of the political parties represented in the Riksdag (the Swedish parliament), two national organizations concerned with domestic violence, two umbrella organizations representing a wide range of women's interests and a member of the Commission which investigated prostitution.

THE 1998 *SEXKÖPSLAG*

In 1991, researchers informed the Swedish government that prostitution[1] had declined by 40 per cent in the 1980s (*Dagens Nyheter* 1991). One year later it was on the increase (*Dagens Nyheter* 1992). Although it was claimed officially that the numbers of prostitutes in Sweden remained low compared with other Western European countries,[2] concern about the increase resulted in the setting up of a Commission in 1993 to investigate the issue and to suggest any necessary changes in the law. The justification for a new investigation – there had been one in 1982 – was that the character and form of prostitution were changing. The membership of the Commission was comprised equally of men and women drawn from a range of backgrounds. The members included civil servants, administrators, police officers, social workers, academics and the manager of a rehabilitation home for prostitutes and drug users. It was chaired by a civil servant from the Ministry of Justice, Inga-Britt Törnell. The Commission collected evidence and made visits to a number of European cities. Its report, published in 1995, recommended that both the selling and buying of sex should be made criminal offences (SOU 1995).

Those found guilty of exploiting another person:

> in an occasional relationship for financial or similar payment are to be sentenced for trading in sex and fined or imprisoned for up to six months. The same shall apply to those who make themselves available for such a relationship. If the crime is serious the sentence will be a maximum of four years. The judgement of whether a crime is serious will depend on whether youth, lack of judgement, vulnerability or dependent status is involved. (p. 33)

Trading in sex was to include making a pornographic film for financial gain where those involved were paid to have intercourse.

One member of the Commission had already resigned when he realized that this was going to be the majority view. An administrator from the Health and Social Affairs Board, Socialstyrelsen, dissented from the main report, arguing that criminalization would drive the

problem underground and exacerbate it. The manager of the rehabilitation home wrote a dissenting report of her own arguing that only the
punters[3] should be punished. However, it was this view which was to
prevail in the subsequent public debate.

The response of judicial organizations – including the police, the
courts and the public prosecutor – argued against the idea of criminalization largely on ground of its impracticability. A number of national
administrative boards (such the one for health and social affairs) agreed.
The Conservative and Liberal parties argued that criminalization would
only drive the problem underground. However, all other political parties
and the vast majority of women's organizations supported the view that
only the buying of sex should be criminalized. It was felt that the
Commission had come up with the right evidence and arguments but
had reached the wrong conclusions. At the 1997 Congress of the Social
Democratic Party, the women's section managed to persuade the
majority of delegates that the punishment of punters only should become party policy. The chairperson of social democratic women, Inger
Segelström, was delighted: 'It is fantastic. It is the first visible proof
that every other politician is a woman ... What is unbelievable is that
the men were with us all the way' (*Dagens Nyheter* 1997).

One year later the Social Democratic government introduced a *sexköpslag* proposal. Its passage through the legislative process was the
combined responsibility of ministers for justice, employment and health
and social affairs – all women. The Social Democratic, Left, Environment and Centre parties gave the new law their overwhelming support
(*Riksdagens Protokoll* 1997/8). The Conservatives and liberals voted
against the measure but it passed by a ratio of 2:1. It came into force
in January 1999.

Two years on, various reports have criticized the new law for its
ineffectiveness and for being counter-productive. The police claim that
there are problems getting evidence sufficient for a prosecution pointing
to the paucity of unsuccessful cases; that prostitution has not decreased
since the passing of the Act; and that they need more powers to enforce
it efffectively (*Svenska Dagbladet* 2001a). An investigator in Malmö
claimed that the situation of prostitutes had deteriorated since the
passing of the new legislation (*Dagens Nyheter* 2001a). They had become
more exposed to violence and perverse acts; were less likely to use
condoms; and had to work for less money. The Committee on Sexual

Crimes has complained that the law is too vague and was not sufficiently well thought out (*Dagens Nyheter* 2000). Public support for the law, however, remains strong. Over 70 per cent of both men and women supported some form of criminalization with only 21 per cent of men and 7 per cent of women wanting to see the law abolished (*Svenska Dagbladet* 2001b). Fifty per cent of those asked said they thought the law should be strengthened. Meanwhile, continuing stories were being reported of increases in the amount of migrant prostitutes coming into all parts of the country (*Dagens Nyheter* 2001b and 2001c).

We have to ask why it is that Sweden has chosen to react to prostitution in this way when elsewhere in Europe a more pragmatic and liberal approach is being adopted. Part of the answer lies in the strength of the women's movement and its objection to prostitution generally, and part in a more widespread public fear about migrant prostitution in particular.

THE WOMEN'S MOVEMENT

Popular movements have a long and impressive history in Sweden. The temperance, labour and non-conformist church movements of the nineteenth and early twentieth centuries spearheaded the social reforms which resulted in the welfare state. Today, the anti-drug and feminist movements are having a similar impact on more specific aspects of social policy. In the popular movement tradition, interest groups around a particular set of issues co-operate with each to achieve collective goals (Alsén 1978). They network with each other to combat what are seen as the adverse consequences of an economy based upon free enterprise. They are linked with each other through a variety of institutions including the study circle tradition. The women's movement is no exception. There are a number of umbrella organizations which help to bring various strands of opinion together. Within the Riksdag itself women from all political parties meet regularly with the minister for equality and co-operate on measures affecting women.

Sweden sees itself as being the most gender equal society in the world, with women constituting half of the cabinet and 40 per cent of the Riksdag. A high proportion of women are employed and have rights to independent taxation and social insurance benefits (Sainsbury 1993). Their working role is underpinned by comprehensive policies on child care and parental leave, the care of the elderly and the disabled. It is difficult not to be impressed by the status of women in Swedish society. However, critics point to deficiencies in the degree of gender equality. Radical feminists in particular have long been cynical about the degree of gender equality and are dismissive of the claims of reformist women to be feminists.[4] It was ROKS, the radical organization behind shelters for battered women, which first began to mobilise women's opinion behind a new way of looking at gender issues back in the 1980s. Women, it was claimed, were still subject to male patriarchy through the tolerance of domestic violence, sex crimes, pornography, incest and prostitution. Prostitution was seen as yet another form of violence against women.

By the 1990s, aspects of ROKS radical thinking had permeated the wider women's movement and finally mainstream public opinion. The women's sections of all political parties except the Conservatives supported the criminalization of punters. Even the female Conservative I interviewed on the subject was certainly behind the radical feminist view. Prostitution was seen as unacceptable in a society which claimed to lead the world in gender equality.

MIGRANT PROSTITUTION

The growth in prostitution in Sweden in the early 1990s was attributed by the Commission to developments overseas. Its report described the growth of the sex industry generally. Organized crime and the Internet were both factors in this development. Pornography, trafficking in women and the sexual exploitation of children were on the increase. Developments in neighbouring European countries were a cause for concern. Commission members visited Oslo, Copenhagen, Helsinki, St Petersburg, Tallinn, Brussels and Amsterdam and were shocked by what they saw. In an interview with one of them, it was stated that developments in Eastern Europe were seen as a potential threat. Without them, he said, there would have been no change in the law. The Commission did not want Sweden to become a market for prostitutes from abroad.

Although some of the Swedish feminists interviewed denied that this 'fear of the foreign' was of crucial importance in their own campaign, it was used by some. Cecilia Bodström, an advocate of the criminalization of punters, in an interview published in a tabloid newspaper, referred to the hundreds of brothels in Estonia, the 8,000 prostitutes in St Petersburg and the 100,000 migrant prostitutes in the EU (*Aftonbladet*

1994). Sweden's other national tabloid, *Expressen*, published another interview with two social workers who claimed that:

> Without exaggeration one can say that there is an invasion of foreign girls ... They are exploited by pimps, mistreat by their clients and spread life-threatening diseases ... Girls from the east have no tradition of using protection. Condoms are simply too expensive in their own countries. They are used to unprotected sex and bring this tradition further into Sweden. (*Expressen* 1998)

The influx of migrant prostitutes and the consequent risk of infection was also raised by Markström, a leading member of the women's section of the Social Democratic Party (Markström 1998).

Månsson, one of the country's experts on prostitution, in his concern about the 'increased flood of pimp-managed prostitutes from the Baltic countries, Poland and Russia' claimed that few Swedish men used prostitutes. However, 80 per cent of those who did so went abroad and half of them became infected with HIV (*Svenska Dagbladet* 1999).

CHOICE AND FORCE

It was not just the threat posed by foreign prostitutes that was raised by those who favoured the criminalization of prostitution. Fears were also expressed about the influx of foreign liberalism. The liberal view that prostitutes should be free to carry out sex work was unacceptable. It was seen as a view that had arisen in those countries where the problem had become overwhelming. By refusing to adopt such a permissive attitude, Sweden could avoid the fate of countries such as the Netherlands. One interviewee expressed the view that the Dutch 'acceptance' of prostitution was a product of their history of colonial exploitation. Another, a Conservative, said: 'We don't discuss whether or not people want to be prostitutes. What sort of freedom is it to choose to sell your body?'

Women, it was said, were forced into prostitution by pimps and those dealing in the contemporary slave trade in women; by poverty, because they were powerless as in the case of minors and the mentally disturbed; or because of their dependence upon illegal drugs. A social work journal claimed that international research had shown that between 40 per cent and 70 per cent of all prostitutes had experienced sexual assault (Martinell 1995: 7). The Commission itself had claimed that most prostitutes:

- Had been sexually abused as children;
- Had got off to a bad start in life;
- Had been deprived of their self respect at an early age and had acquired a negative self image;
- Had developed mental disorders; or
- Had been the victims of assault and rape.
  (SOU 1995: 25, 142)

The Commission was disturbed by the liberal view on prostitution which was spreading throughout the EU. 'Sex work' was becoming socially acceptable with prostitutes establishing trade unions and achieving rights to social insurance. Prostitutes' organizations made a big distinction between forced and voluntary prostitution. As far as the Commission was concerned such arguments were simply devised by those in the sex trade who were seeking to legitimize their activities.

Nor was any support for a liberal line expressed by any of the members in the Riksdag debate on the *sexköpslag*. Demands originating in the Netherlands and the EU that prostitutes needed to be included within the mainstream labour force were explicitly rejected by a spokesperson for the Environment Party. Even in the public debate about the *sexköpslag*, the liberal perspective was expressed very rarely. A prostitute who had been politically active for 20 years and a spokesperson for sex workers' rights denied that prostitution was characterized by violence abuse and drugs (Andersson and Östergren 1998a and 1998b). The sex industry was not synonymous with misogyny and gender inequality, they stated, and seeing women involved as victims was puritanical. They criticized feminists in Sweden for ignoring the publications and reports produced by prostitutes themselves. In other, more liberal countries, they claimed, prostitutes were not censured, pathologized and made invisible. Moreover, organizations representing sex workers abroad were horrified by the developments in Sweden.

Another writer criticized the advocates of the new law as 'neo-moralists' (Bard 1999a). Social fascists were deciding how other people should lead their lives. He claimed that drug dealers, the homeless and immigrants had already been cleaned from the streets. The city had been 'disinfected' of alternative lifestyles. In the tradition of the 'People's Home' and the Myrdals, the state was deciding what was best for people. What was the significance of your body, he asked, when the state could take away your control of it? He denied that all sexual services were the result of coercion. Since there were already laws against violence and rape, he argued, there was no need for an additional law to criminalize punters (Bard 1999b).

PROSTITUTION AND DRUGS

The spur to my own interest in Sweden's sex-buying legislation arose not out of involvement in feminist debates or research into prostitution, but out of my work on Swedish drug policy (Gould 1989, 1994a, 1994b). There seemed to be strong links between the two issues.

The development of Sweden's *restrictive* (i.e. anti-liberal) line on illegal drugs has been documented by a number of researchers (Tham 1991, 1998; Van Solinge 1997; Goldberg 1999). The restrictive line developed in the 1970s and 1980s through the evangelical organization of the National Association for a Drug-free Society, RNS and Parents Against Drugs and drew its inspiration from the ideas of Nils Bejerot (Bejerot and Hartelius 1984). Basically he believed that drug misuse would spread throughout society like an epidemic unless measures were taken to prevent people, particularly young people, experimenting with drugs in the first place. The aim of the restrictive line is a *drug-free society* which stands in stark contrast to the aims of harm reduction and de-criminalization policies advocated by many drug agency workers in the rest of Europe. In the 1980s, the compulsory care of adult addicts and alcoholics was made more strict, syringe exchange schemes were rejected and, in 1993, the *use* of drugs was made an imprisonable offence. All use is regarded as misuse and no distinction is made between soft drugs and hard drugs. As the debate on prostitution emerged in the 1990s, it seemed to me that there were a number of similarities between the Swedish approach to both issues.

It is not surprising that parallels can be drawn between the issues of prostitution and illegal drugs. It is often said that prostitutes use drugs in order to cope with the risky business in which they are involved. It is also known to be the case that many women who become dependent on drugs choose to be prostitutes as a way of paying for their habit.

These connections would obviously assume importance in a country such as Sweden, where the aim is to become a drug-free society. Segelström expressed the concern clearly when she said:

> We know that half the prostitutes on the streets do it to finance their drug misuse. We know through in-depth interviews that many of them are at risk. It is our duty to intervene. (*Dagens Nyheter* 1998)

In the Riksdag debate, a spokesperson for the Environment Party challenged the argument that prostitutes had a right to choose what to do with their own bodies by asking whether someone had a right to destroy themselves with drugs. Since Sweden has a law which prohibits the consumption of drugs, the answer was, obviously, no. The fact that one of the dissenting voices on the Commission was a manager of a home which looked after prostitutes with drug problems was also of some importance.

The parallels go further than the direct connections between the two issues themselves. They extend to the policies devised to deal with them, and indeed to the very discourse through which they are discussed. As women were said to be *forced* into prostitution, so drugs *forced* users to maintain and increase their habits. As migrant prostitutes were said to be *flooding* into the country, so the same was said of illegal drugs. A social work journal drew another analogy between the two issues when it stated: 'Experience shows that prostitution is a form of *misuse* with a similar negative *dependence* and the way back is often laborious with unavoidable *relapses*' (Martinell 1995: 9, my italics).

Both sets of policies are focused upon the *consumer*. Sweden's restrictive line on drugs is based upon the assumption that only by curtailing consumption can the market in drugs be contained. As we have seen the new law on prostitution also singles out the buyer for punishment. And both policies are being pursued internationally – particularly through the European Union (Gould 1999, 2000).

Another significant parallel between the two issues was the way in which other countries and Sweden itself were portrayed. Countries – such as the Netherlands and the UK – were seen as too liberal. Their adoption of pragmatic approaches to the two issues indicated that they had *capitulated*. Sweden by contrast had created model policies which other countries wanted to adopt. As Sweden was *unique* in pursuing the goal of a drug-free society, so it was *unique* in criminalising the purchase of sexual services (Månsson and Roos 1998).

ANALYSIS

The policy analyst faced with the Swedish approach to both prostitution is faced with a seeming contradiction. Here is a society renowned for being progressive and pragmatic on a wide range of social issues, opting to reject and actively oppose the liberal approaches of other Western European countries. In order to understand why, we have to look at Sweden's past, its culture and its recent economic development.

Sweden's reputation for being liberal and pragmatic coincided with the golden age of welfare. In the 1950s and 1960s Sweden was regarded – and regarded itself – as a model society. It boasted the most advanced welfare state in the world and its economy had grown impressively following the Second World War. On most international league tables, Sweden was the leader or close to the top. From the mid-1970s, however, this reputation began to falter and the economic difficulties of the 1990s led to welfare retrenchment and high unemployment. The 'Swedish model' as something for other countries to emulate no longer existed. The pride which many Swedes had felt in their country's national achievements was severely dented. There was a vacuum to be filled by those who wanted to turn their pet political issues into issues of national identity.

Swedish culture and national identity consisted of a number of interrelated features. Swedes themselves were seen as softly spoken, undemonstrative, in control of their feelings (Daun 1996). Their society was clean and organized. Politics proceeded by consensus. 'Sobriety' and 'conscientiousness' were used to describe typical Swedish behaviour (Ambjörnsson 1989; Holgersson 1994). An adherence to the values of rationality, discipline and order had helped to create a 'People's Home' and the belief in a strong state. There was a paternalistic element in all of this. As there was in a temperance movement that had almost achieved the prohibition of alcohol in 1920, and had influenced a restrictive policy which continues even today to limit the availability of alcohol and keep prices high. Sweden's tradition of social engineering – represented by the works of Gunnar and Alva Myrdal – is now described as wanting to 'put people's lives in order' (Hirdman 1989). This perfectly describes the current approach to prostitution.

This 'People's Home' – a society and a culture described by some as an earthly paradise – had been achieved in an age of modernity. In the postmodern era, it had come to be threatened by alien forces – the irrationality of unfettered market capitalism; an influx of immigrants and refugees; the use of strange drugs by hedonistic young people; a European Union which wanted to liberalize alcohol policy. From being a 'model' for others to follow, Sweden was fast being sucked into a globalized morass.

It is against this background – which I have exaggerated for effect – that I would suggest both the pursuit of a drug-free society, and the criminalization of buying sex, need to be evaluated. Faced with threats – real or imagined – to its national identity, certain groups within Swedish society have sought to link their political aims with a need to re-establish the claim of Sweden to be a model for others to follow and to defend Swedish values and traditions. The debate about prostitution was an excellent example of what Billig describes as *banal nationalism* (Billig 1995). Billig suggests that most social scientists have concerned themselves with 'outbreaks of "hot" nationalist passion, which arise in times of social disruption and which are reflected in extreme social movements' (p. 44). Hot nationalism is 'an extraordinary, emotional mood striking at extraordinary times'. It is the stuff of national wars, terrorist activities and movements of national liberation. *Banal* nationalism occurs when:

> In so many little ways, citizens are daily reminded of their national place in a world of nations. However, this reminding is so familiar, so continual, that it is not consciously registered as reminding. The metonymic image of banal nationalism is not a flag which is being consciously waved with fervent passion; it is the flag hanging unnoticed on the public building.[5] (p. 8)

The debate about prostitution was full of such reminders. Migrant prostitutes were a threat to Swedish public health; migrant prostitutes were flooding into Sweden; foreign men used prostitutes more than Swedish men; Swedish men who went abroad to use prostitutes returned infected with HIV; the liberal attitudes of other countries were a consequence of colonialism or a conspiracy by the sex industry. Sweden was unique in advocating the criminalization of sex. Sweden was a model for other countries to follow. How could Sweden be a leader in gender equality and accept the right of women to sell their bodies? Throughout the debate there was this constant reminder of the threat of the foreign and the need to protect Sweden.

The association of a political or social issue with the national interest or national identity entails the risk that it will not be discussed dispassionately. 'Moral panic' rarely leads to good policy-making. If much prostitution is forced and prostitutes themselves are the victims of violence, this is a matter of justifiable concern. But if attempts to deal with the problem make it worse, then they are counterproductive. Katarina Lindahl, the general secretary of the RFSU (National Association for Sexual Education), put it well when she said she believed that prostitution would become less visible and more pimp-governed as a result of criminalization and that it would make women more vulnerable. She claimed that prostitution was a social problem which could be reduced only by social measures and changing attitudes – not by legislation. It was not right 'to send out signals when they hurt those they are meant to help and that is what I think this law will do. Prostitutes will pay the price so that politicians can send out signals against something from which society already distances itself' (Brink 1999: 11).

What Lindhal was proposing was a pragmatic approach. She was arguing for measures that would help rather than damage prostitutes. The Dutch have also taken a pragmatic line. They have applied the principles of harm reduction and normalization to a number of social issues including drugs and prostitution. The harm reduction principle argues that it may be unhelpful to prohibit certain kinds of damaging behaviour. It is preferable to find ways of ensuring that society and the individuals involved learn to minimise the harm done. By making the activities of prostitutes more open and more tolerable – by 'normalising' them – the risk of infection, coercion and violence may be reduced. Education and health care stand a better chance of succeeding and the individuals involved can make a contribution to and benefit from society's social insurance arrangements.

CONCLUSION

The principles of normalization and harm reduction are not unknown to Swedish social policy. The former has been practised to the great advantage of people with disabilities. The latter is now the basis of the country's alcohol policy (Gould 2001: 161). However, they are resisted in terms of illegal drugs – as the refusal to adopt syringe exchange schemes demonstrates – and prostitution. The law criminalising punters is the latest attempt to 'put people's lives in order' by authoritarian means. Policy-makers have allowed an important public issue to become yet another object of banal nationalist politics. Swedish feminists may have done an excellent job in bringing the plight of some prostitutes to public attention, but they are doing their sisters no favours by increasing their vulnerability. Instead of driving the problem underground, it would be better if the women's movement concentrated its efforts on making existing laws against violence, force and slavery more enforceable rather than creating new laws which are not.

NOTES

I am extremely grateful to the Nuffield Foundation for funding the research visit to Sweden which enabled me to gather the information on which this chapter is based. I would also like to thank Ylva 'Elvis' Nilsson for her help, insights and encouragement in the early stages of the research.

1. Although the law on prostitution is equally applicable to male and female prostitutes, much of the debate and concern in Sweden was about women. For the rest of this chapter I shall, by 'prostitutes and prostitution mean female prostitutes and prostitution.

2. It was estimated by the Commission that there were 2,500 prostitutes in Sweden, 650 of whom were on the streets (SOU 1995: 10).

3. There are no unambiguous substitutes in English for the rather clumsy term 'buyers of sex'. Swedes have the word *torskare*, but the most acceptable words in English seem to be *johns* and *punters*.

4. When an earlier version of this chapter was presented at the London School of Economics, a radical Swedish feminist objected to my saying that feminists had had a considerable influence on policy. Most of the politicians who claimed to be feminists, she said, were nothing of the sort. Sweden remained a male-dominated country.

5. It is interesting in this regard to mention that in Sweden the national flag is flown outside people's homes more frequently than in other countries. Its 'flying' is also governed by very strict rules (Swedish Institute 1999).

REFERENCES

Aftonbladet (1994) 'Legalisering skadar främst kvinnor. Sex blir bara något för män', 12 July.

Alsén, H. (1978) *Behöver vi folkrörelserna?* (Stockholm: Tidens Förlag).

Ambjörnsson, R. (1989) 'The Conscientious Worker: Ideas and Ideals in a Swedish Working Class Culture', *History of European Ideas*, 10(1): 59–67.

Andersson, L. and Östergren, P. (1998a) 'Ny lag förvärrar för sexarbetare', *Aftonbladet*, 11 May.

— (1998b) 'Slutrepliken med lögner blev sexarbetarnas kunder kriminella', *Aftonbladet*, 15 June.

Bard, A. (1999a) 'En sexarbetares bekännelser', *GT-Expressen*, 10 January.

— (1999b) 'Min kropp är min', *GT-Expressen*, 3 February.

Bejerot, N. and Hartelius, J. (1984) *Missbruk och motåtgäder* (Stockholm: Ordfront).

Billig, M. (1995) *Banal Nationalism* (London: Sage).

Brink, J. (1999) 'Därför säger RFSU nej till torsklagen', *Arbetaren*, 7: 8–11

Dagens Nyheter (1991) 'Prostitutionen minskar', 13 September.

— (1992) 'Ökat antal kvinnor på gatan', 30 March.

— (1997) 'Köpa sex blir kriminaliserat', 14 September.

— (1998) 'Politiker försvarar kriminalisering', 3 August.

— (2000) 'Sexbrottlagen skärps', 12 November.

— (2001a) 'Gatuprostitutionen minskar I Stockholm', 16 February.

— (2001b) 'Här lockas kvinnor till sexjobb I Sverige', 16 February.

— (2001c) 'Prostitutionen breder sig ut I Norrland', 16 February.

Daun, Å. (1996) *Swedish Mentality* (Pennsylvania: Pennsylvania University Press).

Expressen (1998) 'Invasion av prostituerade', 2 April.

Goldberg, T. (1999) *Drugs Demystified* (Basingstoke: Macmillan).

Gould, A. (1989) 'Cleaning the People's Home: Recent Developments in Sweden's Addiction Policy', *British Journal of Addiction*, (84)7: 731–41.

— (1994a) 'Sweden's Syringe Exchange Debate: Moral Panic in a Rational Society', *Journal of Social Policy*, 23(2): 195–217.

— (1994b) 'Pollution Rituals in Sweden: the Pursuit of a Drug-free Society', *Scandinavian Journal of Social Welfare*, 3: 85–93.

— (1999) 'A Drug-free Europe: Sweden on the Offensive', *Druglink*, 14(2): 12–4.

— (2000) 'Swedish Social Policy and the EU', in Miles, L., *Sweden and the EU Evaluated* (London: Continuum).

— (2001) *Developments in Swedish Social Policy: Resisting Dionysus* (London: Palgrave).

Hirdman, Y. (1989) *Att lägga livet tillrätta* (Stockholm: Carlssons Förlag).

Holgersson, L. (1994) 'Building a People's Home for Settled Conscientious Swedes', *Scandinavian Journal of Social Welfare*, 3(3): 113–20.

Månsson, S.-A. and Roos, J. (1998) 'Döm inte ut lagen mot könshandeln', *Göteborgs-Posten*, 20 August.

Markström, E. (1998) 'Könsköp oförenligt med det samhälle vi eftersträvar', *Arbetaren*, 12: 16.

Martinell, E. (1995) 'Viktigt våga undersöka gränserna', *Socionomen*, 4: 7–11.

Riksdag och Departementet (1998) 'Köp av sexuella tjänster blir straffbart', No. 19.

Riksdagens protokoll 1997/8: 114 Riksdagen, Stockholm.

Sainsbury, D. (1993) 'Dual Welfare and Sex Segregation of Access to Social Benefits', *Journal of Social Policy*, 22(1).

SOU 1995: 15 *Könshandel*, Socialdepartementet, Stockholm.

Swedish Institute (1999) *The National Emblems of Sweden*, Fact Sheet, Stockholm.

Svenska Dagbladet (1999) 'Folkhälsoinstituets insatser inte alltid politiskt korrekta', 27 May.

— (2001a) 'Sexköpslagen döms ut', 15 February.

— (2001b) 'Starkt stöd för skärpt sexlag', 7 February.

Tham, H. (1991) 'Narkotikakontroll som nationellt projekt', *Nordisk Alkoholtidskrift*, 9(2): 86–97.

— (1998) 'Swedish Drug Policy: a Successful Model?', *European Journal on Criminal Policy and Research*, 6: 395–414.

Van Solinge, T. B. (1997) *The Swedish Drug Control System* (Amsterdam: CEDRO, Uitgeverij Jan Mets).

CONCLUSION

Where Do We Go from Here?

BANDANA PATTANAIK

§ Unlike many of the contributors to this anthology I have not carried out academic research on prostitution in any specific country at a given period. Like some others, however, I also work in a non-government organization. It is my work over the last three years with the Global Alliance Against Traffic in Women (GAATW), that has put me in touch with sex-workers and their organizations in various parts of the world.

Why does GAATW, which is an anti-trafficking group, work with sex-workers? In order to explain our involvement I need to outline the history of the term 'trafficking' and the contemporary activism around it. The earliest use of the term referred to the 'white slave trade', primarily describing the Caucasian women who were allegedly coerced or cheated and transported to the colonies to provide sexual services to white male officers. It is important to note that no comprehensive study exists to determine how many of those women were fleeing discrimination at home, how many were going to take up other jobs or, indeed, how many among the sex-workers had made a decision to accept the offers themselves. It is also significant that the term 'trafficking' was never used to describe the large number of men and women from the colonies who were recruited at that time as indentured labourers to other colonies, even though the promises made to them at the time of recruitment were rarely kept and who had little choice in determining their destinies.[1] By 1904 there was an international agreement to suppress 'the white slave trade', which meant cross-border movement of women for an 'immoral purpose', i.e. prostitution. Six years later the agreement was modified to include in-country movement as well but the links to slavery and prostitution remained. In the post-war years the link was strengthened further as can be seen in the problematic Convention for the Suppression of the Traffic in Persons and the Exploitation of Others (1949).

The late 1980s and the 1990s saw a renewed interest among activists in addressing the issue of trafficking in women. Obviously, by then the scale of female labour migration had increased tremendously. By then it was women from developing countries and countries which were experiencing civil and political unrest who were migrating to the developed world in search of a better future. Labour migration from country to city had also increased and many of these new migrants were women, often single. Given the gender inequity in most societies, especially in the developing countries, many of the women were entering the informal sector, including prostitution, where labour protection is non-existent or minimal. Given the stringent migration laws of many developed countries which cater only to the high skilled category of workers, many women migrants were seeking out alternative means by taking help from agents, entering into paper marriages with foreign nationals and even using false travel documents. Often these women entered highly exploitative situations; they were cheated, coerced, kept in slavery-like conditions and under debt bondage. The 1980s also saw a number of developing countries stepping up their tourism industry and opening up entertainment venues to cater to the tourists. Again, young women, many from poor families in the country, came or were brought to the cities to work in these entertainment places. Thus terms such as 'sex tourism' and 'transnational prostitution' became common parlance in the 1980s. The international community responded to the situation by trying to step up measures to stop abuses against women. Predictably, the term which was used to describe the ensuing abuses in the process of migration was 'trafficking'. Efforts to stop trafficking and attempts to abolish prostitution often went hand in hand. In other words, the conflation of trafficking and prostitution received yet another boost. The 1980s was also a time when the prostitutes' rights movement was growing in several parts of the world. Women in prostitution were organizing themselves and voicing their demands for recognition of sex work as work. Understandably, they were extremely critical of anti-trafficking policies which saw all sex-workers as 'victims of trafficking' in need of rehabilitation.

GAATW was launched in 1994 as a network. The need for such a group became clear when an action research project looking into the process of female labour migration from Thailand was completed and its findings were presented to an international audience. The project aimed to empower women, giving their experiences a voice. Findings from the research revealed the complexities of the female migration process; the low level of information and skills among women, their desperate need to take up any paid work, and the absence of any protection against abuses for migrant women in the informal sector. It was evident that policies were needed that would not restrict women's mobility but protect them from abuses should they occur during or after migration. In the mid-1990s there was no internationally agreed definition of trafficking. In fact, the 1949 convention which aimed to stop trafficking did not define the term.

One of the earliest projects of GAATW, therefore, was an international survey that sought to analyse the process of migrant women's entry into and stay in various sites of work in the informal sector. Our research revealed that sites of trafficking included prostitution, forced marriage, domestic work, factory work, begging and work in several other informal sectors. We realized that excessive focus on the sex sector tended to overlook abuses in other areas of work. Regarding the claim of many activists that all sex-workers were trafficked women, we felt that the best way to test its veracity would be to listen to the experience of women in prostitution themselves. As such, part of our work on trafficking became organizing consultations with women in prostitution in order to understand the reality of their lives.[2] Much of this direct interaction has been in the Asian region because of our location in Asia and also because of our limited human and financial resources.

Admittedly my work does not bring me into contact with the whole range of sex-workers in the Asian region. There are women who do sex work but do not want to be seen as sex-workers. There are others who are not keen on political activism. There are also many women in sex work who do not have the freedom to come forward and organize themselves in groups. Much of our work, therefore, has been with sex-workers who have formed their own organizations and/or are with supportive women's groups. While their personal narratives have enriched my understanding of the lives of women often in very difficult circumstances, their political struggle has opened my eyes to the insensitive attitude of mainstream society and the hypocritical policies of our governments. Whenever I have been asked to speak or write anything on prostitution, I have based it on my interaction, albeit limited, with sex-workers.

Much discussion has taken place around prostitution over the last few years. In the non-government sector, aside from anti-trafficking forums, interest in sex-workers has come from health professionals, especially from those working on HIV/AIDS prevention. Although some anti-trafficking and HIV intervention programmes have facilitated self-organizing among sex-workers, many have contributed to a simplification or stereotyping of their lives.[3] While the anti-trafficking activists have chosen to see sex-workers as victims, AIDS workers have by and large seen them as carriers of the disease. There have also been many conferences in academia on the issue of prostitution, bringing together people with a diverse range of opinions.[4] Focus on prostitution, whatever the motive for it, has also created a body of literature on prostitution. And many people have used qualitative methods to research into the subject; listening to different stakeholders, mapping and observing the places of sex work, reflecting and analysing the situation.[5]

Since much of the existing writing on prostitution, including my own, has also been based on interviews with sex-workers, I shall begin with some observations on that. I shall then move on to the contemporary debate on prostitution and highlight some of the points of contention. Finally, I shall describe the current scenario of self-organizing among sex-workers and their demands for protection and promotion of their basic human rights. I would conclude by proposing that these demands be supported by the feminist community.

TALKING TO SEX-WORKERS AND WRITING ABOUT THEM

I welcome the trend towards qualitative research on prostitution and applaud the fact that many women are trying to understand the reality of prostitution from the point of view of sex-workers.

However, qualitative ethnographic research with marginalized groups is often fraught with tension, especially if sexual behaviour is one of the reasons for marginalization. Let us look at a typical scenario. Many of us grow up believing that sex work is immoral. Many also find it difficult to believe that sex work could be an informed choice for some women. In several parts of the world a large number of sex-workers live in relative isolation. They live in brothels, many of which may be inaccessible to non-sex-worker women. In countries like India and Bangladesh the isolation is such that a non-sex-worker woman living in a neighbouring area may have never seen what the brothel area looks like.[6] So when we start our work or research with sex-workers, for most of us the areas where the women live and work, as well as the women themselves, may strike us as unfamiliar.[7] It is at this point that honesty and clarity about our own beliefs, prejudices and notions become extremely important. If we aim to describe the situation from the perspective of the women in it, we will have to learn to be non-judgemental and clearly distinguish between our own feelings and beliefs and the stories which the women tell. Privileging the hitherto unheard voices often results in muddying the waters. They make it impossible for us to arrive at neat theories. Powerful stories often confuse us because they are not homogeneous. The choice which many researchers face then is between articulating their confusion honestly, with respect for others, and making quick generalizations and recommendations. The issue of prostitution is so steeped in myths and notions that the researcher may need to re-examine even the most common assumptions. For example, it is commonly assumed that sex-workers are particularly vulnerable to violence from clients. However, interviews in India and Cambodia have identified the police as the main perpetrators of violence. Sex-workers have also spoken about violence from non-client local people. Migrant sex-workers have reported violence and racist attacks from local sex-workers.

Since no research involving real people can remain neutral or merely at the level of abstraction, we need to take care that our impassioned studies do not have a negative impact on the lives of those who spoke into our tapes. In other words we need to take responsibility for what we are saying about prostitution. In fact, I would like to emphasize that since much prostitution research tends to make policy recommendations, mere 'listening and recording' may not be enough. We need to create spaces for consultations with sex-workers before making recommendations regarding legislation which would govern their lives. In certain countries, before we can ask women about the impact of the existing laws on their lives, we may need to make them aware of the existing laws. Often the police are the face of the law for the women and the dividing line between law enforcement and abuse of the law is very thin.[8] Policy recommendations would also have to be based on an analysis of the impact of the existing laws. 'Rehabilitation' plans for women who were forced into prostitution and would like to leave it will have to be realistic.[9]

As we have seen in the essays in this collection, careful listening and non-judgemental attitudes towards sex-workers result in narratives that neither glorify sex work as liberatory nor denigrate it as soul-destroying. What we hear are the daily struggles and everyday courage of sex-workers which are not very different from the experiences of many other working women in the informal sector. The specific details of those daily struggles and courage may be different depending on the material context. But if we wish to work with sex-workers to end the exploitation and violence in their lives, we need to have realistic starting points within those contexts.

WHOSE SIDE ARE YOU ON?

I shall now move on to elaborate on some of the unresolved issues around prostitution that have divided the feminist community. By highlighting the points of non-communication, my intention is to extend the line of interaction which our authors have already traced. I would like to clarify at the outset that I write from a pro-sex-workers' rights perspective. I shall use examples from countries that I am familiar with but wish to point out that there are sex-workers' groups/support groups in several parts of the world now; before we make any comment on prostitution in a particular country we need to consult them and take their position into account.

Choice or force? Much of the debate around prostitution has concerned the question of choice. Can a woman choose to be a prostitute? Isn't she a victim of trafficking? Or, if not of trafficking, is she not a victim of the social system or of poverty? The difficulty in understanding choice arises when we meet migrant sex-workers, sex-workers who live in very difficult conditions and those who were forced into prostitution.

In order to understand the concept of choice we need to look at what Jyoti Sanghera (1997: 22) describes as 'the multitudinous shades of grey which stretch out extensively between the black and white'. We would need to acknowledge that 'necessity is a factor in all existential choice'. In other words, we need to see what the woman's options were, and what her options are now. The choice could have been between begging and prostitution, could have been between equally badly paid and unsafe work, where they may be coerced into providing unpaid sex to an employer, and being openly in the sex trade. Sometimes it may be a temporary need. To my mind the term 'informed decision' explains a woman's voluntary entry into prostitution far better than dichotomous use of words like choice and force. Further, data from many sex-workers point to the fact that even though they were 'forced' at one time to enter prostitution they prefer to stay in it now rather than returning to mainstream society. This decision, the women explain, is not only because they have not acquired any useful skills for earning a living. It is certainly not because there is easy money in prostitution. In many cases the decision is made on the basis of their experience of having tried to get back and lead a 'normal' life and then not being able to cope with the stigma. Life in brothel areas at least gives them a sense of community within which they are not being judged by others.[10]

Work or exploitation? The other vexed question which has divided activists is whether prostitution can be called work. One of the basic demands of sex-workers' groups around the world is for recognition of sex work as work. The difficulty in accepting sex work as paid work comes from the belief that sex is affective, is between two equal partners and cannot have an exchange value. The fact that some women (or men) can sell sex and give the power to some men (or women) to buy it is somehow seen as demeaning for all human beings. Sex-workers' groups maintain that the demand to recognize sex work as work should be seen as an extension of the feminist demand to recognize all kinds of reproductive labour as work.[11]

My own position on the issue of sex work is that unconditional support should be extended to recognize and validate the reality of the women who are working in prostitution. I am aware, however, of the theoretical difficulties in categorizing sex work. Just what kind of work is prostitution? There are two different suggestions in this regard.

Prostitution can be seen as reproductive labour, akin to the work performed by all women under a diverse range of social relations. Pointing out that the non-recognition of women's reproductive labour creates conditions for women's exploitation, Jyoti Sanghera reiterates:

It is important to state that whether performed within the confines of the household under family relations or in the market under commercial relations in exchange for a wage, all reproductive labour is work; it describes fundamentally necessary work undertaken in order for human society to multiply itself and to reproduce its capacity to work, and exist as human beings. (Sanghera 1997: 33)

Another suggestion made by sex-workers' groups is to see sex work as similar to the work of an artist or a therapist, as a kind of service performed by skilled people. This description best fits the *geishas* and courtesans of yesteryear and can also be linked with today's sex-workers who see themselves as entertainers. It might also be pointed out that many women performing artists were seen as 'immoral' because of their alleged liberal attitude to sexual codes. The description of sex work as entertainment work takes prostitution beyond the paradigm of demand and supply or the framework of necessity (survival for women and gratification for men) and assumes a certain level of skills in the prostitute.

There is also a formulation that sex-workers should be seen as entrepreneurs (see Joan Phillips in this collection). Similarly, some sex-workers in India see themselves as 'business women' or 'women in the trade'. According to this way of conceptualizing sex work one does not need to have an employer.

To me it appears that each of these categories describes certain kinds of sex work, therefore the difficulty of bringing sex work under one specific labour law may remain.

Much has been written about sexual exploitation. Some feminists have seen prostitution per se as sexual exploitation. Before marking prostitution as a primary site of sexual exploitation, we need to examine the situation of women within marriages and relationships and note what degree of freedom they enjoy with their sexual partners. Many women in prostitution have reported that they had much less negotiating power with their husbands and boyfriends and had been forced to have unprotected sex with them. Another aspect to explore would be to examine information about the sexual behaviour of men and women in different societies. Thus, situation analysis of women in prostitution, to find out about the level of exploitation and/or violence, needs to be contextualized. This is not to deny the existence of violence and exploitation within prostitution but to question the exclusive focus on it as a primary site.

ORGANIZING FOR EMPOWERMENT

The last few years have seen the setting up of a large number of sex-workers' rights groups in different parts of Asia. There are sex-workers' groups in Bangladesh, Cambodia, Hong Kong, India, Indonesia, Malaysia, Taiwan and Thailand and possibly in other countries of Asia too. They are at various stages of autonomy; few are fully autonomous, with their own fund-raising and programming status. Many are closely supported by sister NGOs. There are also regional and national networks, such as All India Forum of Sex Workers and the Asia Pacific Sex Workers' Network. As I have mentioned, these groups do not represent the whole range of sex-workers in the region. It might be correct to say that the groups consist of women with relative freedom and political awareness.

The activities of these groups are wide-ranging. Often they start by organizing need-based programmes. For example, many groups have on-going practical skills programmes such as language and literacy classes, non-formal education, money management training including micro-credit schemes, informal banking facilities, health and hygiene classes, legal awareness workshops and training for alternative employment. Although the efficacy of such training depends on many factors, these schemes provide the women, often for the first time, with a space to be together and discuss their situation. Being part of a collective helps them raise their voices against the violation of their basic human rights.

In fact, sometimes a blatant violation of rights may even act as an impetus to form a group. For example, when more than 5,000 sex-workers in a brothel area in Bangladesh were evicted by the state government, the incident provided a rationale for group formation. Later the women fought and won a law case against their own government. The fact that many women in prostitution have no legal awareness whatsoever has made the groups organize awareness-raising workshops. Now they understand that the money which they used to pay the police as a fee was only a bribe. Recently, when the government of Cambodia proposed closure of entertainment venues, many sex-workers protested and demanded that alternative employment provisions be made before taking such decisions. Recognizing that street-based sex-workers are more prone to physical violence, the sex-workers in Bangladesh took training in self-defence and the martial arts. In addition, where the context is not too hostile sex-workers are participating in local forums, writing about social issues and in general claiming their space as citizens of their country. The sex-workers in Nepal are demanding that their children be given citizenship even if the identity of their fathers is not known.[12] Sex-workers in Calcutta have set up their own task force against trafficking and child prostitution.

None of these activities would have been possible without a collective forum. Forming collectives, to my mind, has been particularly beneficial to women working in not too oppressive settings and those who already have a sense of community. Collective strength has proved effective in many developing countries where various kinds of social oppression combined with stigma had left the women with no sense of self-worth. Sometimes an organization which was formed in one brothel area has created a snowball effect and women from other brothel areas have been encouraged to form similar groups. Many sex-workers have reported that they no longer feel isolated and have been able to help each other in times of crisis.

As for the support workers, I think, coming in close contact with sex-workers has made them understand the situation of the women in a more realistic way. While earlier, we had only notions or stereotypes to go by, now it is possible to note the similarities between so-called good and bad women. It has been possible to understand the concept of sexual exploitation within a broader context. Contact with sex-workers has opened our eyes to the other forms of exploitation and discrimination which the women face. For example, that they are often victims of custodial rape, and that they and their children are denied health-care in hospitals and admission to schools, are facts only now being talked about and addressed.

Difficulties The self-organizing of sex-workers in India, in particular, reminds me of the Dalit movement in the country whereby a vast multitude of lower-caste and untouchable people have rejected the token sympathy and patronizing attitude of the dominant classes. Admittedly, no linkages have been established between the Dalit movement and the sex-workers' movement. Nor has there been any link between women in other informal sectors and the sex-workers. For example, anecdotal evidence suggests that there is considerable sectoral mobility among domestic workers, factory workers and sex-workers but there has not been open alliance among these groups. On the contrary, activists report that a very palpable tension exists between them. This, I think, is because sex-workers are by and large seen as sexual deviants/bad women or victims of sexual exploitation.

Migrant sex-workers remain the most vulnerable group among sex-workers. Going by the available data, it could be said that most sex-workers are migrants even when they are within their own country. Seeking anonymity to flee social stigma they often prefer to work away from their place of origin. In many countries migrant sex-workers constitute a very large part of the entire sex-workers' population. While cross-border migration to neighbouring countries may sometimes result in better earnings, as in the case of Vietnamese sex-workers in Cambodia, their illegal status may make them more vulnerable as in the case of Shan women in Thailand. When the cultural and economic differences between countries are strong and visa rules are stringent sex-workers often have to put up with abusive treatment. The case of Thai sex-workers in Germany and Denmark as described by some of our contributors are cases in point. Within the legislative context, migrant sex-workers are primarily dealt with under migration legislation. Since they are often illegal migrants they bear the brunt of repressive prostitution laws as well as strict border control policies. As the TAMPEP (Transnational AIDS/STD Prevention among Migrant Prostitutes in Europe Project, 2001) position paper on migration and sex work puts it, 'the social and political inclusion of migrant sex-workers is an important preventive measure against trafficking in women, a prerequisite of the social inclusion of migrant sex-workers, including transgender sex-workers, is the recognition and implementation of their human rights: as women, as migrants and as sex-workers'.

My work also takes me to newly urbanized communities. It is evident that many bars and other entertainment venues have come up over the last few years. Parents, educators and the general public show concern about the 'loss of moral values in society'. Some of these people even find it difficult to say the word 'prostitute' or 'prostitution' and use euphemisms like 'bad work' and 'women who do bad work'.While working with community groups in northern Burma, for example, we were told that the number of prostitutes has risen over the last few years. Initially the reason which both our male and female participants gave us was that some women are greedy, after easy money. However, closer analysis brought to light factors such as privatization and loss of jobs for local people. The fact that women often have fewer opportunities for education and training was also mentioned. People in many developing countries also express concern over rising middle-class prostitution where some women do prostitution in order to be able to buy expensive cosmetics, fashionable shoes and clothes. The link between prostitution and poverty, lack of opportunity and political conflict on one hand and consumerism on the other is quite obvious.

CONCLUSION

So, when we defend the rights of sex-workers, are we also promoting prostitution? When we say, together with the sex-workers, that sex work is work, are we encouraging women to enter prostitution? Living and working in the developing part of the world and knowing that many women would not have entered prostitution if they had had other opportunities, I certainly cannot say that prostitution is the kind of work young women should aspire to. For me, supporting the sex-workers' rights movement is to recognize that millions of women work in prostitution and they have human rights like anyone else. Respecting their choice to stay in it is recognizing that they have a right to self-determination.

Although at this moment the sex-workers' groups may look more like communities of dissent and may indeed have an adversarial relationship with mainstream society, they are in fact an integral part of society. The political organizing of sex-workers has broken the silence of several women and has initiated a dialogue between a marginalized group and the mainstream society. Understandably, this dialogue has been fraught with mistrust and tension. In fact, if we look back a few years at the history of feminism, we will realize that similar demands to speak for themselves have been made by lesbian women, women of colour and women of the Third World at different points in time. If such a demand is now being made by sex-workers, should we not support it? Many of the battles for the realization of the human rights of sex-workers are still to be fought and won. But a beginning has been made and there is room for hope.

NOTES

1. I am referring to the movement of people from one British or Dutch colony to another to work in sugar, banana, teak and rubber plantations, for example.

2. GAATW held the first consultation on prostitution in 1997, documented in Moving the Whore Stigma (GAATW 1997). A subsequent meeting was co-organized by GAATW, Asian Women's Human Rights Council and SANGRAM in 1999 which brought together several sex-workers from the Asian region. In 2000 a follow-up meeting was held with representatives from sex-workers' groups to look into the working conditions of sex-workers in Asia. Currently we are working on a videography project with sex-workers from five Asian countries to train them in video documentation of their own situation. In addition we have facilitated the participation of Asian sex-workers in several international meetings.

3. An example of anti-trafficking research resulting in the formation of sex-workers' organizations is the Cambodia Prostitutes Union which is an off shoot of an action research project jointly carried out by the Cambodia Women's Development Association and GAATW. Similarly, Durbar Mahila Samanwaya Committee, possibly the largest sex-workers' group in the world, is the result of Sonagachhi HIV/Aids Intervention Project.

4. Many of the essays in this anthology were originally presented at a conference in Aalborg University. Although many of us felt strongly that the absence of sex-workers was a weakness, the conference did bring together a range of academics and NGO activists.

5. As Susanne Thorbek has already pointed out in her Introduction, it is also a feature of this anthology. While I recognize the relevance of writing which does not require the researcher to interview sex-workers, I am just noting interview-based writing as a widely used practice.

6. I recall the shock of the taxi driver when one evening colleagues of mine and I wanted him to take us to Falkland Road, one of the red-light areas of Bombay. He was extremely curious and wanted to know why we were going to the 'dirty areas'. I also recall that friends who lived not very far from Sonagachhi, one of Calcutta's oldest brothel areas, had never been there.

7. Or, on the contrary, if we have gone expecting them to be very different from us, we might be surprised by the similarities.

8. Many sex-workers in Cambodia, Bangladesh and India reported that they had to pay fines to the police because they were in 'illegal work'. On further investigation it was clear that police were abusing their authority and taking bribes from the women.

9. I do not recommend the use of 'rehabilitation' because of its connotations. Instead I prefer the term 'recovery' or 'reintegration'.

10. These data come from GAATW's research with sex-workers and their

children conducted in India, Nepal, Bangladesh and Cambodia. Women who have been in prostitution for several years and are currently living in a relatively open brothel system spoke about the discrimination directed at them and their children by so-called 'good' people. Many were unhappy that their children have reluctantly entered prostitution but felt that their own community could act as a safe haven.

11. Joint Statement of Sex Workers' Meeting, *GAATW Newsletter*, 14, July 2000: 11. Joint Statement from the International of Sex Workers, *GAATW Newsletter*, 15, December 2000: 17–18.

12. The constitution in Nepal denies citizenship rights to persons whose father's identity is not known.

REFERENCE

Sanghera, Joyti (1997) *In the Belly of the Beast: Moving the Whore Stigma* (Bangkok: GAATW).

Index

media - programmes glamourising it

Race